Car
- An

Dealer 750
Description ICARUS
Rising 8⁰⁰
Price $

D0351089

CHASING ICARUS

CHASING ICARUS

The Seventeen Days in 1910 That Forever
Changed American Aviation

GAVIN MORTIMER

WALKER & COMPANY
New York

Published by Walker Publishing Company, Inc., New York

All papers used by Walker & Company are natural, recyclable products made from wood grown in well-managed forests. The manufacturing processes conform to the environmental regulations of the country of origin.

LIBRARY OF CONGRESS CATALOGING-IN-PUBLICATION DATA HAS BEEN APPLIED FOR.

ISBN-10: 0-8027-1711-X
ISBN-13: 978-0-8027-1711-5

Visit Walker & Company's Web site at www.walkerbooks.com

First U.S. edition 2009

1 3 5 7 9 10 8 6 4 2

Typeset by Westchester Book Group
Printed in the United States of America by Quebecor World Fairfield

For Margot

CONTENTS

IN THE FALL of 1910 no one could agree on what to call this daring new breed of men in the heavier-than-air flying machine. *Aviators* and *fliers* were the most popular (and prosaic) monikers, but journalists trawled their imaginations to come up with more colorful descriptions. Browsing through the newspapers on any given day, one might read of "birdmen" or "man birds," "dragon fliers" or "flierlings." Those reporters with a more lyrical bent opted for "wizards of the sky" or "flying gladiators." Those less predisposed to melodrama simply called the men at the controls "jockeys," "riders," "chauffeurs," or "navigators of the upper regions." Just about the only word not deemed appropriate was *pilot*. Therefore, in keeping with the times, I refer to the men throughout the book either as *fliers* or *aviators*, and never as *pilots*. Similarly, *aeroplane* was as common as *airplane*, but for expediency I stick with the latter.

In addition, the International Aviation Cup, or the Coupe Internationale d'Aviation as the French called it, was sponsored by Gordon Bennett, publisher of the *New York Herald* newspaper. He also put his name to the International Balloon Cup. The trophies were often described by newspapers as the Gordon Bennett Aviation Cup and the Gordon Bennett Balloon Cup. To prevent confusion, I refer at all times to the International Aviation Cup and the International Balloon Cup.

The value of life lies not in the length of days,
but in the use we make of them.

—MICHEL DE MONTAIGNE, 1580

The Biggest Events Are Yet to Come

ALL OF AMERICA was excited. The first Aviation Meet was about to take place on American soil, and the nation's newspapers were in no doubt that a new chapter had begun. It was front-page news across the country on Sunday, January 9, 1910, from the *Billings Daily Gazette* to the *Nevada State Journal* to the *Indianapolis Star*. Monday in Los Angeles dawned with a clear blue sky and what one newspaper described as a "mere zephyr of breeze that floated rather than blew up from the sea, and over the valley between the snow-capped mountains." Across the city thousands of people wolfed down their breakfast before riding the Pacific Electric trains fifteen miles south to what had once been called Dominguez Junction, but was now named Aviation Field. As they poured out of the cars onto the platform, children tugged at their fathers' sleeves and asked what was that strange noise. Their fathers weren't sure. Automobiles, most probably, belonging to the rich who had motored out from the city. To some dads, those who had fought in the Spanish-American War, the noise brought back memories of heavy machine guns in action.

None had ever before seen a heavier-than-air flying machine, and they had only read about them in newspaper articles illustrated not by photographs but by sketches of these newfangled inventions that seemed not much more than muslin, wood, and wire. In one such report, published in the *Chicago Daily Tribune* the previous fall, under the heading WHY AN AEROPLANE FLIES, the paper had explained to its readers, "An understanding of what holds an airplane in the air can best be reached by going back to the old familiar kite. A kite is kept elevated by running with it against the wind, or by allowing the wind to blow against it. When the kite flies two forces work against each other; one, the force of the wind, the other, the weight of the kite. It is exactly the same with an airplane, with the exception that instead of waiting for the wind to blow against it, the airplane drives itself against the wind." This was done, continued the paper, by a propeller driven by a motor engine, which, for all the thrilling potential of the airplane, held the key to its development. "If the propellers could whirl rapidly enough they could create an absolute vacuum in front and have thirty pounds per square inch on every inch of their back surface. If this condition were possible, or if engines powerful enough and propellers strong enough to withstand that pressure could be made, an aeroplane, according to such experts as the Wrights, could be sent through the air at a rate of 500 miles an hour." The principles of flight were lost on many among the crowd scurrying toward Aviation Field, but they didn't care. It wasn't the mechanics that mattered, it was the fact that man could fly. They all gasped when they saw the grandstand with its tiers of boxes already filling up quickly. It was fifty feet high and ran for seven hundred feet along one side of the field, its flags gently fluttering in the zephyr. On the opposite side were a row of giant white tents and a huddle of smaller tents at the far end of the field.

The crowd queued patiently to get onto the field, shuffling ever closer to the sign that hung at the entrance and boldly proclaimed in chalk letters a foot high THE BIGGEST EVENTS ARE YET TO COME. They handed over their $1 admission fee (approximately $16 today), clicked through the turnstiles, then rushed to seek out the best vantage points. Once they were happy with their spot, they sat on the grass and waited for the meet to start at one P.M. They shaded their eyes from the sun with their hands and looked toward the large tents, from inside which came the gentle whir of dirigible engines being tested. Farther down the field, nearly a mile away, were the smaller tents, and from inside came that strange noise again. The crowd could see men scurrying in and out of the tents, like rabbits in their warrens, and once or twice, just for a fleeting moment, they caught a glimpse of some strange contraption.

All through the morning Aviation Field filled with Americans come to witness with their own eyes the miracle of what some people called the heavier-than-air flying machine, and others the airplane. Between eleven o'clock and noon three-car trains left the city every two minutes, and the thousands of people that they disgorged were corralled from the station to Aviation Field by three hundred deputy sheriffs, many of them on horseback.

Governor Gillett of California took his place in the grandstand, in among the elite of Californian society, who had arrived in the hundreds of automobiles that twinkled under the midday sun. The governor was publicly welcomed to the field by Dick Ferris, the master of ceremonies, who then declared the meet officially open. Few people in the crowd of fifty thousand were looking at Ferris as he spoke. Instead their attention was riveted on the monoplane that had been wheeled out from one of the tents onto the elliptical racetrack. A lean man, a mustache the only extravagance on a serious face, climbed up onto the seat. Ferris turned and introduced America's own Glenn Curtiss, the greatest flier in the world, so he declared, who had gone to France the previous year and stunned Europe by winning the prestigious International Aviation Cup. The vast throng clapped and whistled, then rose to their feet in wonder as Curtiss's airplane bounced along the racetrack and climbed slowly into the air. Around the racetrack flew the thirty-one-year-old, at a height nearly as great as the flags on top of the grandstand, before landing with a bump and a jolt twenty-eight seconds later. After a moment's pause as the crowd struggled to absorb what they had seen, they shouted their approval. A watching reporter for Utah's *Ogden Standard* wrote that with that one flight Curtiss had "dissipated any doubt that the fragile contrivance of rubberized silk, canvas, and bamboo could really fly."

Ferris allowed time for the audience to recover their poise, then announced that Charles Willard would attempt to circle the official course, which was a trifle more than a mile and a half in length. With a collective intake of breath from the crowd, suddenly Willard was off, soaring up to seventy feet as he approached the halfway mark. Then with a

cough, and a splutter, Willard's engine died. He glided down to earth accompanied by groans of disappointment, but his mechanics soon had him
airborne so he could finish the lap. Ferris bubbled with excitement as—
overlooking the ten minutes Willard had spent waiting for his engine to be
fixed—he reeled off the aviator's lap time: one minute and twenty-three
seconds. How about a round of applause, Californian style, for a splendid
showing? Ferris asked the crowd.

Soon a canopy of dark clouds covered the field and the zephyr had become a bracing breeze. Some of the more knowledgeable of the crowd,
those who kept abreast of aviation matters in the newspapers and science
journals, began to fret. The stronger the wind, the less likely the chance of
seeing a flying machine in action. "Where's Paulhan?" they shouted. "We
want Paulhan!"

Ferris raised his hands apologetically. "We can't do anything with that
Frenchman," he boomed into his bullhorn. "He pays no attention to rules
and regulations, nor to the course laid out for flights. I would not be surprised to see him appear suddenly on his machine through the top of his
tent."

Instead of Louis Paulhan, Ferris gave the spectators two of America's
mightiest balloonists—Lincoln Beachey and Roy Knabenshue. To a smattering of polite applause they began to pilot their small dirigibles around
Aviation Field. It took them five minutes to lumber round the one-and-
a-half-mile course, while parents laid out their picnics and children made
airplanes with their hands. No one paid much attention to the lethargic
dirigibles.

Meanwhile Louis Paulhan and his four French mechanics had wheeled
his Farman biplane out of the rear of his tent and down into a gulley out of
sight of the stands. The Frenchman's poodle yapped at his heels as his wife
handed him his gray cap and yellow cloak. The daring self-taught aviator
had been one of the favorites for the 1909 International Aviation Cup but a
crash had wrecked his dream; now he planned to have his revenge by up-
staging Curtiss in front of his own people.

Up in the grandstand the reporter from the *Indianapolis Star* was idly
watching the dirigibles pass in front of him when "there was a sudden
shout and out of the gulley shot Paulhan, the motor of his Farman humming at a tremendous rate. He swung around the course and came down

before the grandstand at high speed. He gesticulated first with his right hand and then his left, and at times he let go the steering wheel and waved both arms and shouted to the multitude. Circling the full course once Paulhan then began a second round, but stopped with the halfway pole to cut across the field straight for the grandstand. Suddenly veering he described another circle, finally disappearing from view to the north behind the grandstand."

Paulhan was soon back, flying so low over the uncovered grandstand that people ducked in fear of their lives. For eight and a half minutes he buzzed around Aviation Field, covering nearly four miles in total and climbing to 150 feet. "Paulhan was cheered madly," wrote the correspondent for the *Boston Daily Globe*. "Men shouted themselves hoarse, while women applauded and waved handkerchiefs." The Frenchman had stolen the thunder of Curtiss and the other American pilots. Curtiss went back in the air, followed by Willard, and then Charles Hamilton, an aviator with a lingering whiff of danger about him, but the name on everyone's lips that evening as they rode the trains back home was Louis Paulhan.

When the meet ended ten days later Paulhan had won more than $15,000 in prize money and set new world's records for both endurance and altitude, records that took the breath away. He had flown 75.77 miles in one hour and fifty-eight minutes and attained a height of 4,165 feet, seven hundred feet higher than the previous best.

Across America the Los Angeles event was hailed as a resounding triumph. "Aviation has suddenly developed in the United States as a great show enterprise," ran an editorial in California's *Oakland Tribune* on January 21. "The first meet on American soil . . . has been an immense financial success [and] the sum of $75,000 expended in prizes has proved to be a mere drop in the bucket. The meet has given Los Angeles millions of dollars' worth of free advertising the world over."

Even the Wright brothers, Wilbur and Orville, were impressed by the reaction of the American public. They had shunned the Los Angeles meet, considering it tawdry and unworthy of anyone with a serious interest in aviation. But soon Wilbur had dispatched a telegram to Roy Knabenshue, who had for several months been badgering the brothers to form an exhibition team. The message was brief: COMPANY READY DISCUSS EXHIBITION BUSINESS SERIOUSLY. WHEN CAN YOU COME DAYTON.

The *Oakland Tribune* said that dozens of cities had already begun to petition the Aero Club of America for the right to stage the International Aviation Cup race in the fall, when Europe's finest aviators would come to America to compete for the title that Curtiss had won in 1909. "That the bidding will be high and the competition strenuous goes without saying," wrote the *Tribune*, "for aviation fever has developed in every community . . . and the desire is whetted to see it practically demonstrated by the world's best exponents of the art."

But Paulhan couldn't agree. As he packed up his airplane, a nagging sense of unease was in his soul. How swiftly the attitude of the crowd had changed during the meet, he reflected, from the idiotic amazement of that first day when he swooped over the grandstand, to the bored indifference of the final few days. Even his race around the course with Curtiss for the speed prize—which the American had narrowly won—had failed to evoke more than a halfhearted cheer.

Paulhan expressed his concerns in an interview with the *Weekly Sentinel*. "They [the crowd] are ennui," he sighed. "I shall have to do something to remove that blasé feeling." The reporter asked whether Paulhan was proud nonetheless to have set a new record for altitude flying. "No!" he exclaimed, throwing up his hands. "I have forgotten that. Records, more records, better records, until, pouf! the breath goes out and I really find that path to paradise—or to Hades."

CHAPTER ONE

It's Europe or Bust

Saturday, October 15, 1910

WALTER WELLMAN WAS WOKEN by a knock on his door at four A.M. The fifty-two-year-old Ohioan groped for his spectacles, fitted them to his sleepy face, and padded across the floor. Standing outside the door was the night manager of the Chalfonte Hotel in Atlantic City, who apologized for the intrusion, then relayed a message he had just received over the telephone. Melvin Vaniman had requested Mr. Wellman's immediate presence at the balloon house. Conditions were favorable. The news was like a splash of cold water to Wellman's face, and a few minutes later he was in his khaki flying suit busily instructing the night manager to telephone the city's fire and police departments.

Once that was done, he took an automobile to the balloon house, arriving just as the eastern sky began to be illuminated by the first streaks of dawn and the hogsheads of fog drifting toward the shore at the head of a southeast breeze became visible. Vaniman, a failed opera singer who was the airship's second-in-command, briefed Wellman on the latest telegrams from the weather bureau in Washington and assured his captain that the hurricane ravaging Cuba was too far south to affect them. In his opinion, and that of the weather bureau, they were good to go. But still Wellman hesitated as he stood in front of the balloon house gazing out to sea. His voyage to reach the north pole in a dirigible the previous year had ended in humiliation, and he couldn't bear the thought of more public ridicule. "Perhaps we'll make a trial flight first," murmured Wellman. Vaniman's patience snapped: "Not much you won't! There will be nothing doing right now but the trip all the way across. We've delayed too long already and the weather is too good to miss now. It's Europe or bust."

Wellman regarded his chief engineer in silence. Those newspaper reports were never far from his thoughts, the ones that accused him of being a phony and a fool, deriding his talk of crossing the Atlantic in an airship as nothing more than "hot air" (and how they loved the pun). "Okay," said Wellman eventually. "Let's go."

A little before seven A.M. the canvas doors of the balloon house were pulled back by Wellman and his five crew members, and two hundred police officers and firefighters flooded inside. They knew the drill. Quickly they surrounded dozens of tightly packed steel drums of gasoline, all strapped together to form a thirty-three-foot-long rectangle, and lifted it onto their shoulders. It was heavy, over two tons, and the men's legs ached under its weight as they shuffled slowly toward the water's edge. Wellman and his crew called it the airship's "equilibrator," but that was plain gobbledygook to everyone else, who called it the ballast.

The equilibrator was an ingenious contraption constructed by Wellman and Vaniman. At the end of the gasoline drums was a series of forty heavy wooden blocks, each twenty inches in length, which would compensate for the gradual diminution in the equilibrator's weight as gasoline drums were hauled up and poured into the tank in the floor of the passenger car. Under normal conditions it was hoped the *America* would sail at a height of two hundred feet with the lower end of the equilibrator trailing in the water. Then, when the gas expanded and raised the airship, the weight of the equilibrator increased. When the gas contracted, on the other hand, more of the equilibrator would rest on the water. That was the theory, at least, but it had yet to be put into practice because there hadn't been time to try out the equilibrator.

With the equilibrator on the beach, the volunteers returned to the balloon house. On Wellman's command, they carefully untethered the guy ropes that anchored the airship to the ground. Up close, the men holding the guy ropes could see where the seams of the envelope's cotton and silk layers had been cemented with three emulsions of rubber. If they looked closely they could even make out where extra strips had been glued to cover the needle holes and prevent the escape of hydrogen. In his subsequent account of the expedition, Wellman described how the gas bag worked by inviting readers to

> measure off with your hands what will approximate a cubic foot of air. It is apparently impalpable, without substance or weight. Yet our physics tell us this cubic foot of air has a weight approximating 1.2 ounces.
>
> Now if we have a box containing exactly one cubic foot of air, and if we force the air out and put in its place hydrogen weighing only .1 ounce per cubic foot, the box is 1.1 ounces lighter than it was before. If the box should be made of a substance so flimsy that its weight was only one ounce, it would rise in the air because it and its contents together are lighter than air. Multiply our one cubic foot by 345,000— the volume of the gas reservoir of the airship *America*—and what do we have? We have taken out 345,000 cubic feet of air, weighing 414,000 ounces, or 25,800 pounds; and we have put in 345,000 cubic feet of hydrogen weighing 34,500 ounces, or 2,150 pounds. By this simple means we have gained a lifting force of 23,650 pounds—the difference between the weight of the air displaced and the gas which displaces it. In the case of *America* the gas bag, with its valves, inner balloons for air, and other appurtenances, weighs approximately 4,700 pounds; hence, the net lifting force is 18,950 pounds. In other words, the gas can carry the weight of the balloon and a load of nearly 9½ tons besides.

The men walked forward on Wellman's order, and as the nose of the 228-foot-long airship appeared at the hangar entrance like some great mythological monster emerging from its cave, the bystanders outside gasped in astonishment. "The crowd, constantly augmented in numbers, as the news of the proposed flight spread through the city, lost its skepticism when they saw the balloon move from the hangar," wrote a watching reporter from the *Fort Wayne Daily News*. Suddenly everyone began to believe that Wellman was serious in his intention to sail across the Atlantic.

Vaniman and his two assistant engineers, twenty-four-year-old Lewis Loud and Fred Aubert, climbed into the 156-foot-long steel passenger car that was directly underneath the *America*'s gas bag [envelope] and secured to it with 188 hempen cords. The car was enclosed but had several celluloid windows, and in its floor was the gasoline tank. To the rear of the car was the engine room, connected to the pilot's seat by a speaking tube. The lifeboat was suspended six feet under the car, and Jack Irwin, the twenty-nine-year-old Australian wireless operator, hopped in and made a final check that the *America*'s Marconi wireless installation, housed in one of the watertight compartments, was properly functioning.

Scores of spectators gathered around, oohing and aahing as they caught sight of the wireless. Three months earlier a Marconi had been responsible for apprehending the notorious Dr. Crippen in mid-Atlantic as he fled England for his native America on board the *Montrose*. At this very moment the doctor was on trial in a London court for the murder of his wife, and to most people the Marconi wireless was only marginally less fascinating than a flying machine. Fascinating, but incomprehensible. People couldn't begin to understand that the steel frame of the car would act throughout the voyage as the wireless radiator and the equilibrator cable as its earth connection. The lifeboat would also be the ship's galley, though in reality this was nothing more than a gasoline stove with aluminum utensils. Wellman shooed away the crowd from the boat and ran through the inventory of food packed in another of the watertight compartments: bread, beans, bacon, coffee, malted milk, boiled ham, eggs, tinned meats. Enough provisions for thirty days, at a stretch.

The crew grudgingly posed for a photograph, scornful of the pressmen who had for thirty days insinuated they were charlatans. Only Irwin appeared to take it all in stride; he stood in the center of the group, hands in his pockets, beaming for the camera. Murray Simon, the English steamship officer who had been hired as a navigator, was dressed as if he were going for a punt on the river Thames, dapper in a tie and wing collar, and a straw boater that surely wouldn't last long once they were in the air. Wellman's salt-and-pepper mustache bristled as he fielded the first question from the press pack. Was it true that the French motor expert Jean Jacon refused to fly because he had not been paid?* Wellman wouldn't be drawn into a war of words. How long did he estimate it would take him to reach England? He replied that he counted on covering the three thousand miles in ten days. One or two of the reporters gave a whistle of surprise. Why, that would mean three hundred miles a day? It was possible. And did he regard the trip as dangerous? "We do not know," said Wellman. "That there is in it some risk to life is apparent. How great this risk must remain an unknown quantity till we have put it to the test. Once well on our way, the danger of fire or explosion will be ever present in our minds. The combination of a ton of inflammable hydrogen, nearly three tons of gasoline, sparking motors, electric light, and wireless is not one to inspire confidence."

Wellman added that they had taken all possible precautions, insulating the engines with steel gauze and asbestos, placing the gas valve far aft, and carrying the exhaust from the motors well out from the gasoline tank. But they could do only so much. "Lightning may strike the ship and fire the hydrogen," he explained. "Our equilibrator may not ride well in heavy seas and by its shocks injure the airship, or it may possibly foul some ship or fishing vessel. Both engines may break down . . ." Wellman's voice trailed off as he spotted his wife, Laura, and two of his five daughters in the crowd. Their doleful countenance told him he had said enough. They, like the other crew member's families, were all too familiar with the fate of Oscar Erbslöh, the celebrated German balloonist who, along with his crew of five, had been killed three months earlier when their airship exploded in midair.

Wellman smiled at his wife as he addressed the pressmen: "Our lifeboat is hung with an instantaneous releasing device and is at all times kept fully equipped . . . We aim to follow as closely as we can the steamer lane from New York to the English Channel, and if we should be so fortunate as to be able to keep fairly on the course, help would not be far away in case of accident."

---

* Jacon claimed he had been hired by Wellman during the summer for $50 a week, plus expenses, but that no money was forthcoming after the first week. Then, on October 14, Jacon received his back pay, but it was only $30 a week.

Wellman's farewell to his family was brief. Three kisses, a few words, and then he was gone, too distressed to steal a backward glance. Fred Aubert, the youngest member of the expedition, tried to look as bold as his twenty years would allow as he climbed the ladder. He turned, exchanged shy glances with Rebecca, his sweetheart—one of Wellman's daughters—then he, too, was gone.

Last up was Vaniman. For a few seconds he stood at the foot of the ladder arguing with Wellman about the airship's cat, Kiddo. The chief engineer could hear the gray tabby meowing pitifully from the car. "I don't want that cat on board," he shouted. "Blasted thing will keep me awake." Simon reminded everyone that it was considered bad luck to let a cat leave a ship, but Vaniman didn't care a fig for maritime traditions. He pulled himself aboard and threw the cat into a bag. "Cast off!" yelled Wellman at the same moment, and before Vaniman had a chance to lower the bag on the end of a rope, the *America* began to rise. It was five minutes past eight and Simon marked their departure with an entry in the log: "Now we will make these blooming critics eat their own words. They have been hammering us for the last month, ridiculing our 'worn-out gas-bag,' an 'old coffee-mill for motor,' telling us we should never leave sight of land . . . now let those landlubbers who are afraid of their own shadows and who like to criticize others, let the blighters go to blazes."

At about the time the *America* lifted into the fog, a compatriot of Simon's was rising gingerly from his bed in a Washington, D.C., hotel room. Claude Grahame-White examined his bruises and counted his blessings. The day before he had nearly lost his life when his airplane was caught on the beam by a gust of wind as he took off from Washington's Benning racetrack, hurling him from the track at sixty miles per hour, through one fence, then another, before coming to rest in a muddy field. His escape, so the morning newspapers all agreed, had been nothing short of a miracle. Grahame-White was pleased to read that most papers had condensed details of the crash into just a couple of paragraphs, appended to the main report about his visit to the White House earlier in the day. It was the lead story in the *Washington Post*, accompanied by a series of dashing photographs. The paper called the stunt "the most remarkable and daring landing ever made from such a height by an aviator, either native or foreign." It then described how thousands of people had deserted their offices, stores, and factories and watched openmouthed as the white-winged biplane circled first the Washington Monument, then the dome of the Capitol, before making a perfect landing on the asphalt of Executive Avenue and rolling to a stop a few feet from the White House gates. President Taft had been away on business, but the first man to help Grahame-White down from his seat was Admiral Dewey, the hero of Manila. "A wonderful piece of work you have just performed," boomed the admiral. "I want to congratulate you on the remarkable feat."

A cluster of other high-ranking military officers had quickly arrived on the scene, among them Brigadier General James Allen, head of the Army Signal Corps, and the man responsible for military aviation in America. Grahame-White was soon on his way to the Metropolitan Club for lunch and more handshakes, while back on Executive Avenue soldiers encircled the biplane and kept inquisitive citizens at bay.

Grahame-White's social call to the White House hadn't been impromptu; like everything else in his life it was meticulously planned. Together with an American friend, Clifford Harmon, a property tycoon turned amateur aviator, and his business manager, Sydney McDonald, Grahame-White had concocted the visit as a way of promoting the airplane, and himself. Harmon was on good terms with the chief of the Washington police, and he'd arranged for traffic to be barred from Executive Avenue between eleven A.M. and midday on the Friday.

That the police agreed was a mark of the esteem in which Grahame-White was held in the United States, a mere six weeks since his arrival. He had come from England bearing a formidable reputation, with the *New York Herald* calling him the "greatest all-round aviator in the world." In April 1910 he had raced Louis Paulhan from London to Manchester (a distance of 185 miles) for a newspaper prize of $50,000; Grahame-White had lost, but only after he had become the first man to fly cross-country at night in a desperate attempt to overtake the superior airplane of the Frenchman. "The race, not of the century, but the centuries!" trumpeted New York's *Evening Post*, which saluted the Englishman's gallant flight.

Overnight, quite literally, the thirty-one-year-old had become a sensation, the incarnation of the belle epoque, the decade before the outbreak of war in 1914 when gaiety and glamour reigned. From an early age Grahame-White had been fascinated by stories of flying found in the pages of penny dreadfuls,* such as *Deadwood Dick's Electric Coach* and *The Voyage of the Flying Dutchman*. Obsessed with flying, Grahame-White used the family wealth to purchase a hot-air balloon. He went up a few times, usually with a picnic hamper and a pretty girl in tow, but the novelty soon wore off because "it was impossible to go where you wanted as one was compelled to go in the direction in which the wind carried you."

Automobiles were more to Grahame-White's liking, and he became an avid racing driver, striking up a keen friendship with the Honorable Charles Rolls (one of the cofounders of the motorcar company Rolls-Royce). In 1905 Grahame-White opened an automobile showroom in Mayfair, one of London's most exclusive addresses. He plastered his office walls with the mottoes that would drive him through life: DO IT NOW!, HUSTLE LIKE HELL!, and his favorite: WHEN TRYING ANYTHING, TRY SOMETHING BIG! Soon business was going so well Grahame-White branched out. He bought a speedboat, called *Gee Whizz*, in which he took the pretty girls for a spin at speeds of 50 mph. Later he invested in a more leisurely vessel, a large yacht, which allowed Grahame-White more time to attend to the needs of his shipmates. He christened the yacht *L'Amoureuse*, or "love life."

However, the arrival in France in 1908 of an American whose character was diametrically opposed to Grahame-White's changed the Englishman's life. Wilbur Wright lived almost puritanically. The son of a bishop in the Church of the United Brethren in Christ, the forty-one-year-old bachelor had never touched a drop of liquor. He didn't gamble, didn't womanize, he didn't even talk that much. His enjoyment came from hard work and aviation.

In the summer of 1908 Wright had come to France to show skeptics that he and his brother, Orville, had indeed invented the airplane with

---

* Penny dreadfuls were cheap and sensationalist novels popular with the British working classes and schoolboys.

the first flight at Kitty Hawk, on December 17, 1903. On August 8 he flew for 107 seconds before a spellbound audience. Nothing like it had ever been seen in Europe, and the Wrights were acclaimed as the true inventors of the flying machine. For the next few months Wilbur Wright—the *homme-oiseau* (birdman), as he was labeled by the French press—gave regular demonstrations at Camp d'Auvours near Le Mans.

Grahame-White was in a party of British flying enthusiasts who motored down from London one sunny September day to watch Wright in action. After the flight the group of Englishmen were introduced to the aviator, and Grahame-White was awed by the "ascetic, gaunt American with watchful, hawklike eyes." It would be the one and only time the two men met on friendly terms, and on the journey back across the Channel Grahame-White thought of nothing else but the Wright invention.

The following year Grahame-White was one of the half million spectators who attended the Rheims Aviation Meet, the first international event of its kind. While most people were content simply to marvel at the skills of Glenn Curtiss and Louis Blériot, Grahame-White yearned to emulate them. Passing himself off as an official member of the British military delegation that had been invited to Rheims by their French counterparts, Grahame-White gained access to the hangars and buttonholed Blériot. In flawless French he commiserated with Blériot on his failure to win the International Aviation Cup but said how impressed he had been with his eponymous airplane. He would like to buy one and learn to fly. The Frenchman took an instant liking to the intruder, whose self-assurance was more Gallic than Anglo-Saxon. Within a few weeks Grahame-White had installed himself in Blériot's Parisian factory and was overseeing the construction of his airplane. He christened it the *White Eagle*, and by early November it was ready to fly. Unfortunately for Grahame-White, Blériot was out of town at a flying exhibition, so instead of waiting for tuition, he and a friend decided to learn on the job. "It's a flying machine, isn't it?" he said to his accomplice. "Then let's see if it can fly."

It did, and the news that Grahame-White had soloed without a single lesson received widespread coverage in the French newspapers with one running the headline UN VOL SENSATIONNEL! When Blériot returned, he gave a rueful shake of his head at the impertinence of the grinning

Englishman, but secretly he was deeply impressed. Over the next fortnight the pair flew together often with Blériot demonstrating to his passenger the skills that he had used on his historic flight across the English Channel four months earlier.* Then on November 25 the *White Eagle* suffered a catastrophic malfunction as they passed over Blériot's new aerodrome in Pau, southern France, at 60 mph. The rudder control failed as Blériot banked to turn away from trees, and the small biplane flew straight on. Blériot remained unperturbed as he opened the throttle and gained a precious few feet of height, skimming so low over the trees that Grahame-White could have reached down and plucked a leaf from a branch had he not been holding on for dear life.

Having just cleared the trees, Blériot belly flopped down into a dried-up riverbed, incurring nothing more serious than a few bruises and a damaged ego. It would be the most important flying lesson of Grahame-White's life, one that added another motto to his collection. "A man who keeps his head can never be injured through a fall," said Blériot, as the pair scrambled up the riverbank and began to trudge home toward the aerodrome.

Grahame-White's love of flying was only one of his passions. He had two others: money and women. After completing his flying instruction with Blériot, he returned to England and unsuccessfully competed for the London-to-Manchester prize. A fortnight later, with his star in the ascendancy, Grahame-White had hired Frank Marshall to act as his press agent with specific instructions to "circularize the whole of the British and foreign press to give the flights every publicity." Marshall, however, hadn't circularized to Grahame-White's satisfaction, so he fired him and gave the job to Sydney McDonald. When Marshall took his former employer to court for alleged breach of contract (which suit he won), the British press rather looked down their noses at Grahame-White. Were not English gentlemen renowned the world over for their modesty and self-effacement?

---

* On July 25, 1909, Blériot became the first man to fly across the English Channel. Leaving France early in the morning in a monoplane of his own design, he touched down in England thirty-seven minutes later.

Perhaps, but those two qualities were of little use in the lucrative and competitive business of aviation. Grahame-White had seen the money being offered to those men bold enough to risk their lives chasing records. Blériot was $5,000 better off after his Channel flight, Curtiss's victory in the 1909 International Aviation Cup race had enriched him by a similar amount, and now Paulhan had pocketed the big one, $50,000 for being first to Manchester.

But where Frank Marshall had failed to sufficiently promote the Claude Grahame-White brand, Sydney McDonald succeeded. Throughout the summer of 1910, the flier "scooped the pool," as the British press were wont to say, accepting a $10,000 retainer for a series of exhibition flights in the north of England and winning $5,000 in a distance race in Wolverhampton.

As for Grahame-White's third passion, that required the least effort. He could handle the female of the species far more deftly than he could an airplane, and women were prone to go weak-kneed at the sight of his athletic six-foot frame in the same way men were the moment they spied a flying machine.

He was disarmingly handsome, with a strong mouth, full lips, and deep brown eyes, and he would tuck his shock of dark hair under his cap, then turn the cap back to front. To women, it was another sign of Grahame-White's rakishness; to those of his own sex it was yet more evidence of his insufferable vanity. The man was preposterous, they seethed, more in love with himself than anyone else. But in truth it wasn't so much Grahame-White's undeniable ego that grated on many men, but his perfection. Tall, beautiful, debonair, witty, courageous, rich, talented . . . he damned well had the lot.

At an aviation meet in June at Brooklands racetrack, twenty miles southwest of London, Grahame-White had been at the center of an unseemly squabble between two women who should have known better. For many years he had been on friendly terms with Pauline Chase (to him she was Polly, to her he was Claudie), a twenty-five-year-old American actress with golden hair, a pert nose, and a gleam in her blue eyes that suggested that perhaps she wasn't quite the ingenue she appeared to be at first glance. She certainly knew what she wanted from a man, and it wasn't a good heart or a worthy talent. "I've no time to waste on duffers with no position or money," she had once famously told a reporter.

Chase had made her stage debut at age thirteen at the Casino Theater in New York, but apart from a colorful role as the Pink Pajama Girl in the racy Broadway show *Liberty Belles*, her early career was uneventful. Then in 1904 she was offered the part of First Twin in a new production about to open in London called *Peter Pan*; audiences were captivated by the play and its writer, James Barrie, was similarly entranced by Chase. She became his goddaughter when she was christened in 1906, and the same year Chase was elevated to the title role in *Peter Pan*. The *Times* of London considered that she brought a certain "delicate grace" to the part, and the *Chicago Tribune* found her "distractingly pretty." Her name became synonymous with the little boy who wouldn't grow up, and Grahame-White had lost count of the number of times he had sat in the front row of the Duke of York's Theater scowling at Captain Hook.

On the June day in question, Grahame-White had promised Chase over lunch that he would take her for a spin in his Farman biplane later that afternoon.* Chase was thrilled. Her self-promotion was as ardent as Grahame-White's, and she could picture the following day's headlines: PETER PAN FLIES FOR REAL.

Unfortunately for Chase, when she arrived at Brooklands she was confronted by an indomitable English aristocrat, Lady Abdy, a "rather massive but handsome woman . . . who had taken a violent fancy to Mr. Grahame-White." So violent was her fancy that Lady Abdy had bid £150 ($750) for the chance to fly with her very own Eros in a lunchtime charity auction held in Grahame-White's absence. As he helped Chase up into the seat of his biplane, Lady Abdy thundered across the racetrack and "with an evident dislike of his attractive companion, angrily and abusively asserted her right to the first flight." Grahame-White tried to explain to her ladyship that he needed first to go for a quick test flight, but she was having none of it. Did he really expect her, Lady Abdy, to

---

* Few women had ever flown up to this time, and only one, Baroness de Laroche of France, had her pilot's license. The first American woman licensed was Harriet Quimby in 1911. Before the decade was out, both women were killed in flying accidents.

play second fiddle to a common American actress? Fearing the English-woman might physically assault Chase, Grahame-White "gave in and took-off in a foul mood, with Lady Abdy triumphantly ensconced behind him." Within seconds of taking off, however, the airplane's engine stalled (probably unable to withstand the weight of the "massive but handsome" passenger), and Grahame-White had to crash-land in the sewage farm that bordered the racetrack. Both walked away without a scratch, much to the relief of Pauline Chase, who, with a perfumed glove over her nose, inquired ever so solicitously after the well-being of Lady Abdy.

Grahame-White's charismatic appeal in Europe hadn't gone unnoticed by the promoters of American aviation meetings, and neither had his fondness for Pauline Chase. That she was coming to New York to star in a Broadway production of *Our Miss Gibbs* at the Knickerbocker was doubtless used by the promoters as another reason why Grahame-White should accept an invitation to tour the United States. He sailed from England at the end of August, a few days after he had been paid $50,000 for putting on a show in Blackpool on the northwest coast of England. Hundreds of his fans, mostly female, were quayside to wave him off, and only after several minutes did they quiet enough for him to say a few words to the press corps. "I hope to give a good account of myself in the various competitions," Grahame-White began, at which point a young woman pushed past the reporters and thrust into his hands a good-luck sprig of white heather, asking nothing more in return than a kiss. "I am confident," he continued, "of being able to maintain the reputation of Great Britain, which I regard as being in advance of America with reference to aerial navigation."

When Grahame-White arrived in a rainy Boston on September 1, dozens of American reporters were there to greet him. "Fine flying weather for ducks," he joked, adding that he was eager to get into action at the Boston Meet in two days' time. Ever the consummate showman, Grahame-White patiently answered every question with a smile, and he was particularly attentive to the female correspondents who had braved the weather. His diligence paid off handsomely. The *Boston Post*'s sob sister wrote that Grahame-White "is possessed of a fine athletic figure and is the best set-up man in the whole flock of birdmen who have en-tered the Meet. Unlike the silent, mysterious Americans, who seem to be out of their element on the ground, Grahame-White is thoroughly at home with his two feet everywhere." Another reporter, Phoebe Dwight (this was her nom de plume, her real name being Eleanor Ladd), had a warning for the men of Boston: "If you want your lady-loves' hearts true to you, it's hardly safe to amuse them by taking them out to the avi-ation Meet. For before you know it these hearts may be fluttering along at the tail of an airplane, wherein sits a daring and spectacular young man who has won the title of the matinee idol of the aviation field, Claude Grahame-White."

Dwight's prophecy came to pass, and by the end of the Boston Meet women were falling over themselves to fly with the Englishman. For Grahame-White it was the opportunity to combine several of his pas-sions, and he instructed Sydney McDonald to charge $500 for a five-minute trip. Dozens of women were happy to pay this enormous sum, from Katharine Reid, "a spinsterish schoolmarm who arrived accou-tered for the air in outsize motoring goggles, legs swathed mummywise in burlap," to Marie Campbell, who, in the opinion of the *New York Her-ald*, was "an uncommonly attractive young woman . . . with comely features."

Of even more interest was the sight of Miss Eleonora Sears being helped up into the seat behind Grahame-White. Instantly, the American newspapers identified the twenty-eight-year-old brunette as Grahame-White's feminine equivalent. Sears was a Boston socialite, the great-great-granddaughter of Thomas Jefferson and the daughter of a father regarded as one of the wealthiest men in America. She had many other attributes: good looks, charm, talent, and an insatiable energy. The pre-vious spring she had walked 108 miles in two days from Burlingame to Del Monte in California, and barely a day passed without the papers re-porting on her latest athletic feat. As for potential suitors, they couldn't keep up. In the same week that Grahame-White arrived in Boston, the *Chicago Daily Tribune* reported that Sears, "the society girl who plays polo, golf, tennis, rides to the hounds, shoots, hunts and fences, with a vim and a dash that have won her worldwide reputation, has two rivals for her hand."

One, the paper continued, was the arctic hunter Paul J. Rainey, who had traipsed "almost to the north pole to get her some bear pelts," and the other was Harold Vanderbilt, who had first come across Miss Sears in the fall of 1909 when, as a Harvard law student, he unsuccessfully defended her in a Boston court on charges of overspeeding her automobile. Vanderbilt was not a natural athlete, commented the *Tribune*, but so strong was his ardor that he "had to play tennis in the broiling sun, golf till the soles of his feet cracked and try out occasionally a bucking broncho [*sic*], when he would have much preferred reclining upon a silken divan."

But with Rainey now in the snowy wastes in search of more pelts and Vanderbilt touring Europe, Sears saw nothing wrong in broadening her horizons. Of course, she had to put the opposition in the shade, and her flight time of eleven minutes and thirty seconds was a record for a female passenger in America. "It was perfectly heavenly!" she cried to reporters afterward. "Just the finest thing I ever enjoyed . . . Really, honest and truly, I wasn't scared a bit. Mr. Grahame-White just makes you feel that it is all coming out all right. I knew from the time we left the ground until we landed that I wasn't in the least danger when he was driving." Miss Sears autographed a wing of the plane, as was the habit among Grahame-White's admirers, then handed over the check for $500 with a promise that it wouldn't be the last.

One person who hadn't been persuaded to take a trip with Grahame-White—even a free one—was President Taft. He had been a fascinated spectator at the Boston Meet on September 9 but declined the invitation to fly with a quip about his 250-pound size. TAFT INTEREST PLEASES WHITE was the headline in the *Boston Globe*, leaving one to wonder if the Englishman hadn't now usurped the president in national importance. John "Honey Fitz" Fitzgerald, the mayor of Boston (and the grandfather of John F. Kennedy), accepted an offer and later praised Grahame-White's "perfect control of his machine." The three men got on famously, underlining the Englishman's magnetic personality. Princes, presidents, pressmen, Peter Pan—they all appeared to be under the spell of Grahame-White.

But the nine-day Boston Meet had a serious side, and Grahame-White never let himself be distracted by a pretty face or a big name. He was in

America to win, and at Boston he did so spectacularly, taking four first prizes, including in the blue-ribbon event, the thirty-three-mile race from the airfield to Boston Light* and back. That earned him $10,000, bringing his total earnings during the meet to $22,500. At a time when office clerks earned on average $5 a week, store assistants $7, and railway conductors $10, it was a fantastic sum. Boston threw a dinner in his honor, and a starstruck Mayor Fitzgerald handed over the check along with a silver loving cup on which was inscribed FROM BOSTON FRIENDS, IN ADMIRATION OF HIS SKILL AND SPORTSMANSHIP AS AN AVIATOR.

Grahame-White was now arguably the most famous man in America, and the size of the offers he received reflected his enormous pulling power. He accepted a $50,000 contract to fly at the Brockton Fair in Massachusetts in early October (but turned down a series of speaking engagements with the Keith vaudeville agency at $2,000 a throw), then left for New York with his manager to discuss with the event's promoters the possibility of entering the International Aviation Cup race. Of course, he would make sure he found time to take in a Broadway show, perhaps *Our Miss Gibbs* at the Knickerbocker Theater.

A month later, on the morning of Saturday, October 15, Grahame-White had banked his Brockton check for $50,000 and was a member of the three-man British team that would contest the International Aviation Cup against America and France at Long Island's Belmont Park racecourse.† He intended to leave Washington, D.C., in a couple of days, once he'd fulfilled his engagements, among them an appearance as the guest of honor at a party thrown by Mr. and Mrs. John Barry Ryan at the Cosmos Club that evening.

The six weeks he had thus far spent in the United States had been an unalloyed success. Aside from the money he had made and the women

---

* The ninety-eight-foot lighthouse, the oldest in the United States, is on Little Brewster Island in Boston Harbor.

† The Belmont Park of today bears little resemblance to the original. In the 1950s the clubhouse was demolished and rebuilt, and the course closed between 1963 and 1968 for a $30.7 million renovation. The old grandstand suffered a similar fate to that of the clubhouse, and new parking lots and approach roads were constructed.

he had wooed, Grahame-White had enjoyed the American attitude to
life. The Americans' hard-nosed approach to business and their straight-
talking was more in tune with his own personality than that of the petti-
fogging bureaucrats and out-of-touch imperialists who, in his opinion,
held back Britain. He was in a sunny mood when he arrived at the Benning racetrack for another day's flying. A reporter told him that the airship *America* was under way.

What did Grahame-White think of its chances? "I think Walter Wellman has every chance of success," he replied, adding, "If I should say
what I really think about the future of aeronautics, people would laugh at
me. I believe that the time will come when the public will look back upon
such men as I am and wonder how we could have been so foolish as
to trust our lives in the airplane of today . . . the time will come when
transatlantic airships will be as common as steamers are today, perhaps
more so."

A similar question was being asked that same day approximately seven
hundred miles west of Washington in St. Louis, Missouri, by a reporter
for the city's *Post-Dispatch* newspaper. The respondents were some of
the principal players in the field of American aeronautics, gathered in St.
Louis either because they were aviators flying in the meet or because
they were balloonists preparing to take part in the Fifth International
Balloon Cup race. Harry Honeywell and Alan Hawley fell into the latter
category, but neither could rustle up much enthusiasm for Wellman's
chances. "I hate to make a prediction," said Hawley, who then didn't and
mumbled only, "I wish him success but . . ."

Honeywell was hardly any more enthusiastic, musing that he wouldn't
fancy being in Wellman's shoes if the airship's motor should pack up. Fortunately for the reporter, one of the aviators flying for the Wright brothers'
exhibition team was more forthcoming. "Wellman is taking an awfully
long chance," reckoned Arch Hoxsey. "He may make it, if he doesn't encounter storms and if his equipment is absolutely perfect."

It was Hoxsey's twenty-sixth birthday and he could look back on the
past year with pride. In January he had been one of the thousands riding
the train from Los Angeles to Aviation Field to gape in awe at Louis
Paulhan and Glenn Curtiss. That had been Hoxsey's first sight of a flying

machine, but just as Grahame-White had been mesmerized by his encounter with Wilbur Wright in France, so Hoxsey had undergone an epiphany. He had quit his job as a chauffeur to Los Angeles millionaire John Gates, kissed his widowed mother good-bye at the home they shared in Pasadena, and headed east to Dayton, Ohio, home of the Wrights. Orville and Wilbur had had their share of cranks turning up on their doorstep begging them to teach them how to fly, but Hoxsey was different. For a start he had studied automobile mechanics during his youth, which had led to a stint as a racing driver in Europe. Then there was his appearance, his cheerful blue eyes behind a pince-nez balanced on a prominent nose. Marguerite Martyn, a reporter for the *St. Louis Post-Dispatch*, who had visited the St. Louis Meet earlier in the week to see if any homegrown aviators were capable of giving Grahame-White a run for his money, described Hoxsey as "severely correct in his attire, you would take him for some rather ponderous scholar." Miss Martyn was upbraided when she addressed Hoxsey as "Archie." It was "Arch." Hoxsey was clean-living—he wouldn't have been taken on by the Wrights if he had been anything but—and he would even give his machine a good dusting before each flight. Just about his only vice was a fondness for chewing gum. His jaws were always chomping, either on the ground or up in the air when he was performing one of his stunts with his good friend and fellow Wright flier Ralph Johnstone, from Kansas City.

On Saturday evening Hoxsey was presented with a silver plate at a dinner held in St. Louis's Racquet Club in recognition of all he'd accomplished during the meet, particularly the hundred-mile flight from Springfield, Illinois, to St. Louis, a feat that Hoxsey played down. "The credit is due to the biplane," he told the audience of his three-and-a-half-hour trip a week earlier. "Several men could have made the trip." Then Ralph Johnstone and another of the Wright team, Walter Brookins, received gold medals and warm words of appreciation for all their efforts. Johnstone had entertained the estimated sixty thousand at Kinloch Park that afternoon by flying "repeatedly close to the people in the pavilion, sometimes passing within 10 feet of them. Once he headed straight for one of the pavilions at a low altitude about 5 feet from the ground. For a moment it seemed that he would crash into the light fence and the crowd behind it, but when he was within 15 feet of it, he tilted his elevator and shot up over the people's heads."

The thirty-year-old Johnstone collected his medal and returned to his table, where his wife, a former actress, greeted him with a kiss. This was a rare night off for the couple, a break from their six-year-old son, Ralph junior, who was back at the Jefferson Hotel in the care of a nanny. The pair had met a few years earlier when Johnstone toured America and later Europe as a trick cyclist, earning a decent wage, but nothing compared with what he raked in now as an aviator. Even though he'd been one of the Americans eclipsed by Grahame-White at the Boston Meet, Johnstone had still earned $5,000 for nine days' work. Unfortunately for him, it all went to the Wrights, as did every last dime of prize money won by one of the brothers' exhibition team. In return the aviators were paid $20 a week and a further $50 for every day they flew. The fliers had at first refused the terms, to the amusement of the Wrights. No contract, no airplane. So with a grumble the men all signed, promising as they put pen to paper that they would also not drink or gamble during a meet.

Johnstone had been taught to fly six months' earlier by Walter Brookins on Huffman Prairie in Ohio, where the Wrights had experimented so often with their invention in 1904–5. They made for an odd couple, Brookins and Johnstone, even though they enjoyed one another's company. The twenty-two-year-old Brookins had singularly failed to impress Marguerite Martyn, the *St. Louis Post-Dispatch* reporter, who reckoned that Brooky, as the Wrights called him, was a chip off the old brothers' block, though that was no surprise for Brookins had grown up in the same neighborhood and had been taught at public school by their sister, Katharine. "It may be that the Wrights have succeeded in converting him into one of their perfectly adjusted pieces of machinery," wrote a dismayed Martyn. She found the dark-eyed Brookins "unapproachable" and "diffident" and, worst of all, he displayed "genuine boyish scorn for all things feminine." No, concluded Martyn, Walter Brookins was most definitely not heartthrob material. Johnstone, on the other hand, showed potential. "He is quite the most 'showy' in his personality," wrote Martyn, "and he is the handsomest of the [St. Louis] aviators, and fits the popular description of a matinee idol, but his qualifications are signally reduced by the fact that he has already succumbed to the net we would weave for him." In other words, Johnstone had a wife.

At the St. Louis dinner Johnstone was his usual ebullient self, "happy go-lucky . . . big-hearted, good-natured, one always found him joking and smiling." But it was all an act. In reality his bonhomie was like a bandage that concealed from his wife his sense of impending doom. Neither she nor little Ralph was allowed near his hangar in the final few minutes before a flight because it was there, as he prepared to go up into the air, that Johnstone's fear began to seep out like blood through the bandage. First he became quiet, then mournful, and Hoxsey, though the younger of the pair, would play the part of the mother Johnstone had lost in his youth. Don't worry, Ralph, he would tell him with a tonic smile. Remember what they call us, we're the "Stardust Twins," the best stunt fliers in the world. Nothing will happen to us.

When Brookins collected his gold medal from Albert Lambert, president of the Aero Club of St. Louis, he declined to make a speech: "I do not care to speak quite as much as I care to fly." If Grahame-White had been present, he would have choked on his cognac at such a missed opportunity for self-promotion, but Brookins had the Englishman very much in his sights that evening, even though he was seven hundred miles east in Washington. Brookins still seethed at the memory of his recent role in Boston's Claude Grahame-White show, where, on the orders of the Wrights, Brookins hadn't contested the race to Boston Light and back. "The course is too dangerous for our machines," Wilbur Wright had told reporters later when asked why no American had challenged Grahame-White. The admission humiliated Brookins and the Wrights, as did the sound of thirty-five thousand American voices singing "God Save the King" when Grahame-White stood on the winners' podium. But the hour for revenge was fast approaching, and as Brookins endured the small talk of his fellow diners he was confident that in exactly two weeks' time, on the day of the International Aviation Cup race, Grahame-White would get his comeuppance. The Wrights had just finished testing their latest airplane, and the results had even put a smile— albeit momentarily—on the faces of Wilbur and Orville. Vague news of these trials had leaked out to the press, but as *Fly* magazine reported at the start of October, no one could yet shed much light on the matter: "Orville Wright has been flying at Dayton with a new machine so swift that it recently got away from him, ending its flight in a smash. Nothing definite is known of this machine except that its planes have been trimmed down to their lowest margin of lifting capacity. Who will drive the machine is still a mystery." Not for Brookins, it wasn't.

For Albert Lambert, president of the Aero Club of St. Louis, it was hard to decide which was preferable: the reticence of Walter Brookins or the jabbering of the European balloonists. There was just no shutting them up during Saturday's dinner. One of the French balloonists, forty-one-year-old Alfred Le Blanc, was kicking up a fuss about the Laclede Gas Light Company, the official race suppliers. If the company stuck to its promise to start filling the ten balloons tomorrow and not on Monday, race day, the gas would be stale and the race a disaster. Lambert told Le Blanc he would speak to the company first thing tomorrow. Next in the complainants' queue was Captain Hugo Von Abercron, a short, stocky German with an unmissable mustache who demanded to know why no cash prize was on offer. In Europe such rewards were mandatory, he avowed. Lambert calmed the German and assured him that negotiations were in progress with several prominent businessmen and an announcement would soon be made.* Then Lambert erred by drawing attention to the magnificent silver trophy for which the balloonists were competing. Surely that, a winged female figure with bare breasts and flowing hair, holding the torch of progress in one hand and supporting a elongated gas balloon on her back, was all the incentive required. The Swiss pilot Emil Messner couldn't believe what he was hearing. "It is a beastly work of art," he spluttered. "It looks like a German sausage!"

A ruckus then erupted when Lambert was asked to clarify what would constitute a technical landing during the race: when the balloon's drag rope touched the ground or when the balloon basket did? The correspondent

---

* Nearly $5,000 was collected at the eleventh hour, with $3,000 coming from Gordon Bennett, but donations also came from the Aero Club and $500 from the brewing magnate Adolphus Busch, founder of Anheuser-Busch.

from the *St. Louis Post-Dispatch* looked on in bemusement as "at once a ba-
bel of German, French, Swiss and English arose." Lambert quieted the
confusion by calling for a meeting of the aeronauts the following morning
at the Jefferson Hotel, but the beleaguered president's problems weren't
quite over. "In the midst of the tumult," reported the *Post-Dispatch*, "the
German entrants could be heard calling for hay."

Lambert looked nonplussed. Why on earth did they need hay? To
keep their feet warm, they replied in unison, explaining that it could get
very cold during a balloon race. Lambert guaranteed them that they
would have all the hay they needed. Once calm had been restored to the
dinner, a second round of speeches began. Von Abercron proposed a
toast to his compatriot Oscar Erbslöh, winner of the 1907 International
Balloon Cup race and recently killed in an airship accident. Then one of
the American balloonists, Alan Hawley, rose to his feet and on behalf of
the United States wished everyone a safe race. "The best advice I can offer you," he said, "is to keep close to the ground." The final speaker was
the Swiss balloonist Colonel Theodore Schaeck, at fifty-four the oldest
competitor in the race. He and Emil Messner had won the cup in 1908
with a 750-mile flight from Berlin to Norway. The voyage had lasted
seventy-two hours, forty of which had been spent drifting across the
North Sea. So sure had they been that they would ditch and die in the
water, Messner and Schaeck had written farewell letters to their families.
Grahame-White might have balked at the vulnerability inherent in a free
balloon, but putting one's fate in the lap of the gods was the beauty of
the sport in Schaeck's view. "The airplane is doing great things," he told
his audience of balloonists and aviators, "but I notice that the spherical
still exists. Besides, your airplane has still to remain in the air seventy
hours or more!"

Some of the balloonists banged their glasses on the table and cried,
"Hear, hear!" casting playful grins at Hoxsey and Johnstone, who smiled
and applauded Schaeck back to his seat. Slowly the party began to break
up, the aviators mindful of a need for an early start tomorrow so they
could organize the transportation of their machines to New York. The
balloonists, too, couldn't afford to wake with a sore head if they had to
be at the Jefferson Hotel at ten A.M. to resolve the question of a technical
landing. But a few men lingered over their drinks, and among the topics

of conversation was Walter Wellman. Had they heard the latest? According to that evening's edition of the *St. Louis Post-Dispatch*, he was making capital progress at fifteen knots an hour. What was more, a wireless message from the airship had confirmed that the engines were working well and the sea was calm.

CHAPTER TWO

Let's Stick by the Ship

Sunday, October 16, 1910

WHEN THE BALLOONISTS began arriving for their meeting with Albert Lambert shortly before ten A.M., the local papers were in the lobby of the Jefferson Hotel. One story dominated the morning news, encapsulated by the headline in the *St. Louis Republic*: WELLMAN'S AIRSHIP MAY BE DESTROYED BY TERRIFIC GALE. Alongside the bleak article was the photograph of Wellman and his crew taken twenty-four hours earlier, just before they climbed up the rope ladder into the car, and underneath was another, slightly smaller headline: 100 DEAD IN STORM THAT SWEEPS CUBA. The hurricane had ripped through the Caribbean on Friday, killing scores and causing over a million dollars' worth of damage in Havana alone when seas broke through the city's Malecón seawall. Now, the paper warned, the hurricane was tearing up the eastern coast and the *America* airship was slap bang in its path.

In the first hours after their departure from Atlantic City, everything had gone according to plan on board the *America*. Wellman stationed himself as lookout in the lifeboat, passing the time with Jack Irwin, the wireless operator, who had on two thick woolen earphone pads. The young Australian sent his first brief message at eleven A.M.: "We have sighted

Long Island and are driving ahead into the northeast." It was picked up by Robert Miller at the wireless station on Million Dollar Pier, where the families of the crew had assembled after the airship had disappeared from sight. Two hours later Irwin informed Miller that the fog was lifting, and at one P.M. he tapped out a message to their support team: "All did nobly. We are doing our best to repay you for your support."

Up in the car Simon was delighted to find that steering a ship in the air was exactly the same as steering a ship in the water. He had cut two circular holes in the celluloid windows to enhance his field of vision, and with the fog now gone he had a magnificent view of the ocean. With Vaniman and his two assistants aft in the engine room, and Wellman and Irwin down below in the lifeboat, Simon was left alone with his thoughts. Conversation was all but impossible because of the noise of the motors, but a few minutes after midday the engines stopped. Vaniman shouted through the speaking tube that it was nothing to worry about, just a bit of sand in the motor. Fred Aubert took advantage of the pause to prepare a round of ham sandwiches, and Wellman asked Irwin to send progress reports to the *London Daily Telegraph*, the *New York Times*, and the *Chicago Record-Herald*.

The rest of the daylight hours had been unexceptional, but dusk revealed a disconcerting sight; illuminating the sky was a steady shower of red-hot sparks from the *America*'s exhaust. The fireworks display was pretty, but if just one stray spark landed in some cranny of the airship, they would be blown to kingdom come. Wellman had rushed into the engine room, but Vaniman had just shrugged and reassured his skipper that they were perfectly safe. Then at eight P.M., as fog thickened, Simon heard a shout from Wellman through the speaking tube that connected the car to the lifeboat: "Ship ahead!" Simon peered through his two small, circular holes and just made out a large, four-masted schooner not more than a hundred yards away. The vessel was the Boston-registered *Bullard*, bound for Norfolk and skippered by Captain Sawyer, who had heard of Wellman but had no idea the epic quest was under way. He and his crew thought the light they could see bearing down on them came from a mast of a large steamer, so they "ran about shouting and yelling . . . hoping that its lookout might see us in time to avoid a collision."

As the sound of the airship's engines grew louder, Sawyer and his men still couldn't see the ship that they now felt certain was going to run them down. The skipper later confessed there had been pandemonium on deck as they braced themselves for the collision. And then suddenly, "out of the darkness and mist shot a big aerial phantom . . . the thing was such a big surprise for all hands that we were knocked off our pins." The sailors dropped to their knees, clasped their hands in prayer, and looked up in terror as the airship passed above them. Over the noise of the engines, Sawyer also heard the airship scraping the topmasts as she veered away. Up in the car Simon knew they had come perilously close to death, but the Englishman in him couldn't resist making light of the incident in his log: "I don't suppose they had heard about us, and I would like to hear their remarks now!"

In the early hours of Sunday the *America* pushed on east at a steady 15 miles an hour. They were on schedule to fulfill Wellman's prediction of reaching England in ten days. At four A.M. the engines were turned off and everyone—save the lookout—got his head down for a couple of hours' rest. Simon crawled into his hammock after a twenty-hour shift, "too tired even to dream," and fell asleep in seconds as the airship drifted peacefully northeast.

Wellman shook Simon awake. The two-hour sleep had felt more like two minutes, but the anticipation of another day's adventure quickly swept the fatigue from his body. As Simon sat down at the controls, Vaniman started the motors and they were on their way once more. By eight A.M. the fog had thinned and Simon spotted a fishing boat, and the ripples of shoal water underneath, "which proved we were in Martha's Vineyard, which is between Nantucket Lightship and the mainland." Wellman was cock-a-hoop when he learned of their position. There would be no humiliation in pulling up short on the coast of New England, and now the broad Atlantic stretched before them. He told Aubert to cook breakfast and to be sure to make it a good one: ham, eggs, and strong coffee all round. Simon reckoned it the finest breakfast he had had in a long time, one that fed his morale as much as his stomach. The biggest unknown before their voyage had been the *America*'s engines, but they had been faultless in the twenty-four hours since their depar-

ture. Why shouldn't they remain so? For the first time, Simon succumbed to temptation and pictured the faces of his friends and family
when he arrived in England.

It was around ten A.M.—just as the balloonists sat down with Albert
Lambert in St. Louis's Jefferson Hotel—when things started to go wrong
for the *America*. Since dawn the weather had been becoming ever more
aggressive, but now the breeze was a wind and heavy gusts from the
southwest struck the airship. Each blow sent the craft shooting forward at
an alarming speed as the equilibrator "jumped from wave to wave, fifty to
eighty feet each leap." Sometimes the equilibrator dived beneath the
ocean, and the airship's cables were pulled taut for a few seconds until it
leaped clear. Then the sudden release of tension sent the car rocking from
side to side with Simon struggling to remain upright in his seat. He looked
fearfully around him as the car creaked and groaned with every fresh gust.
Huddled in the bowels of the lifeboat, Wellman and Jack Irwin felt themselves drop ever closer to the whitecapped waves of the Atlantic.

If the lifeboat hit the surface, they knew it would be torn loose from its
shackles, portending a miserable end to their adventure, and their lives. It
was too dangerous to try to climb back into the car with the wind so
strong, so through the speaking tube Wellman ordered the crew to lighten
the craft's load. Vaniman and this team of engineers jettisoned some gasoline, and for a while the *America* regained its buoyancy. "It's a pity to see
that good fuel going to waste," Simon wrote in his log, "but we have to do
it to save the ship." Then he added as an afterthought, "I would like to
have some of those longshore 'old women' here with us now."

At noon they dumped more gasoline to lighten the sagging *America*,
but by two o'clock on Sunday afternoon they had passed through the eye
of the storm, and a relieved Wellman and Irwin scurried up the ladder
into the car. The strain of the last few hours was etched into every one of
their faces, and Vaniman in particular seemed upset by their tribulation.

Wellman asked Simon for an estimate of their position, and he replied
that they had covered 140 miles since the sighting of the fishing boat at
eight A.M. In the last couple of hours they had been pushed northeast and
were drawing near to the transatlantic shipping lanes. Vaniman gave a
nervous cry and asserted that the time had come to issue a Mayday over

the wireless and to then launch the lifeboat. Wellman disagreed, accepting that while they didn't now have enough gasoline to get them across the ocean, they could still make a run for England if the wind changed to out of the west. Vaniman laughed, a short disbelieving laugh, and challenged his captain to put it to the vote. Wellman turned to the first man, Lewis Loud, and asked if he wished to abandon ship or remain aloft.

"Let's stick by the ship," said Loud.

"I am with you for fighting it out," said Simon.

"So am I," said Irwin.

"And I, too," said Aubert.

To lift the spirits of the crew Wellman told Aubert to rustle up a hot meal. Later, as they sat back replete and momentarily relaxed, Aubert spoke wistfully to Simon of his girlfriend. How he wished he were back in Atlantic City, the two of them on the hotel veranda holding hands. He looked Simon in the eye and asked, "What our are chances?"

"Very good," replied Simon with a reassuring smile.

Darkness brought a drop in temperature and in height as the cold contracted the airship's gas. As they began to dip toward the sea, Wellman ordered the smallest of the three motors, the twelve-horsepower donkey engine, to be broken up and heaved overboard along with more gasoline. Then he joined Irwin in the lifeboat, and for a long time the pair crouched in the swaying vessel trying to establish contact with a shore station or passing ship. Frequently they heard their signal letter *W* repeated over the airwaves, but they were out of range to reply. All they could do was listen impotently as ships flashed back the same message to one another: "Any news of the *America?*"

Exasperated, Wellman began to climb the ladder to the car. Suddenly his sheath knife snagged on one of the rungs, and as he tried to free himself, he slipped, losing grip with both hands and feet. Only the jammed knife prevented his falling into the ocean. It felt to Wellman that his legs dangled a long time above the Atlantic, but in seconds Loud and Aubert reached down and hauled him up. For a minute or so no one spoke as they all recovered their breath, then the two engineers began to laugh. Simon joined in, and so did Wellman, his relief giving way to exhilaration at his narrow escape. "This crew seems to be made up of the right kind of men," wrote Simon in his log, shortly after he came off duty, "and I never wish to be shipmates with a better bunch."

When the meeting of the balloonists at the Jefferson Hotel broke up at lunchtime, there was, to the undisguised relief of Albert Lambert, unanimity, with not a disgruntled European to be seen or heard. They had all agreed on the definition of a landing during the race, and Lambert dispatched one of his assistants to type out a press release on the subject:

- *If the basket touches the ground, a landing is made.*
- *If the drag rope becomes entangled in trees or trails along the ground for fifteen minutes, a landing is constituted.*
- *If a balloon alights in a lake or a river, a landing is made.*
- *If a balloon descends in salt water, it is disqualified.*

Lambert had also happily informed the ten teams that the Laclede Gas Light Company had agreed to reschedule the inflation of the balloons from Sunday afternoon to early Monday morning. This news, coupled with the announcement that the winner of the race would receive $2,000, the runner-up $1,500 and the third-place balloon $1,250, sent the balloonists off to lunch in great cheer. One of the French competitors, Walther de Mumm, a scion of the champagne family, produced a couple of bottles with which they celebrated a harmonious morning's work.

After lunch the men retired to their rooms and the comfort of soft beds and clean linen. All of the ten two-man crews were experienced balloonists, gloomily aware that that they might not get the chance to lay their head on a feather pillow for several days.

If the men couldn't sleep, then they checked and rechecked their provisions and equipment. Had they the right quantity of coffee and an adequate number of canned soups? Would it be better to take more apples and fewer oranges? Should they pack a quart of whiskey or a bottle of crème de menthe? They cleaned their revolvers for the umpteenth time, made sure they had the correct maps, included a spare pair of gloves (just to be safe), and laid out on the floor of their room the most precious items of all: barometer, thermometer, compass, barograph, and an air-recording aneroid barometer. They lovingly cleaned and polished each one, then repacked them in their cases.

A little while later they'd unpack everything and do it all again, just to occupy their minds and ward off the inevitable feelings of apprehension that collected in the hollows of their imaginations like pockets of mist on a fall morning. As one of the American entrants busied himself on Sunday afternoon, he stoutly refused to entertain thoughts of the fate that had befallen him in the 1908 International Balloon Cup race. Instead, thirty-six-year-old Augustus Post, copilot to Alan Hawley in the balloon *America II*, pored over a large map of the Great Lakes region, supplied to him the previous week by Major Hersey of the Milwaukee Weather Bureau.

Post was handsome, with black hair and eyes and a goatee that made him look more like a French musketeer than an American balloonist. His personality was just as exotic. He was a poet, raconteur, singer, an entertainer who could imitate the sounds of everything from airplanes to canaries, and an actor who had appeared in theaters across America.

Having graduated from Harvard Law School, Post had returned to his native New York City and bought a Waverley electric car, reputed to be the city's first horseless carriage. A few years later at the 1900 Paris Exhibition he took to the air for the first time in a balloon, and in 1905 Post became not only one of the founding members of the Aero Club of America, but also its first secretary. Among his friends he counted the Wright brothers and Glenn Curtiss, and that fact alone—his ability to be on good terms with these implacable enemies—was proof of his affability. Everyone liked Augustus Post, except his estranged wife, Emma, who in October 1910 was waiting for their marriage to be annulled in a New York court. To her, Post was nothing but a showboater, a man who "loved the limelight . . . [and] the society of other women."

Post wasn't troubled by his wife's vow to squeeze him for every last penny. Whatever happened, it couldn't be worse than what he'd experienced on October 11, 1908.

There were many ways to die in a balloon, as the *New York Times* had insensitively pointed out in July 1910 when it listed the thirty-five fatalities in the last four years. One could drown, as Paul Nocquet had in April 1906 when his balloon dropped into Gilgo Bay in Long Island; one might be struck by lightning, as poor Lieutenant Ulivelli was near Rome in 1907; one could explode in a ball of fire as two British balloonists had during an exhibition in London in 1908; or one might be swept out to sea, to vanish forever, as was the case with Frank Elkins in 1909, last seen heading out over the Pacific Ocean.

Perhaps the most terrifying prospect of all was the plummet, the sudden fall from the sky with the balloonists powerless to do anything but scream. Aviators could, at least, struggle with the controls of their machine, allowing themselves a sliver of a sense that their fate was in their own hands.

When Augustus Post had been invited by Holland Forbes to be his copilot in the 1908 International Balloon Cup race, Post had accepted without hesitation. Forbes was a good man in Post's estimation, the vice president of the Aero Club of America, and an accomplished sportsman who owned his own balloon, the *Conqueror*. The pair sailed to Germany, spending much of the voyage with their heads in a series of foreign-language phrase books they had been sent by the race organizers. Taking off from Berlin, the contestants were liable to end up anywhere from Scandinavia to the Sahara, so it was advisable to be as much of a polyglot as possible.

The day of the race was a Sunday, warm and sunny, and Berlin was teeming with spectators. The *Conqueror* was the ninth balloon to start, and at 3:40 P.M. it rose into the air to a great cheer. When the balloon reached four thousand feet, Post noted the height in his logbook and also entered the barometer reading. He heard Forbes cluck with delight and say, "How nicely it works!" Suddenly Post felt the basket tremble. He looked up and saw the bottom of the balloon beginning to shrivel as a large tear appeared on one side of the varnished cotton. "She's gone," said Post calmly. As the gas rushed out of the tear "like the blowing off of a steam boiler," Post jumped to his feet and reached for the appendix cord, a rope that acted as a safety mechanism and tightened if pressure was lost so the balloon would keep its shape and not fold up. But the appendix cord hadn't been designed for such a catastrophe as they now faced. With the balloon holed, turning it into a giant parachute was their only small chance of survival. Post slipped the cord through its knot and it rose inside to the top of the balloon.

To the tens of thousands of spectators on the ground death appeared assured. A woman standing close to the correspondent from the *New York Times* screamed, "They are killed!" and turned her face from the sky. The reporter watched transfixed as for two thousand feet they "shot down like a bullet." In the basket Forbes began to cut away the bags of ballast sand that hung from the four corners in a pathetic attempt to halt their descent. Post queried, what about the spectators below, might not they be hit by falling bags? Forbes ignored Post and continued to off-load their ballast. Post looked up at the balloon, begging it to come to their aid, and suddenly it did. The *New York Times* reporter gasped with thousands of others as "the envelope appeared to take, first, a triangular shape, and then was transformed into a sort of parachute at the top of the net, and the progress of the wrecked balloon was considerably ar-rested." Post and Forbes felt they were under a large mushroom as the netting over the balloon held firm against the cloth, which struggled to get through its meshes. They were no longer traveling at the speed of a bullet, but as the wind pushed them away from the field toward the city, it seemed to Post "as if some great giant was hurling buildings, streets, churches, up at us with all his might." For several moments they skimmed the rooftops of first one street, then another, with Post and Forbes clinging for dear life to the concentrating ring above their heads. The basket smashed at an angle into a chimney, bounced upward, and dropped through the tiled roof of No. 7 Wilhelmstrasse in the suburb of Friedenau. Neither man dared move in case their descent had been only temporarily checked. Warily they got to their knees and peered over the basket's rim. They appeared to be stuck fast in a hole in the roof with the cloth draped over the chimney. Forbes clambered out onto the flat roof, unslung his camera, and started to take some photographs: of the bal-loon, of the house, of Berlin. "The whole world," he had decided, "looked beautiful."

It was the last time Augustus Post had worked with Forbes, a balloonist Post had come to realize was dangerously cavalier. One of the sandbags cut from their basket had landed on a baby carriage, and only the infant's nurse's quick grab of the child in it moments before the impact had prevented a ghastly accident. Moreover, why had the balloon dropped in the first place? When the pair arrived home a fortnight after their miraculous escape, Post refused to comment on the incident but his partner had plenty to say to the press. "It is inexplicable to me why the balloon should burst," Forbes told reporters on the quayside. "None of the aeronautical experts to whom we referred the matter can find any reason for it." Then he embellished the story with an untrue account of their crashing through a roof and finding themselves in a woman's boudoir. "The lady," he said with a chortle, "was unfortunately out."

Unbeknownst to Forbes, Gaston Hervieu, a respected French balloonist, had widely been quoted in the American press attributing the calamity to "the length of the appendix, which increased the pressure at the top of the balloon and caused it to burst. I consider such experiments dangerous before proper experience has been acquired." In other words, Forbes had recklessly endangered his life and Post's with his foolish tampering.

Post's enthusiasm for aeronautics hadn't dimmed with his near-death experience, but he vowed to choose his partners with more circumspection. In one of the many articles he wrote for aviation publications, Post declared, "The successful make-up of a team in a long-distance balloon-race depends on many qualifications, mental almost more than physical. For many hours perhaps, two men, cut loose from the earth, sharing a profound solitude, must have one mind and one motive, and must act instinctively with a precision that admits of no hesitation and no discussion . . . Your companion must be one with whom you are willing to share a great memory—and that is in itself something of a test of one's opinion."

By the summer of 1910 Post was as much an aviator as he was a balloonist. Earlier in the year he had become the thirteenth American to solo in an airplane, and he had not long acquired his flying license when Alan Hawley appeared at the door of his Manhattan apartment.

Hawley had a job persuading Post to join him as his copilot in the balloon *America II*. Even though they had flown together—and finished fourth—in the 1907 International Balloon Cup race, Post now had other ambitions. He was about to journey to Boston to compete in the Boston Air Show, and was of half a mind to enter the Chicago to New York airplane race, for which the prize was $25,000.*

Hawley lacked Post's flamboyance. Where one had an exotic goatee, the other had a modest mustache. Post was a poet and an actor, a man who went running each day to keep in shape; Hawley was a sober-suited stockbroker, less impulsive and more cerebral than his friend, and his portly frame betrayed his fondness for a long lunch. The two were opposites in physique and temperament, but they complemented one another perfectly.

What won Post over was the revelation that the balloon would be the *America II*, which had won the USA the International Balloon Cup in 1909. It was considered a "lucky balloon," and Post couldn't resist its pull. He agreed to join Hawley after the Boston Air Show, and in the second week of September they were reunited in Indianapolis.

On September 17 the *America II* and eight other balloons rose into the air hoping to win the right to represent the USA in the International Balloon Cup the following month. The selection procedure was simple: the three balloons that covered the greatest distance before landing would be chosen. One by one the balloons came to earth, first the *New York* after only 185 miles, then the *Pennsylvania II*, then *Hossler* . . . until only the *America II* remained airborne. Post and Hawley finally landed in Warrenton, Virginia, 450 miles east of Indianapolis, after a flight time of forty-eight hours and twenty-three minutes. It was a new American endurance record for a balloon, and Hawley told reporters they could have gone on longer but came down "for fear of being blown into Chesapeake Bay." It had been a memorable trip, but, he added, "While we were passing above Noble County, Ohio, on Sunday evening I distinctly heard two bullets whistle past my ears . . . The government should take steps at once to protect balloonists who are likely to be killed at any time by ignorant or vicious countrymen who persist in firing at them as they fly above farms." That he and Post had

---

* The *New York Times* had offered $25,000 to the winner of the Chicago to New York airplane race, but the daunting nine-hundred-mile distance deterred everyone.

not been shot down was pure luck, and for that they thanked the continued good fortune of *America II*.

In New York there was little interest in the balloon race about to start in
St. Louis, nor was there much enthusiasm for Walter Wellman and what
the *New York Sun* called his "mad enterprise." All eyes were on Belmont
Park and the forthcoming International Aviation Meet, even though it was
still a week away. The Sunday edition of the *New York American* carried a
photograph of Glenn Curtiss greeting two of the French aviators, Count
Jacques de Lesseps and Hubert Latham, as they stepped off the steamship
La Lorraine twenty-four hours earlier. Both men had expressed their pleas-
ure to be in New York and their eagerness to begin tuning up their aircraft.
The race organizers took the Frenchmen to lunch at the Café Martin, and
later, when the six-foot-tall count, who was the tenth child of Ferdinand de
Lesseps, builder of the Suez Canal, arrived at his apartment at the St. Regis
Hotel, he was asked by a reporter what had impressed him most about
New York. "Your Fifth Avenue and the constant stream of pretty women
passing along it," replied the twenty-seven-year-old, with the earnest appreciation of a connoisseur. "I think your American women are the per-
sonification of elegance and 'chic.' They are admirable."

Hubert Latham had checked into the the Knickerbocker Hotel (now
known as 6 Times Square), an Astor establishment on the corner of
Broadway and Forty-second Street, and he was soon sitting at the bar admiring the magnificent twenty-eight-foot-long mural, *Old King Cole and
His Fiddlers Three*, by Maxfield Parrish,* and chatting to the bar steward in
flawless English. Born in Paris in 1883 to an English father and a French
mother, Latham was a slim, well-dressed man with a pallid complexion,
visible evidence of his consumption. A Parisian physician had given him a
year to live—eighteen months ago. Latham's grip on life was still strong,
and he intended to keep squeezing until the pips squeaked. He was rarely
to be seen without a glass in one hand and his long ivory cigarette holder
in the other. The ivory reputedly came from the tusks of an elephant shot
by Latham during an expedition to the Sudan in 1905. Big game had been

---

* Parrish received $5,000 for painting the mural in 1906. In 1935 it was moved to the
St. Regis Hotel, and in 2007 it was restored at a cost of $100,000.

Latham's first love upon graduating from Oxford University in 1904, but in 1908 he witnessed one of Wilbur Wright's flights at Le Mans and, like Claude Grahame-White, fell in love with the airplane. He bought shares in Gastembide & Mengin, a struggling company set up by a French mechanical engineer called Leon Levavasseur, who had constructed a lightweight monoplane that had crashed in every trial. Latham cut a deal with Levavasseur: "I will try the machine for you and continue flying with it, no matter how often I smash it. If I am killed, all the better—but you must repair it for me."

The crashes were frequent in the first few weeks of the partnership, but Latham survived each one, crawling out from under the wreckage with one hand already reaching for his cigarette case. Steadily, Levavasseur ironed out the flaws in his airplane (christened the *Antoinette* in honor of the wife of Monsieur Gastembide) until, in June 1909, Latham flew fifty miles without a hitch. The following month he'd left France in an attempt to win the $5,000 prize on offer for the first man to fly across the English Channel. Thousands cheered his departure and thousands waited for his arrival, but it was not to be. Six miles off the French coast the airplane's fifty-horsepower engine coughed like a consumptive and died. Latham made a perfect landing on a flat sea, and as the wooden machine bobbed gently up and down, he lit a cigarette and waited for his rescue.

Latham was one of several aviators whose photograph appeared in the *New York Sun* on Sunday alongside an article that listed the names of the twenty-six fliers slated to appear at the meet. The paper also gave details of the money on offer: "The cash prizes amount to $72,300 [approximately $1,152,500 today]. The aviators will also receive a percentage of the gate receipts. One special prize of $10,000 is offered for a flight from Belmont Park to the Statue of Liberty and back. Another prize of $5,000 will be awarded to the aviator who reaches or exceeds an altitude of 10,000 feet. Other prizes will be given for duration, distance, speed, cross-country flights and passenger carrying."

But the *New York Herald*, which was owned by Gordon Bennett,* was

---

* Gordon Bennett was the then sixty-nine-year-old publisher of the *New York Herald*, the paper founded by his father. Though Gordon served in the navy during the Civil

keen to point out that the Belmont Park event would be more than just a "Show," a few days of inconsequential entertainment given over to playboys and stuntmen. Much more was at stake, proclaimed the paper in an article headlined NATIONS BATTLE FOR AIR CHAMPIONSHIP:

"So great is the interest in the secrets that are expected to be revealed that army officers, not only of this government, but of France, England and Germany, will be students of what takes place there. The first practical use of the flying machine being for military purposes, this demonstration of types designed by the greatest constructors in the world will add something like a final word on their relative values."

The contingent of American army officers planning to attend at Belmont Park wished they could share the *Herald*'s bullishness, but they had encountered too many shortsighted, penny-pinching bureaucrats of late to hold out much hope for the "final word."

In February 1910 the *New York Times* had run an article about the visit to the White House of a delegation of American aviation specialists, including Cortlandt Field Bishop, president of the Aero Club, and Brigadier General James Allen, chief signal officer of the army. Their goal was to persuade President Taft to increase the spending on airplanes and dirigibles, and the paper stood squarely behind them, even going so far as to print the respective aerial strengths of the major powers in the hope of shaming the government into action: "Germany has now in military service 14 dirigibles of six different models and 5 airplanes; France has 7 dirigibles and 29 airplanes; Italy 3 dirigibles and 7 airplanes; Russia 3 dirigibles and 6 airplanes; Austria 2 dirigibles and 4 airplanes; England 2 dirigibles and 2 airplanes . . . the United States has just 1 dirigible and 2 airplanes."

Taft had lent a sympathetic ear to the delegation but refused to accede to their request. Let's wait and see how aviation develops in the next year or two was the gist of his demurral. A motivating factor in Taft's decision was his wish to concentrate the United States' energy and finances on Latin America and Eastern Asia, what he called his Dollar Diplomacy. The USA was heavily investing in both regions in an attempt to create

---

War, he gained a reputation as something of a playboy in later years, and in 1877 a New York socialite ended their engagement after a particularly debauched evening. He spent the rest of his years in Paris and died in 1918.

stability, while at the same time promoting American commercial interests at the expense of European ones, and Taft saw no reason why he should divert money to the purchase of airplanes. That Europe was becoming increasingly unruly—what with Serbia recognizing Austria's claim to Bosnia, Turkey suppressing unrest in Albania, and an arms race between Britain and Germany—was of little interest to Taft. In his opinion war in Europe would not affect the United States.

Yet a month later American papers reported that the French Senate had agreed to increase their military aviation budget by $145,000, and in June the *Baltimore American* carried a dispatch from Berlin stating that $3 million was being spent by the German military in preparation for large-scale aerial maneuvers later that year. The correspondent warned, "German military experts are visionaries . . . their imaginations teem with the dreams of the future in the air. They see the heavens crowded with aerial crafts of all sorts . . . [a] complete aerial navy consisting of big battleships with tubes for casting down explosives, swift clippers of the clouds, corresponding to the present high-speed naval cruisers, small torpedo craft and transport vessels."

The army asked Glenn Curtiss to put on a display during an Atlantic City meet in July. Curtiss was happy to oblige, only too aware of the potential riches that lay in store for his airplane manufacturing company if the government's head could be pried from the sand. On July 12 Curtiss climbed up onto the small, hard seat of his biplane and took off toward the Atlantic coast in search of the anchored yacht *John E. Mehrer II*, which, for the purposes of the demonstration, would be an enemy battleship. The oranges heavy in the pockets of Curtiss's jacket were his bombs. Flying at 45 mph, he approached the yacht at three hundred feet and dropped the first orange. It landed three feet from the officials gathered on the deck. The remaining "bombs" were released with similar accuracy, and later Colonel William Jones told the *Chicago Daily Tribune*, "The air machine has proved its efficacy."

Emboldened by the success of Curtiss's trial, Major General Leonard Wood, chief of staff of the army, announced that efforts to obtain funds from Congress "at the next session for an equipment of airplanes would be doubled." Wood let it be known he was demanding nothing short of half a million dollars for what he called an urgent need.

Alarmed at the prospect of a cut in its funding, the U.S. navy launched an offensive against the airplane. Rear Admiral Robley D. Evans wrote a column for the *Boston Sunday American* in early September in which he ridiculed the idea that the airplane posed a threat to the navy. "A few oranges or confetti bombs have been dropped from a height of a hundred or a hundred and fifty feet [*sic*]," he wrote, "much to the amusement of the nursery maids and children who saw the experiment . . . Any good baseball player would have caught the oranges, and at the distance from which they were dropped the aviator would have been unseated by the return throw." Rear Admiral Evans concluded that the experiments were "absolutely futile" and asserted to Americans that, provided they trusted his expertise, "they will not consider the danger to battleships very serious."

Congress agreed with Evans and turned down Major General Wood's demand for more funds, but the American army found an unlikely ally in Claude Grahame-White. Before leaving England he had berated the British government for exhibiting similar backwardness, and in America he continued to warn that a frightening new chapter in warfare was about to be opened, and it wouldn't be confined to Europe. At a dinner given by the National Press Club in Washington in early October, Grahame-White had told his audience of reporters and high-ranking military figures, "Eventually the airplane will be the feature in all wars. Guns and powerful bombs will be carried on them, and the greatest of the modern battleships will be useless."

On the afternoon of Sunday, October 16, however, Claude Grahame-White had far more pressing matters on his mind than the role of the airplane in future wars; there were women to be entertained, so he spent the afternoon at the Benning racetrack doing just that. The *New York Herald* described how Grahame-White stopped his motor at fifteen hundred feet "and made one of his sensational sweeping dives in front of the club house lawn, landing lightly on the ground just as Miss Katherine Letterman, social secretary to Mrs. Taft, cried out some words of encouragement." Leaving Miss Letterman blushing like a besotted schoolgirl, Grahame-White shot back into the air and repeated the stunt to a thunderstorm of wild applause. The correspondent from the *Herald* was as rapt as everyone else, but nonetheless he couldn't help but notice that among the onlookers was Pauline Chase, and she appeared to have one eye on the sky and the other on Marie Campbell, the "uncommonly attractive young woman" who had ridden with Grahame-White at Boston. Curiously, Miss Campbell had now turned up in Washington.

CHAPTER THREE

A Sort of Bleeding to Death

Monday, October 17, 1910

IN THE EARLY HOURS of Monday the wind picked up and shifted direction from the northwest to the northeast. Beneath the *America* the empty lifeboat sparred with the ocean, sometimes getting caught by a rising wave, on other occasions swaying just out of reach. The crew jettisoned more gasoline, and as Wellman watched it stream down into the sea, he silently accepted that with it went their chances of ever reaching England. He knew as well as Vaniman that it was ludicrous to imagine they could drift three thousand miles across the Atlantic and pop in for tea with the king at Buckingham Palace. But Vaniman wouldn't end up in the metaphorical stocks, pelted with public scorn when—if—they returned home having done no more than flirt with the Atlantic. He alone, Walter Wellman, the man whose much publicized attempt to reach the north pole by airship in January 1909 had lasted a mere thirty-three hours, would have to endure another rubbishing in the press, similar to the one he'd suffered the year before when, among other things, he'd been labeled a "fake" and "a four-flusher." He eased himself into his hammock, removed his spectacles, and rubbed his weary eyes. Death or humiliation, that was the choice he faced.

As Wellman fell into a troubled sleep, Murray Simon, the English navigator, took the watch. At four A.M. he wrote in his logbook, "The wind has eased considerably and things begin to look joyful again. While I'm on watch everybody else is asleep. All the crew wake up one by one and I assure them all is well and there are prospects of a fine day." With the engines off and the wind down, the silence of the night was matched only by the magnificence of the dawn. Even in their parlous situation, Simon felt moved to comment on "a beautiful sunrise and I quite enjoyed it." Uplifted by the sight, he descended the rope ladder into the lifeboat and cooked himself breakfast.

Wellman woke at six thirty A.M. to the first piece of good news since they'd left Atlantic City two days earlier—the sun was out.

At midday Simon took advantage of the sun to calculate their position: thirty-eight degrees six minutes north, sixty-six degrees twenty-one minutes west, "about 400 miles east of the Hampton roads," as he noted in his log. Half an hour later Jack Irwin picked up two shore stations calling the *America*'s signal letter, one in Siasconset and the other in Cape Cod. Over and over they repeated the *W*, but Irwin was unable to make himself heard no matter how loud he shouted into the receiver or how hard he banged the side of the boat in frustration. The rest of the crew joined him in the lifeboat and listened mutely as they heard one of the shore stations "tell us great anxiety exists on land regarding our welfare."

When the distant voice died, all they could hear was the soft smack of the swell against the hull of the lifeboat. Thoughts of home cast a shadow over them far greater than that of the airship, until eventually Wellman broke the silence with a request for lunch. Fred Aubert dished out six plates of smoked ham and dry biscuits, and afterward Simon sat back in the lifeboat and enjoyed a quiet smoke as Wellman outlined their plan.

For the last few hours the *America* had been running fifteen to eighteen knots per hour with a southeasterly wind, which meant they were headed toward Bermuda. They would hold the remaining gasoline in reserve for what Wellman called "the final struggle" to reach the island. Simon suppressed a laugh for the sake of the others. He admired Wellman's calm determination, but as a sailor long in the tooth he knew that the chances of reaching Bermuda were negligible.

While the rest of the men napped in the warmth of the afternoon sun, Simon retrieved from the car his logbook and camera. First he took a snapshot of the airship, then one of Kiddo the cat stretched out contentedly in the lifeboat. Simon opened his logbook: "The *America* airship will die from sheer exhaustion, a sort of bleeding to death, and before the last comes we must take to the boat," he wrote, demolishing his skipper's plan in a sentence. That prospect held no fear for Simon, who was experiencing a nostalgic yearning for the old-fashioned type of ship. "I am looking forward with pleasure to three or four days in the lifeboat. It is well stocked with provisions, water and tobacco. It contains several sleeping berths, sea anchor, and wireless plant. That lifeboat has always looked good to me. It is the most complete little craft for its size I have ever seen and reflects credit upon Saunders of Cowes, who built it. My favorite sport is boating, but whether my longshore shipmates will regard two or three days in an open lifeboat in the Atlantic in the light of sport I do not know."

However, launching the lifeboat presented a problem large as well as dangerous. Simon described it succinctly as "that blessed equilibrator." The lifeboat was suspended between the airship and the equilibrator; to launch the lifeboat the equilibrator would need to be submerged, but the moment they released the lifeboat's shackles, the reduction in weight would pull the equilibrator up out of the water and . . .

It didn't require much imagination to picture the damage that a two-ton, thirty-three-foot-long equilibrator could inflict on a twenty-seven-foot-long lifeboat. But instead of contemplating their grisly demise, the men's thoughts turned to ways of solving the problem. Lewis Loud suggested the most obvious solution—to get rid of the equilibrator. How exactly? they asked. Easy, replied Loud. He proposed to sit in the boatswain's chair while the others lowered him down and he cut the cords that held it. Brave, said Wellman, and bold, but also impractical; the loss of the equilibrator would create such an imbalance that after a rapid rise the *America* would gradually sink down into the water.

The other two solutions were dependent on factors outside their control. They could wait for a calm sea and still breeze before launching the lifeboat, so that they stood less chance of being hit by the equilibrator, or they could sit it out in the airship until they made contact with a passing vessel.

They decided to sit it out, to keep headed toward Bermuda for as long as possible while they scanned the endless ocean for a ship. Their best chance of salvation in the opinion of Irwin lay in the regular steamer that left Bermuda each Monday bound for New York. Taking their charts and plotting the steamer's probable speed, they reckoned it should be under them sometime on Tuesday morning. The information passed around the men like a mug of strong rum, warming them with hope. But soon the feeling faded and each contemplated the risks they faced during the night if the wind got up or rain fell. Then the equilibrator would drag them down, but they no longer had the reserves of gasoline to lift themselves clear of danger; instead they would have to take to the lifeboat, in the darkness and on a heavy sea, and with the equilibrator eyeing them like some ruthless monster from the deep.

Wellman spent the late afternoon locked in the watertight compartment of the lifeboat, his eyes glued to the barometer in case the reading should start to drop. But by six P.M. the weather was still fair, so Wellman gave the order to throw overboard whatever they could spare. Simon tossed away a five-pound box of sugar, several jars of bacon, and some biscuits. What a waste! young Aubert thought, laughing, as he looked on. The sharks won't think so, said Simon, and who knows, perhaps they'll be so full they won't eat us. The joke wasn't appreciated.

They had a feast for supper of cold bacon, biscuits, and malted-milk tablets, then lay back in the lifeboat smoking and spinning yarns. There was no talk of equilibrators or engines; instead, the tales were of "fair damsels left behind," and of their slim ankles and silken hair.

Despite the uncertainty of what lay ahead, there was no anxiety in the boat; rather there was a serenity, the sort experienced on the eve of a battle by soldiers who have put their faith in a higher power. Simon marveled at the night sky and wrote that in the bright moonlight "millions of stars are twinkling and the water below gleams like silver. Flying fish hover around our strange craft, and below big batches of gulf weed drift lazily by. It's perfectly calm, peaceful . . . we all feel elated—the reaction, possibly, after tremendous strain during the last two days. We have no fears for our immediate future."

Several hundred miles west of the airship *America* the moonlight was drawing out the lyricist in the *New York Herald*'s correspondent as he sat in the empty press stand at Belmont Park. It had been a slow day thus far, and the pages of his notebook were as empty as the seats around him, save for a few quotes from Count Bertrand de Lesseps, brother of the aviator, Jacques, about the exorbitant rates demanded by Lloyd's of London for the insurance of spectators during the forthcoming air show. With a suit for damages having recently been filed against the Asbury Park Meet organizers,* American companies had recoiled at the idea of underwriting the Belmont Park Meet. Lloyd's hadn't, however, though they'd charged $500,000, and the organizers had also taken out a $2,500 policy to insure the hangars and other temporary structures. Each airman had been asked to pay a 1 percent premium, and Bertrand de Lesseps was outraged. "For the same amount of premium demanded for the time of this meet I could take out a much larger policy for a year in France," he'd muttered to the *Herald* reporter.

Jacques de Lesseps was happy to leave such administrative minutiae to his brother. Of greater concern to him was the course around which he would have to fly. He and Hubert Latham had arrived at Belmont Park on Monday afternoon and blanched at what they had seen. Houses, trees, railroad tracks, and telegraph poles all skirted the hexagonal five-kilometer circuit, yet the biggest hazard to the aviators' safety, in their view, lay at the western end of the course, where the final turn before the grandstand was alarmingly tight.

As they came around the back straight of the racecourse, inside the row of twenty wooden hangars that had been erected, the aviators would have to angle left, almost at ninety degrees, past a tall red-and-white pylon that was less than a hundred yards from the grandstand that flanked the home straight. Latham told de Lesseps that the English expression for such an acute corner was *dead man's turn*.† Latham advised the *New York*

---

* On the first day of the show in August 1910 Walter Brookins crashed his Wright biplane, injuring himself and Maurice Gorvel, who suffered a broken arm. Gorvel claimed $15,000 in damages against the Wrights and the Asbury Park Motor and Aero Club, the first ever suit for damages involving an airplane.

† In the early years horse races at Belmont Park were held in the English fashion, that is to say clockwise. Thus dead man's turn would have been the first corner for the jockeys as they rode away from the grandstand. But the aviation course was to be held counterclockwise, meaning that the pilots had to negotiate the corner while avoiding the grandstand.

Herald that "while there were conditions that he did not approve of he would nevertheless compete." However, added the Frenchman, tapping a cigarette on his silver case, what the reaction would be of his compatriot the more . . . how could he put it? . . . "excitable" Monsieur Alfred Le Blanc, when he saw the course, Latham wouldn't care to imagine.

Latham and the de Lesseps brothers, accompanied by their ravishing sister, Countess de la Bergassiere, left their worries behind and lunched at Manhattan's elegant Café Martin on Twenty-sixth Street and Broadway. Later in the afternoon Jacques de Lesseps caught a train to Canada to visit a young woman to whom he had taken a fancy during an aviation show in Montreal the previous month. He would return in a few days, he told his brother, but in the meantime he issued strict instructions: keep an eye on our sister—Grahame-White is on his way to New York.

Once the de Lesseps had departed Belmont Park, the *New York Herald* correspondent spent Monday afternoon kicking his heels as he waited in the vain hope that an aviator might arrive to take his machine for a spin, but none appeared, and instead of the thrilling sound of a hundred-horsepower engine, the only noise was the hammering of nails as workmen rushed to finish converting the 650-acre Belmont Park from a horse track into an aviation field. With the start of the tournament just five days away, the transformation was all but complete, and the organizers were confident that the half million spectators expected to attend the weeklong meet would be accommodated without problem.

The betting ring under the grandstand now resembled a "covered and inclosed amphitheater, where an exhibition bazaar and trade show will be conducted. Airplane motors and other accessories and appliances for air craft, automobiles, motor boats, and all other things used in connection with outdoor sports will be exhibited." In front of the green-and-yellow grandstand the once immaculate lawn had been overlaid with two hundred corporate boxes, and what little remained of the grass had been churned to mud by a combination of heavy rain and workmen's boots. A temporary stand had been added to one end of the grandstand, increasing the number of spectator boxes to five hundred, and a press stand had also risen from the turf with a hundred individual desks and telegraph instruments at the reporter's right hand.

The racecourse itself had also been altered, so much so that "should any of the old followers of horse racing enter Belmont Park now they would think that they had never seen the place before." The fences had been removed, the jockey board taken down, the timers' stand had vanished, replaced by a judge's box in the shadow of dead man's turn. Opposite the grandstand on the other side of the racetrack was a vast scoreboard fifty feet long and thirty feet high with ladders for the scorers. The infield jumps and wings had been uprooted, and the track and infield sod leveled. Eleven red-and-white pylons, each thirty-five feet tall surmounted by a twenty-five-foot flagpole, marked out the route of the five-kilometer course, and incorporated into this circuit was a smaller two-and-a-half-kilometer course, staked out with additional pylons. In the northwest corner of the grounds, near the clubhouse, a number of chestnut trees had been felled and towering canvas screens erected along the high fence to prevent people from watching the show for free. The clubhouse had been given a makeover for the influx of Belmont Park's exclusive members with a lick of paint and some new furnishings, and for the first time in months all the electric elevators were functioning. Automobiles would be parked on the grass either between the hangars and the clubhouse or at the eastern end of the field, but how organizers would cope with the demand had yet to be resolved. They had received nearly five thousand applications for parking spaces for the first day alone, five times the number available. All but the fabulously rich and famous were politely being requested to take the Pennsylvania railroad to Belmont Park, but the organizers' headquarters on the eleventh floor of an office block on Fifth Avenue was already inundated with furious complaints from people whose social standing was at stake—a certain type of New Yorker would not countenance riding the railroad.

The twenty wooden hangars (plus four canvas ones that had been requested by the Wright brothers) stretched in a line north from the clubhouse for more than fifteen hundred feet. Each hangar was fifteen feet high and spacious enough to house the airplane, its spare parts, and a team of mechanics. On Monday afternoon the names of the airmen had been put in a hat along with the numbers 1 to 27. There was no number 13—that was considered the kiss of death by the airmen—but the thirteenth name to emerge from the hat had been Claude Grahame-White.

Now in the fading evening light the workmen were adding the numbers to the front of the hangars, which had earlier been painted green.

No doubt about it, thought the *New York Herald* correspondent as he tested his seat in the press stand, Belmont Park was unrecognizable from that May day in 1905 when forty thousand hysterical race-goers had seen the little bay Sysonby finish in a dead heat with Race King in the Metropolitan Handicap. So busy was the *Herald* reporter musing on the past that he didn't spot the small figure away to his left ease himself into his monoplane; the first the reporter knew that his day might not entirely be wasted was when he heard the gnarl of the machine's engine.

For the next twenty minutes the reporter, and the workmen who had set down their tools, were engrossed in the impromptu flying display. When the show finished, the reporter scampered across the grass to discover the airman's identify; with that done, he rushed back to the press stand and began his copy for the next day's edition: "Sysonby's ghost stood at the far turn of Belmont Park as the heavy shadows of dusk were fading into the mystic light blues of early moonlight last night and gazed wistfully at a weird, batlike thing that flitted in swooping circles back and forth across the widespread infield. In the air was the herald of a coming day for Belmont Park that is in a fashion ghostly or unreal. Darting swiftly about the field and wheeling around the pylons as swiftly as a swallow turns, Mr. John B. Moisant of Chicago . . . was tuning up a brand new 'flat plane' Blériot racer."

But he had done more than tune it up, exclaimed the reporter, he had performed "one of those things that other aviators will tell you cannot be done." He explained how the propeller of a Blériot monoplane turned clockwise, which, in theory, meant it was only possible to bank left. But in twenty minutes Moisant had turned that theory on its head by executing "one of the prettiest figure eights ever seen and [he] made the turn to the right with as little trouble as though directing the flight of a pigeon."

America had impatiently been waiting for the return of John Moisant from Europe. This enigmatic man had been the toast of England and France during the summer, after becoming the first aviator to cross the English Channel with a passenger in his airplane. One of the first reports to reach the United States appeared in the *Chicago Daily Tribune* on August 18 under the headline CHICAGOAN IS "KING OF THE AIR." The reporter, having interviewed Mr. Moisant, assured his readers that he spoke "with an accent which stamped him undoubtedly as more American than Spanish, as he had been generally supposed to be." Moisant had laughed at the idea that he was anything other than an American, telling the *Chicago Daily Tribune* and other newspapers that his family were of French descent but that he had been "born in Chicago thirty-five years ago." He fed the press other tidbits as he stood in a field of oats six miles from Dover on the south coast of England, alongside the French mechanic who had been his flying companion. Moisant had studied architecture at university; for every flight he wore Japanese paper underwear underneath his overalls to protect against the cold; he'd arrived in Europe in 1909 and spent time in Italy and Switzerland, but this was his first time in England. The most astonishing revelation—given that he had just become the first aviator to fly across the Channel with a passenger—he saved to last, and it left the reporters openmouthed: "I took up flying as a hobby eight or nine months ago, and this is the sixth time I have been in the air, and the machine I am using is the only one I have ever flown in."

How on earth could a novice pull off such a feat? Moisant shrugged, it was nothing really, just a bet he had with some friends a fortnight earlier. But how had he navigated if he had no knowledge of the Channel or its coastlines? "I found my way by compass entirely. Set my direction by it, allowed for the wind, and here I am." You do realize, said the *Daily Mirror* representative, that "all airmen have previously asserted that their compasses have failed owing to the vibration of the machine?" Moisant led the reporters to his airplane and pointed out the compass, which was insulated in glycerin and lay on the floor in front of his seat. "That's what took me straight to Amiens [from Paris] last night and right on to Calais this morning."

Moisant was lauded on both sides of the Channel with the French newspaper *France Patrie* hailing his "energy, audacity and intrepidity," and *France Presse* saying he had "won the admiration of the whole world." He was headline news in all the London papers with the *Daily Chronicle* carrying his exclusive account of the voyage under the legend REMARKABLE FLIGHT BY UNKNOWN MAN.

The British in particular were fascinated by Moisant, a man so unlike their own aviators, most of whom were in a similar mold to Claude Grahame-White—tall, handsome, and dapper, with the suave self-confidence of the privileged. The American was five feet three inches and 135 pounds, with a hairline in rapid retreat, but as the *Westminster Gazette* told its readers on August 18, "One would expect that this journey of his [across the Channel] would knock his nerves up, but he maintains a calm equal to that of the Trafalgar Square lions." The *Daily Express* called Moisant "chivalrous to his fingertips," another paper considered him "the most self-possessed of aviators," and the *Pall Mall Gazette* was struck by his "keen brown eyes," which took in everything and everyone around him. Once, just once, it was noted, the eyes flashed with anger, when a group of spectators had begun pawing at the wings of his monoplane.

In the second half of August the fascination for Moisant was transplanted to endearment as his stated intention to reach London turned into what the British loved best—a series of glorious failures. His landing in the field of oats on August 17 had been just a temporary stop to fix a slight problem with his engine, but the fault proved to be more problematic than at first thought, and it took Moisant another three weeks and seven flights to cover the seventy miles to the British capital. But he still received a two-foot, silver-plated cup from the *Daily Mail* newspaper for being the first aviator to fly from Paris to London, along with the affectionate tributes of a nation whose people were impressed that his "cheerfulness of temperament does not seem to have been in the least degree impaired by the chapter of accidents which befell him." Moisant returned the compliment, telling the *London Evening Standard*, "I have been treated right royally here in England, and I cannot sufficiently express my gratitude for all the kindness shown me. Such hospitality I have never met with in my life before." The paper then inquired what his intentions were now his epic flight was over. "I have no plans for the future," replied Moisant. "I am a happy-go-lucky sort of fellow and never know twenty-four hours in advance what I am going to do."

But someone else was planning Moisant's future, even as he spoke to the *Evening Standard*. The president of the Aero Club of America, Cortlandt Field Bishop, had been in Europe since early May negotiating for the services of several French aviators for the Belmont Park Meet, and he made sure he was in London to greet his compatriot when his airplane finally touched down. On September 15 the British press broke the news that Moisant would shortly return home to challenge for the International Aviation Cup. After entertaining the British public in a couple of air shows, Moisant sailed from France aboard *La Savoie*, eager to be back in the USA after more than a year in Europe.

Waiting for Moisant's ship at the New York quayside on Saturday, October 8, were a throng of reporters, all scanning the disembarking passengers for the small Chicagoan with the big cup. They pushed and shoved and cursed, but they needn't have bothered because what they all desperately wanted was the answer to the same question—and it had nothing to do with aviation. What they longed to know was if the John Moisant who had flown from Paris to London was the same John Moisant who had led an armed uprising against the president of Salvador.

The moment the *Chicago Daily Tribune*'s report of August 18 hit the newsstands in America, describing Moisant as the new "King of the Air," a reporter for the *Evening Standard* in Ogden had sat back in his chair and started to turn over the name in his mind. Where the hell had he heard it before? Then it came to him. He searched the paper's archives to make sure his memory wasn't playing tricks. It wasn't. He found a short piece from May 13, 1909, headlined CRUISER ALBANY HAS ENGAGEMENT. The opening paragraph began, "Unconfirmed reports were received in shipping circles today that the crew of the United States cruiser *Albany* has had an engagement with a party of emigradoes being led against the republic of Salvador by John Moisant, an American citizen, formerly owner of several plantations. More recently Moisant has been involved in revolutionary movements in Nicaragua and Salvador."

Within a short time the reporter had filed his piece for the evening edition of August 18. It made the front page, under the headline MOISANT'S ROMANCE.

For whatever reason the British newspapers had left the story alone, perhaps because they considered that what an American got up to in Central America was none of their business. So it was something of a shock to Moisant when he descended the gangplank of *La Savoie* to discover that aviation was the last thing on the reporters' minds. When he'd recovered from his surprise, Moisant reacted waspishly to any question he didn't like. "You'll have to find out about that from somewhere else," he snarled at a reporter from the *New York Globe* who asked about his revolutionary activity in Salvador. The *New York Morning Sun* received a similar rebuff from Moisant "with a swift, nervous utterance." On the subject of his nationality, Moisant's patience was wearing thin, and he turned on the reporter who asked if he was of Peruvian origin. That was a new one, Moisant replied with a sarcastic smile. "They [the press] have guessed many times that I was Mexican, Spanish, South American, even French—anything but American, which I am."

Exasperated by the tone of the interrogation, Moisant told the reporters that if they didn't have questions about aviation, then he'd bid them good day. The *Sun* sulkily asked if he was confident of success at the forthcoming meet, at which point Moisant brightened up and rattled off, "I do not expect to win any prizes in the Belmont Park Meet. What chance would I have in my fifty-horsepower Blériot against [Alfred] Le Blanc's hundred-horsepower machine? I came here at the request of and to oblige my friend Cortlandt Field Bishop, and I will leave soon after the meet, as I want to attend to the completion of my new machine, which I believe will be able to make between 120 and 130 miles." Moisant launched into an explanation of his new machine, a monoplane that would be shaped like a torpedo boat and "made entirely of aluminum and steel," but the reporters were already beginning to drift away, uninterested in all his aviation talk.

Unfortunately for Moisant, his wish to focus solely on his aeronautical feats was being undermined at the very moment he left quayside to check into the Hotel Astor, for on the other side of the country, the people of San Francisco were waking up to read the definitive account of John Moisant in the city's *Chronicle* newspaper. The article was headlined THE REVOLUTIONIST FROM SAN FRANCISCO, and its author, J. R. James, had evidently spent weeks on the story, interviewing everyone from the city's collector of the port to former friends and family members, including one of Moisant's sisters, Louise. This brilliant piece of journalism gave the truth behind the legend, and the more people read, the more their jaws dropped. As Moisant had admitted in England, wrote James, he had been born in Chicago in 1875 to American parents, and the family name came from the Normandy region of France. He was younger than his three brothers, George, Alfred, and Edward, and also had three sisters. In the early 1880s they had moved to San Francisco. When their parents died, the three elder brothers went south to Salvador and engaged in coffee planting and banking; soon they were joined by John and the sisters, and the businesses flourished in the years that followed.

Then one morning in April 1907 soldiers had arrived at the plantation in Santa Emilia and a search of the ranch turned up seventeen rifles. George and Alfred were arrested and thrown in jail on charges of plotting to overthrow Salvador's tyrannical President Figueroa. The Moisants protested that it was a plant, a dirty little scheme dreamed up by the government because they didn't like to see Americans doing well for themselves through their own honest endeavors without recourse to bribing corrupt officials.

The family appealed to the American State Department for help, but Secretary Elihu Root wasn't interested, so Moisant set out to free his brothers on his own. He met with Dr. Prudencio Alfararo, a long-standing opponent of President Figueroa's, who was impressed by Moisant. Soon he was outlining his plan in front of José Santos Zelaya, president of neighboring Nicaragua, another man who wished to see the back of his Salvadoran rival.

Moisant was furnished with a Nicaraguan gunboat, the *Monotombo*, and three hundred soldiers. One of the most daring attempts to overthrow a government ever seen then ensued, a tale fit to grace the screens of the movie theaters that were now cropping up all across America. The *San Francisco Chronicle* illustrated the coup with a sketch depicting a bandolier-wearing Moisant marching through the jungle at the head of his army. The accompanying text was every bit as swashbuckling:

> Moisant boldly steamed into the bay of Acajutia, a well-garrisoned, fortified Salvadorean port, at noon on June 12, 1907. Before the commander of the fortress knew what the visiting craft was about, Moisant had trained his guns on the tower of the fortress and in less than five minutes had disabled the defenses so that not a shot could be fired. Then, landing his men, he captured the garrison, imprisoned

the commander and forced 100 Salvadorean soldiers to join his ranks on the pain of death . . . Marshaling his forces, he set out for his avowed purpose of capturing San Salvador, the capital of the Republic, sixty miles from Acajutia. It was there that his brothers were in jail . . . [and] it was there that the flower of the Salvadorean army, 3,000 strong, was garrisoned . . . Giving no heed to the fact that the odds were about ten to one against him, Moisant led his troops on to their second victory. Sonsonate, twelve miles inland from Acajutia, on the way to the capital, was taken after a brief but fierce attack. The invaders caught the Sonsonate garrison off its guard and though desperate resistance was made, the town was soon in the possession of the enemy. Moisant lost twenty-five men in the fighting here; the Salvadoreans lost more than forty . . . Moisant had cut the wires from Acajutia to Sonsonate, but he did not take this precaution promptly enough after capturing the latter place. Before the lines were severed an energetic telegraph operator rushed to a key and flashed the news of the capture of the town to San Salvador.

Rumors had soon spread through Moisant's army that a force of three thousand soldiers was headed their way on special trains with orders to give no quarter. The press-ganged Salvadoreans stole away in ones and twos, and the Nicaraguans began to argue among themselves. Moisant tried to allay the men's fear, exhorting them to remain steadfast so that together they could defeat the president's army. But it was to no avail. Panic set in among his men and Moisant had no choice but to retreat to the gunboat.

President Figueroa derided Moisant as an American *diablo* and put a price on his head. He also declared that the incursion was proof that the whole family had been conspiring against him since the day they arrived in Salvador. The time had come, said Figueroa, to execute George and Alfred Moisant as an example to other would-be American insurgents. The threat finally stirred the United States government into action. President Roosevelt warned Figueroa that if so much as a hair on either American's head was harmed, there would be dire consequences. A cruiser, the USS *Olympia*, steamed into Salvador's waters to demonstrate the seriousness with which America treated threats to its citizens. Within days George and Alfred were released and the embargo on the family coffee plantation lifted, but John Moisant wasn't through with President Figueroa. He organized another coup in May 1909, but word was leaked to the U.S. government, which ordered his interception by the USS *Albany*. State Department officials told Moisant he had become an embarrassment and a nuisance. If he was caught in Salvador in the future, then they wouldn't intervene, he would be left to fend for himself.

Moisant appeared to heed the warning. He settled in Guatemala and opened a bank and for a few months led the life of a respectable business-man. But President Figueroa was never far from his thoughts, particularly as Guatemala bordered Salvador. Then in early 1909 Moisant read an arti-cle in a newspaper about the airplane, and an idea began to take shape in his head. He wrote to one of his sisters in San Francisco and told her he was off to Europe to learn how to fly. She wasn't surprised, her John had "always had an inventive turn of mind." What Moisant didn't disclose in his letter was that when he had learned how to fly, he would return to Sal-vador and finish his revolution by air.

The *San Francisco Chronicle* knew nothing of Moisant's belligerent ambition; the paper just glowed with pride that a man they claimed as one of their own had "in six months mastered the fine points of this new game [flying] as he mastered the arts of business, diplomacy and warfare in the little explosive republic to the south." The rest of the United States was equally in awe of John Moisant following his return home, and it began to dawn on people that they might, just might, have found an aviator every bit as glamorous as Claude Grahame-White and Count Jacques de Lesseps. Of course, Moisant wasn't as handsome as the En-glishman, but while Grahame-White had been selling motor cars in Mayfair, Moisant had been waging war in Salvador. Suddenly Moisant was elevated from unknown to number one, America's best hope for re-taining the International Aviation Cup. His opinion was sought on all things aviation, and Moisant was happy to talk—just so long as the re-porters didn't poke around in his past. On October 13 he used an inter-view in the *New York Evening Sun* to mock those who doubted the military potential of the airplane, saying, "People talk of shooting at fly-ing machines from the ground and warding off an attack in that way. We can travel seventy miles an hour, more than that soon, and can go up five thousand feet or more. Can they hit us under those conditions?" Asked by the *New York Globe* if his dream of building a metal airplane was nothing more than a flight of fancy, Moisant wagged his finger at the correspondent and said, "That's one of the greatest troubles with airplanes today, and the reason they are not safer and a greater commercial possibility. Their construction is too frail and there are too many wires and the wings are too flimsy. Would you expect an automobile to be safe if it had a canvas body and a lot of little wires to work it by?"

On October 12 Moisant had visited Belmont Park for the first time in a dark suit and derby and found the course to be "very satisfactory." He forecast it would be the greatest air show ever seen and caused gales of laughter among the reporters with another prediction, that "the next generation will use airplanes as we use automobiles." Are you serious? they asked, and Moisant's dark eyes narrowed. "There is no great mystery or great difficulty about operating an airplane," he growled. "Learning to guide an airplane is about as easy as learning to ride a bicycle." He cited his own experience in flying across the Channel. "Latham, Le Blanc, and Blériot said I was crazy . . . [and] when I said I was going to take a passenger, they thought I had gone stark mad . . . but I had a map and a compass in front of me and had no difficulty." To the American newsmen Moisant's comments were as welcome as summer rain after the drought of interesting quotes from America's other aviators. The *New York City Post* commented that his public statements "since his arrival in this country have been of extraordinary interest. No one else talks with the assurance and apparent mastery of the subject displayed by the young American."

But Moisant's turns of phrase didn't go down well with his peers, most of whom had read his thoughts as they prepared to leave St. Louis for Belmont Park. In their opinion it was nothing more than a shabby publicity stunt from a loudmouthed novice. If flying was as easy as cycling, then why had nearly twenty aviators been killed since the start of the year, many of them experienced men such as Léon Delagrange, the Frenchman, and Charles Rolls of England?

The Wright brothers' exhibition team refuted Moisant's remarks in interviews with the *St. Louis Post-Dispatch*, with Walter Brookins call-

ing him "foolish" for flying from Paris to London with such little experience. "He's lucky he didn't break his neck . . . an aviator must acquire
a fine judgment of direction, of speed and of distance."

Arch Hoxsey echoed Brookins, labeling Moisant's Channel flight
"miraculous luck." As for flying being as easy as cycling, that was plain
dumb: "If a man on a bicycle makes a mistake in judgment and falls, he
escapes with bruises," Hoxsey asserted, "but an error of an aviator—a
pull on the wrong lever, the warping of the wrong wire—may cost his
life." Only Ralph Johnstone conceded that in the basics of both skills
there might be an element of truth in Moisant's comments, although—
and here a look of thoughtful mischief spread across his face—"it is easier to learn to make the spiral descent in an airplane than to learn to
loop-the-loop on a bicycle."

Newspaper editors rubbed their hands in delight at the public spat,
and the Belmont Park organizers pumped the hand of Cortlandt Field
Bishop. Well done, old man, for getting that Moisant fellow over, the demand for tickets to the aviation meet was now so great they'd had to
open two more box offices at their Fifth Avenue headquarters. From
a revolution in Salvador to a revolution in American aviation, John
Moisant was one of a kind. But what would happen, the organizing committee asked one another gleefully, when Moisant, the American revolutionary, met Grahame-White, the English gallant . . . a repeat of 1776,
perhaps?

John Moisant's brief flight around Belmont Park on the Monday evening
christened the course. Not only was he the first of the competing aviators
to have had a practice spin, but it was also the first time a monoplane had
graced the New York skies. The *New York Herald* correspondent counted
himself privileged, as did the workmen, who resumed their painting
when the display was over, chattering excitedly to one other about the little piece of history they had just witnessed.

On Monday evening most of Moisant's rivals were en route to New
York from either Europe or St. Louis. Those on the train heading East
left behind a city still flushed with aviation fever. The sixty thousand
spectators who on Saturday had peeked through their fingers watching
the death-defying stunts of Ralph Johnstone spent Sunday recovering

before another great spectacle presented itself—the start of the International Balloon Cup race. The twenty balloonists had arrived on the rectangular aero grounds, between Newstead and Chouteau avenues, at two o'clock on Monday morning to supervise the inflation of their twenty-eight-thousand-cubic-feet balloons, and twelve hours later they had been joined by fifty thousand St. Louisians. Police authority began to creak under the sheer weight of numbers, and it was decided to close Papin Street to traffic and turn it into a vantage point for bystanders. Residents in the street, and in Chouteau Avenue, were delighted and started to hawk their houses—come and watch from the comfort of our home, ten cents for a standing spot and twenty-five cents for a kitchen chair. Elsewhere, on the northern side of the field, across the way from a vacant lot, the occupants of a row of brick flats had clambered up onto the roof to watch what to some resembled a field of giant mushrooms. A better view was to be found from one of the two grandstands that had been erected—holding a total of four thousand balloon enthusiasts, who had each paid $1.50 for the privilege—on the east and west sides of the aero grounds. Yet the best spot of all was from the walkway that encircled the base of the four-story-high red gas tank that had filled the balloons. Here a hundred corporate guests of the Laclede Gas Light Company drank champagne, nibbled canapés, and loosened their ties as the temperature climbed into the eighties. With opinions inflated by alcohol, the guests discussed the likely victor and, ever so discreetly, wagered one another. Some went for Alfred Le Blanc and Walther de Mumm in *Isle de France*, a balloon that had the backing of Frank Lahm, the American victor in 1906; others laughed at the idea; in their view it had to be the veteran Swiss crew of Theodore Schaeck and Paul Armbruster in *Helvetia*, the very same balloon that had carried Schaeck across the North Sea two years earlier. The *Düsseldorf II* was fancied by one or two, who reckoned that the fusion of German thoroughness in pilot Hans Gericke, and American chutzpah in copilot Sam Perkins, would be a winning formula. The more patriotic of the guests, having accepted a refill from one of the impressively attired waiters, tipped one of the three American balloons to win. Doubt it, they were smugly informed, haven't you heard the news? Two of the U.S. entries, the two from St. Louis, right enough, were laid out on the field overnight without a tarpaulin covering. Feasted on by grasshoppers. Holes everywhere. They say they've patched them up but . . . well, if I were you, I'd save your money.

A detachment of soldiers from the Signal Corps ringed the balloons to prevent spectators from getting too close, and only a handful of reporters and Aero Club officials were allowed near enough to observe the crews' final preparations. The correspondent from the *St. Louis Globe-Democrat* was curious to discover what supplies each balloon contained. He was startled to find that the European baskets were weighed down with alcohol: on board the *Düsseldorf II* was "a quart of whisky, four quarts of assorted wines, a bottle of cognac, twenty-four bottles of beer"; the second of the three German balloons, *Germania*, piloted by Hugo Von Abercron and his aide, August Blanckertz, carried "eighteen bottles of beer, six bottles of champagne and three bottles of Hoch [beer]"; the *Helvetia* was equipped with beer and whiskey; the Swiss crew of Emil Messner and Leon Givaudan in *Azurea* showed the reporter a small wooden box, inside which were "two quarts of whisky and one bottle each of brandy, chartreuse, Benedictine and crème de menthe." As for the two French crews . . . the reporter had never seen anything quite like it. While the American balloons had only the bare necessities—field glasses, hunting knives, water, and food such as fried chickens, boiled eggs, canned soups, and, in the case of Alan Hawley and Augustus Post, "specially prepared lozenges, one of which is said to be sufficient nourishment for one day"—the French baskets were regally furnished. Jacques Faure, a cousin of Hubert Latham's, and his copilot, Ernest Schmolck, in *Condor* had "a mattress and a pillow, a camp stool, a medicine chest, a bottle of cologne . . . one dozen pint bottles of champagne, two quarts of whisky, one dozen pints of mineral water, three fried chickens, 2 pounds of ham, 2 pounds of roast beef, 1 pound brie cheese, three pots of cheese, one can of corned beef and two loaves of bread." It was harder for the reporter to ascertain the exact contents of the *Isle de France*'s basket, on account of Le Blanc being "very excitable and irritable," but "case after case of champagne were opened and stacked on one side of the basket . . . to the number of about four dozen pint quarts." Not surprisingly, added the newsman, Le Blanc also threw in a bottle of Bromo-Seltzer.

The only balloonist willing to furnish the *St. Louis Globe-Democrat* with a few words was Alan Hawley. He showed the reporter his energy lozenges (they were actually condensed-meat tablets), then explained the water anchor he had designed, which consisted of two life preservers enclosed in a net and would be used on the drag rope if they crossed a body of water to preserve the equilibrium of the balloon. Do you think you will win? Hawley was asked. He flattened down the red tie he was wearing and considered his response. "It's at least forty percent luck," he said at length, "and were it not so, we American aeronauts would stand but a poor chance with the foreign aeronauts here today. What chance would we have with men like Le Blanc, who has made innumerable flights, or Faure, who has made two hundred and seventy-five? I have made forty flights only, and I guess I have made more than any of the Americans entered today."

The reporter tucked his pencil into his pocket, wished Hawley and Post good luck, and went on his way. When he was out of earshot Captain John Berry of the St. Louis Aero Club, who had helped with the inflation of the *America II*, turned to Hawley and asked if he really believed his chances of victory were that slim. Of course not, Hawley replied, grinning: "We are good to stay up seventy or eighty hours and expect to break every record for distance and endurance. I know we are bound for the Canadian wilderness, but no timber shall stop us. We'll sail as long as the balloon has an ounce of lifting power and take our chances on being found."

Shortly after four P.M. officials informed each crew of the latest weather forecast they had just received: the air currents for the next eighteen hours would be from the southwest to the northeast, favorable to the balloonists. The tropical hurricane that had devastated Cuba was now sweeping across the Gulf of Mexico and would have little effect on the weather, but an atmospheric depression over North Dakota might influence their direction.

The starting order of each balloon had been decided two days earlier, and by four thirty P.M. the first crew, Jacques Faure and Ernest Schmolck in *Condor*, had adjusted their ballast so that they were floating inches off the ground. A dozen soldiers from the Signal Corps carried the basket to the starting point, whereupon the timer counted down the seconds and then, at four forty P.M., shouted, "Let go, all!" The soldiers released their grip and stood back as the *Condor* rose into the air. Twelve minutes later the second balloon, St. Louis's own *Million Population Club*, piloted by Louis Von Phul and Joseph O'Reilly, ascended, but within seconds there was a problem. They had started "heavy," their balloon festooned with forty bags of sand, each weighing thirty-nine pounds. For a moment it seemed the balloon would strike the grandstand as it lurched across the sky. Spectators froze in fear or dived under their seats as Von Phul whipped out his hunting knife and slit one of the ballast bags attached to the side of the basket. A shower of sand fell from the sky onto the heads of some spectators, but the *Million Population Club* regained its poise and climbed safely above the grandstand. The next three balloons got away without incident and followed the *Condor* and *Million Population Club* in a north-by-northwest direction. The sixth balloon to rise was *St. Louis No. 4*, piloted by Harry Honeywell and, according to the *St. Louis Globe-Democrat*, "the favorite with the crowd," certainly the one that received the biggest cheer as it passed over the grandstand. It headed north, as did the *Helvetia* and *Düsseldorf II*, which were next to leave.

The penultimate balloon to depart was also the lightest; not only did the yellow-clothed *America II* carry no whiskey or champagne (only a small hip flask of cognac in Augustus Post's coat pocket), but its ballast consisted of just twenty-nine bags, each weighing forty pounds. Standing in the basket next to Hawley, Post could feel his heart thumping as he waited for the starter's order. This was the moment he dreaded above all others, the few seconds when his imagination reminded him of what had happened in Berlin. Once, when asked by an acquaintance what the start of a balloon race felt like, Post had replied that it "must be something like the proverbial 'last moment' of a drowning man. In the instant's pause—literally one of suspense—there flashes through the mind, if not one's whole life, at least all the days and weeks of preparation."

The starter hollered, "Let go, all!" and the *America II* climbed into the air, a great ball of yellow rising like the sun on a summer's morning. Seven minutes later the *Germania* was off, and the aero ground of St. Louis had been harvested of all its giant mushrooms.

The *America II* made good progress, and at six ten P.M., twenty-four minutes after their departure, Post made the first note in the logbook, recording their direction as north, their altitude as five hundred feet, and the temperature as seventy-eight degrees. In the column headed REMARKS he wrote only "moonlight." Twenty minutes later he jotted their first bearings: "17 miles northwest of St. Louis," and at seven twenty P.M. they were "across Mississippi River" traveling northwest at a height of three hundred feet. Fifteen minutes later they crossed another river and inquired of a lone boatman visible on the silvery water below their whereabouts. "This is the Illinois River and you're now in Jersey County," he shouted, nearly losing his balance and toppling into the water as he looked up.

For a while the *America II* followed the Illinois River before they caught a swift stream of air that took them north at nearly 30 mph, through Calhoun County, Illinois.

At nine o'clock the *America II* was still scooting along at a good lick, not far above the tops of trees and the odd farmstead. Keep an eye out for crazy farmers and their shotguns, Hawley warned Post, only half in jest. But the only human voice they heard was from a man who rushed out of his front door, clapping his hands in delight, and yelling, "My God, it's a pretty sight, brother!"

CHAPTER FOUR

Will Launch Lifeboats and Trust to You

Tuesday, October 18, 1910

AT FOUR A.M. Murray Simon was woken from a deep sleep by Lewis Loud, and for a few moments Simon did nothing but "growl like a demon" at being turned out of his hammock. He got scant sympathy from Loud, who told him it was his turn on watch, alongside the skipper.

Simon and Walter Wellman made themselves snug in the lifeboat, lit up a cigarette each, and nattered. The captain of the *America* was old enough to be the father of the twenty-nine-year-old Englishman, but in the chilly night air they were without rank or restriction; they discussed food, weather, future attempts, and the probable whereabouts of the steamer from Bermuda. Then Wellman scanned the night sky and predicted another fine day. "As soon as the sun comes out today, the *America* will go up again well aloft," he said to Simon. "We'll have to let out some more of our gas, which will mean we're about done by sundown." Simon took a long, deep, satisfying drag on his cigarette, then asked, "Why not draw water and fill one of the tanks as ballast so we can keep down during the day?" Wellman liked the sound of that: "Good idea, we'll try it."

Simon finished his cigarette and with a "Cheerio" climbed the ladder into the car and positioned himself in his navigator's seat, still marveling at the sensation of floating in midair in profound silence. Suddenly he heard a shout from below. "Why, there's a ship!" cried Wellman. Simon jumped up and peered through the two holes he'd cut in the canvas. At first he saw nothing and yelled down to Wellman, "Ship be blowed!" But Wellman was adamant, so Simon looked again, and this time he made out the lights of a ship about six miles to their east. All hands were raised, and Irwin tore down the ladder, jumping the last couple of rungs into the lifeboat and unbalancing Wellman, who was in the bow waving his arms frantically in the direction of the ship.

Able seaman Stanley Angel was shivering in the crow's nest of the SS *Trent* when he spotted what he thought was the morning star away to the northwest. The eighteen-year-old Londoner nudged his pal, able seaman George Sangster, and pointed out the "white light up in the sky." The two squinted through the gloom, and suddenly a red light blinked twice to either side of their "star." "So help me God," exclaimed Angel, "it's an airship!" The red lights flashed again, and the lookouts read the Morse code for "Help, Help, Help." Sangster ran aft and breathlessly informed Mr. Fitzgerald, the fourth officer, that an airship was off the port side. If you're being "nutty," he was warned, they'll be hell to pay. Sangster promised he wasn't being nutty, and in a few moments Fitzgerald was wearing his lookout's expression of childlike amazement. Chief Officer Lainson was summoned to see the "phenomenon," and he in turn sent orders to rouse Captain Down, and to fetch signalman Albert Leach. They waited on deck, watching the signals for help that "continued to come from beneath the black blur that was dancing low across the northern sky." Leach arrived with his Morse lamp and was instructed to ask if they had wireless. "Yes," flashed the red lights in reply. Captain Down was now present and, on seeing the affirmative response, dispatched someone to wake Louis Ginsberg, the ship's wireless officer. In the meantime, Leach asked his counterpart where he was from. "The Wellman airship *America*, from Atlantic City, bound for Bermuda," answered the red lights.

With his electric blinker, Irwin identified himself, then asked a question of his own: "Who are you?" Back came the reply: "We are the *Trent* of the Royal Mail Steamship Company, bound from Bermuda to New

York." The six men in the lifeboat punched their fists in the air. Simon threw back his head and roared, "We do love our airship, but, oh, you *Trent*!"

Through his earphones Irwin was serenaded by a symphony of dots and dashes from the hand of Louis Ginsberg:

"Do you want our assistance?"

"Yes. Come at once," Irwin carefully tapped out in response. "In distress. We are drifting. Not under control."

"What do you want us to do?" asked Ginsberg.

Irwin imagined the captain of the *Trent* standing over the shoulder of the wireless operator whispering instructions, much as Wellman was doing in the lifeboat.

"Come ahead full speed, but keep astern, as we have heavy tail dragging."

"Okay," replied Ginsberg. "Am standing by the wireless in case of trouble."

"You will pick us up at daylight. You will be better able to see us then."

"Okay."

As Irwin communicated with the *Trent*, the rest of *America*'s crew were having what Simon described in his log as a "lively debate" about how best to abandon the airship. Their speed was fifteen knots per hour and they were some eighty feet above the ocean with the equilibrator still lurking ominously close. Simon advised dropping into the sea without delay and launching the lifeboat. Vaniman disagreed, saying it was too dangerous, that it would be safer to slide down a rope onto the deck of the *Trent*. Simon rubbished the idea and in urging his plan "used more sailor language than he had used in years past." The outburst failed to win him the day, however, and Wellman told Irwin to radio the following message to the *Trent*: "Come in close and put the bow of your ship under us. We will drop you a line, but do not stop your ship, as you will capsize us."

"Okay," replied Ginsberg.

A more congenial atmosphere prevailed on board the *Trent*. Captain Down thought the passengers might like to see the extraordinary sight, so he sent a steward to knock at their cabin doors. Within half an hour nearly all the ship's 150 passengers were crowded on deck, their night-clothes hidden under heavy coats, gaping in amazement at the sight before them.

As dawn broke, the *Trent* was feet away from the *America*, and Captain Down had "every man in the crew at work now, from stokehole to crow's nest maneuvering about under the airship. Sometimes we had to drive full speed astern to get out of the way of the car and then, as the wind would catch the airship again, we would have to put about and chase her with all the power we could get up."

By seven o'clock the wind had strengthened and was pushing the *America* west at a rate of twelve knots, with the *Trent* in hot pursuit. It was a "crazy chase," Down told his officers, and he began to despair of ever effecting a successful rescue by means of a line. He had been struck by another thought, too: what if, in the *Trent* passing under the airship, some gasoline should drop down the vessel's funnel into its fires? A message was sent to Wellman—launch the lifeboat.

Irwin received the message and passed it to Wellman. Neither he nor anyone else protested; they just wanted the refuge of the *Trent*. "Keep close as possible. Will launch lifeboat and trust to you," replied Irwin. Vaniman trailed a cord from the gas valve down into the lifeboat, and when he was settled inside the vessel, he pulled on the cord and released the gas. Simon and Loud stood at either end of the lifeboat with their hands on the safety clutches, watching the airship begin to lose its shape and waiting for the right moment to spring free.

The *Trent* had taken up a position 150 feet astern of the airship, and Captain Down issued orders for two small launches to be readied. As crewmen prepared the rescue craft, they silently cursed the passengers, who, with their mugs of coffee and their squeals of excitement, clogged the decks. The *America* sent another message, which Ginsberg scribbled down and passed to his skipper: "We have a motor going above. We can't hear your signals now. Will say when I can. We are pumping air into the airship ready to bring her down to the level." Down looked across at the airship and saw that its body had started to sag so that it resembled an animal brought to its knees by a hunter's bullet. The lifeboat was feet above the waves, and two men were fiddling with its cables. Ginsberg pressed a hand to his earpads as another message stuttered across the water: "We are going to launch the boat, stand by to pick us up."

The moment the gas valve was opened, the taut hide of the *America* began to wither. Vaniman scooped up the cat in his arms as the lifeboat dropped slowly toward the ocean. Irwin tapped out his final message, whipped off his earpads, and locked the wireless in the lifeboat's compartment. Then he cut the aerial wires and the earth wires and slipped a life preserver over his head.

Simon looked at Loud, nodded, and yelled, "Let her go!" The pair snapped open the safety clutches, and the boat hit the water with a mighty splash and lurched gunwale under. The six men clung to the lashings of the lifeboat as a wave caught them side on and spun them round. The lifeboat righted herself as the balloon soared skyward. Simon was just about to let out a triumphant roar when the equilibrator rose out of the waves like the terrible sea serpent they had all imagined and smashed into the port bow, "knocking a hole in the forward air chamber and nearly knocking Loud's head off."

Loud had seen the beast lunging at him out of the corner of his eye at the last second and ducked, catching a glancing blow on his shoulder. Irwin cushioned his fall, and the pair lay sprawled at the bottom of the boat for several seconds, until they heard a strangled cry from one of their shipmates. Looking up, they saw the prow of the *Trent* "as high as a church," bearing down on them. There seemed no escape, yet the passengers watching from the rail seemed oblivious of what was about to happen; Simon could hear them cheering. One or two were leaning over the side taking a souvenir snapshot. Simon looked from the rail to the giant propellers whisking the Atlantic Ocean into a welter of white foam. Irwin jumped up onto a seat and prepared to leap overboard as the sound of the propellers grew louder. Then, with a terrifying noise, the port quarter of the *Trent* scraped the length of the lifeboat, peeling off its white paint. For a few seconds they surfed the whirlpool of the ship's propellers, then were clear, though for a few seconds none of them could quite believe it.

The crew of the *America* were treated as heroes when they were finally pulled on board the *Trent*, but they were interested only in a hot breakfast and a hot bath. After both had been taken, the men fell into some bunks, pulled clean blankets over their heads, and slept for several hours. When they emerged in the afternoon, they had the luxury of wearing clean clothes supplied by the *Trent*'s crew, and for over an hour they happily signed autographs and discussed their adventure with the passengers. Captain Down told Wellman he had last seen the airship drifting west toward Cape Hatteras with its nose close to the water. Then Down invited him to give a short talk on their adventure that evening, after the minstrel show.

There wasn't a seat to be had in the concert room when Wellman took the stage to a standing ovation. He gave a brief account of their voyage, in layman's terms, then thanked his comrades for their faithfulness and bravery. He wrapped up his lecture with a tribute to the airship, wherever she might now be: "Good old *America*, farewell," he said, turning from his audience and addressing the ocean. "You played your part in the game of progress. In the years to come many aircraft will cross the Atlantic; and you will be honored as the ship that showed the way."

Also headed for New York, but a day ahead of the SS *Trent*, was the transatlantic liner *Kronprinz Wilhelm*, and on board was a black-haired Frenchman with "a liquid eye and an olive skin." Once or twice during the crossing from Europe, Roland Garros had sat at the piano and dazzled his fellow passengers with his talent. They asked if he was a professional, and Garros had shaken his head, smiled, and explained that he was an aviator on his way to Belmont Park.

It had never been the twenty-two-year-old's intention to fly when he arrived in Paris in 1908 from his birthplace on the Indian Ocean island of Réunion, but an outing to the Rheims Air Show the following year led Garros to send a letter home advising his family of a change of plan.

In March 1910 Garros had his first flying lesson and in July received his aviation license; for the rest of the summer he appeared in numerous European air shows in a Demoiselle, a monoplane made of bamboo and silk. Cortlandt Bishop, president of the Aero Club of America, had signed Garros to appear at Belmont Park the moment he first clapped eyes on his extraordinary machine. The small Frenchman would be the clown of the show, thought Bishop, twirling his small mustache with his index finger, as was his custom; he'd be the flier to put a smile on the face of New Yorkers. Certainly the Demoiselle had caused much amusement in Britain when Garros had flown in a show at Bournemouth on the south coast of England in August. "Nothing so excruciatingly funny as the action of this machine has even been seen," wrote the correspondent of *Aero* magazine, wiping a tear from his eye. "The little two-cylinder engine pops away with a sound like the frantic drawing of ginger beer corks; the machine scuttles along the ground with its tail well up; then down comes the tail suddenly and seems to slap the ground while the front jumps up, and all the spectators rock with laughter. The whole attitude and jerky action of the machine suggest a grasshopper in a furious rage."

Word of Garros's "hummingbird" had been brought to America by returning aviators, and a flock of reporters were in attendance when the *Kronprinz Wilhelm* docked on Tuesday. The Frenchman graciously fielded all questions, ignoring the odd snicker as he explained that his machine weighed 250 pounds and was, as he spoke, being unloaded from the ship's hold in four separate crates. "I will demonstrate the efficiency of my Demoiselle as soon as I get it together and run it out upon the course at Belmont Park," he said. "It rises into the air quickly and, when in the air, can be easily maneuvered. There is no trouble about turning to right or left in this machine. In the matter of speed the Demoiselle can equal any of the heavier type of fliers."

When the newsmen returned to their offices from the quayside to write about Roland Garros, they found waiting for them on their desks a facsimile of a statement telegraphed by Glenn Curtiss from his manufacturing headquarters in Hammondsport, New York, to J. C. McCoy, chairman of the Belmont Park Aviation Committee. The characteristically laconic announcement stated simply that two of his fliers would be operating new racing machines, monoplanes, during the forthcoming meet.* Tantalized by the brevity of the exciting revelation, the *New York*

---

* On October 15 Curtiss had informed the Belmont Park organizers that he wouldn't personally be appearing to defend the International Aviation Cup, which he had won in Rheims in 1909, but he promised nevertheless to send a team to compete. The *World* reported that in the future Curtiss "intends giving up flying except for experimental purposes."

Herald telephoned Jerome Fanciulli, manager of Curtiss's New York office, and charmed some further details from him. "In the lines and the chassis they [the new machines] are essentially Curtiss airplanes," explained Fanciulli, "though the lower plane surfaces are practically eliminated and the surfaces of the upper planes greatly reduced." Yes, yes, said the *Herald* reporter impatiently, but what are the machine's chances of winning the International Aviation Cup for America? "It should be much faster than the racer used by Mr. Curtiss at the Boston meet," reckoned Fanciulli, "which found him somewhat unprepared to compete with Mr. Grahame-White's speedy Blériot. Since the meet, Mr. Curtiss has concentrated his energies on perfecting the new fliers." In conclusion, said Fanciulli, Mr. Curtiss was confident of putting up a good show.

Most of the ten balloons in the International Balloon race had stayed low on Monday night, sometimes skimming no more than two hundred feet above the ground in the cool night air. None thought of jettisoning some of their valuable ballast bags to increase their height; that tactic could be employed later, if they encountered sudden pockets of cooler air during the day (when normally the sun's heat would be expected to expand the gasbags) or if they lost height because of gas seeping out through the stitching of their balloons.

Seven of the crews were confident their balloons were leakproof; these were the ones made from silk and treated with rubber. Hugo Von Abercron had gone even further with his balloon, *Germania*, covering its rubber surface with aluminum dust so that, in the words of the *New York Herald*, "it glistened like silver." Trials in Germany had convinced the forty-one-year-old Abercron that the sheen of metal better deflected the sun's rays. The balloons that hadn't been reinforced with rubber were the French *Condor* and two of the American entrants, *St. Louis No. 4* and *Million Population Club*. They had just a thin layer of varnish covering the silk envelope of their balloons, which was inefficient at preventing gas from escaping but efficient at absorbing rain or dew—just what a balloonist didn't want.

To add to the Americans' woes their balloons had been attacked by

St. Louis's grasshoppers during Sunday night, and it had quickly become evident to Louis Von Phul and Joseph O'Reilly in *Million Population Club* that though they had laboriously patched up as many holes as they could on Monday, gas was escaping at an alarming rate. Throughout Monday night the pair had off-loaded nearly two thirds of their ballast as they headed northeast, and at half past five on Tuesday morning they had only fourteen sandbags remaining. As dawn broke, they could see to their east Lake Michigan, its flat surface the color of marble. So tempting. Younger, rasher, more inexperienced balloonists might have taken on the lake, their common sense giving way to their pride, but Von Phul and O'Reilly knew that to do so would be reckless to the point of suicidal. They'd scrutinized the map by flashlight and cursed when they calculated that they would have to cross Lake Michigan at its widest point—eighty miles from shore to shore. Eighty miles with now just ten bags of ballast. If the weather turned, if the temperature dropped, or if it began to rain, they no longer had enough ballast to prevent the balloon from plunging into the lake.

At seven A.M. they passed north over the lakeside town of Racine, dispensing with another couple of sandbags to ensure they didn't become entangled with a church spire. A few miles farther on was open country, and Von Phul brought down *Million Population Club* within sight of Lake Michigan. The land belonged to John Tramball, not a man who frightened easily, and instead of a shotgun blast he welcomed them with an invitation to his breakfast table. Having demolished a plate of ham and eggs, Von Phul telephoned the race organizers in St. Louis to tell them he'd come down six and a half miles north of Racine, Wisconsin, giving him an estimated distance of 320 miles.

The early hours of Tuesday had also been a little trying for Jacques Faure and Ernest Schmolck in the *Condor*. Progress had been swift at first, and the Frenchmen's hearts began to pump a little quicker when they saw the southern shores of Lake Michigan beneath them. Despite the accoutrements on board—the mattress, stool, cologne, Brie, roast beef, and one dozen bottles of champagne—the balloon soared to ten thousand feet. The pair slipped on their fur-lined gloves and turned up the collars of their coats and congratulated themselves on their impressive start.

Then came the hours of terror, dread, and pain, the effect of which were all too visible when Ernest Schmolck sat before reporters in a Chicago hotel the following evening. With his right arm in a sling and his face heavily bruised, the Frenchman told how "we suddenly struck a zone of air where the temperature was close to zero. The gas in the balloon began to condense rapidly and we started falling."

They fell quickly, and silently. One thousand feet . . . two thousand feet . . . three thousand feet. They cut away bags of ballast, threw out the cologne, the Brie, the roast beef, bottles of champagne one by one, but still they fell . . . four thousand feet . . . five thousand feet. "After a sheer drop of six thousand feet there came a brief halt," explained Schmolck, "and we thought we were safe, but the relief was only for a moment. Again the balloon began to drop." Over the side went some more sandbags and the last of the champagne and the twelve bottles of mineral water. They heard the splash as each hit the black waters of Lake Michigan. Faure told Schmolck it was no good, they were doomed. All they could do was hope to swim to safety. "We were within a hundred feet of the surface of the great lake when we discarded our shoes and coats and clasped our life preservers to our bodies," said Schmolck. And then, he said, shaking his head at the reporters in merry disbelief, "Just when we thought ourselves lost, the balloon was halted in its downward flight." They were forty-five feet above the lake, saved only by the drag rope that hung from the basket and had touched the water, reducing their weight and arresting their descent. If there had been any champagne left, they might have opened a bottle, but instead they breathed a deep sigh of relief and put their faith in the thin length of rope that dangled beneath the basket. And then a stroke of luck: the wind picked up and pushed them southwest, back across the lake, until they sighted land. And the arm, the reporters asked Schmolck, was it injured during the descent? Oh, no, he explained, that came later, after a further mishap. "Our attempt to land was fraught with new perils. The balloon sailed three miles over the rough country at express-train speed, dragging the basket in its wake. The basket was dashed against fences, farmhouses, and three chimneys fell during the onslaught. Fences were bowled over and small trees knocked down. Finally a stout barbed-wire fence caught us and held long enough to throw Monsieur Faure and myself headlong into a marsh filled with muddy water. We half swam and half waded to terra firma."

Schmolck's arm had been lacerated during the landing but fortunately not broken. He and Faure had taken a while to gather their senses before setting off on foot to find help. The *Condor* had come to rest just outside the Wisconsin lakeside town of Two Rivers, forty miles southeast of Green Bay. They'd covered little more than four hundred miles, but neither Schmolck nor Faure cared. They were alive.

During the first night in the *America II*, Alan Hawley and Augustus Post had quickly settled back into the familiar routine that had served them well during the 1907 race. They ushered in Tuesday with a can of hot mutton broth, "heated by putting water upon lime packed about the tin which, in slacking, produced heat enough to bring the soup to a palatable temperature." Once they'd wolfed down the broth, the pair put the cans under their coats and warmed their chill bodies for a few pleasurable minutes.

Hawley and Post drank water from their quart bottles at regular intervals and played a game of animal identification as they passed over endless pastures. The horses, they discovered, chased after the balloon, but chickens and pigs "exhibited their usual panic with noisy sounds and frantic rushing in all directions to escape the great hawk which, no doubt, they thought was going to get them." A little before three A.M. they exchanged greetings with a man on the porch of his isolated house, who told them they were in Whiteside County, Illinois. Hawley decided to turn in for the night and curled up on the bottom of the basket. Post took the first watch, standing on the forward side of the basket and keeping a constant eye on the statiscopes, aneroids, and other instruments. He made the occasional remark in the logbook, noting at four forty A.M. that they were in Stephenson County, Illinois, traveling north by east at an altitude of seven hundred feet. The *America II* was now in perfect equilibrium, and they hadn't needed to add or remove any sand from their ballast tray since eight o'clock on Monday evening. The tray, containing a tin scoop, hung in a corner against the side of the basket, with a fresh sack of ballast underneath in case of a sudden disturbance. Post and Hawley knew not to play idly with the tray, for "in a state of equilibrium, the ballast is put out by the spoonful and even a small piece of paper thrown out will change the delicate balance."

Hawley was on his feet to greet the sunrise at six eleven A.M., just as they crossed the state line into Wisconsin below Newark in Rock County. Forty minutes later they were three miles south of Janesville, Wisconsin, and a ten-year-old girl was shaken awake by her mother and told to get outside quick, something special was happening. The balloon passed low enough for the little girl to make out the red flag of the Aero Club of America on the yellow envelope and the words *America II*.

With the heat of the sun the balloon rose rapidly to two thousand five hundred feet, and at nine forty A.M. Lake Michigan came into sight. They approached the water between Milwaukee and Port Washington, but once they were over the lake the temperature dropped and so did the *America II*. Neither man was concerned about the steady descent as they came to within two hundred feet of the lake. Post threw out the drag rope and for a while they drifted sedately northeast. Soon, however, the wind changed and they were pushed back over the western shore.

They tried again, this time ridding their basket of some ballast and rising to nearly six thousand feet with the strength of the sun aiding their elevation. Out of reach of the cooling influence of the water and with the return of a northeasterly wind, *America II* traversed Lake Michigan without incident and passed over Ludington, Michigan, a settlement on the eastern shore, at two P.M. Fifty miles farther on, Hawley dropped a handwritten message near a farmstead in Thompsonville, addressed to Albert Lambert, president of the Aero Club of St. Louis:

America II passed over this place Tuesday. Course due north. HAWLEY & POST.

Soon it was twilight, then darkness, and Hawley and Post spent some time scooping out sand from the ballast tray to establish an equilibrium now that their gas had contracted with the night air. At four thousand five hundred feet they had to their northeast an invigorating view of

Lake Huron sparkling in the bright moonlight, one of those vistas that makes a man feel privileged. Inspired by the sight, neither Post nor Hawley jibbed at the idea of crossing the water in the dark. They'd had a grand run to date, and they trusted their luck to hold.

CHAPTER FIVE

We Are in Bad Country and Grave Danger

Wednesday, October 19, 1910

WEDNESDAY'S PAPERS CARRIED depressing news for devotees of American ballooning. The stark headline on the front page of the *St. Louis Republic* said it all: BUT ONE AMERICAN BALLOON IN RACE. Underneath was a dispiriting account of the first thirty-six hours of the International Balloon contest, beginning with the capitulation of *Million Population Club*, continuing with the dramatic descent of the *Condor*, and finishing with the sorry saga of Harry Honeywell and J. W. Jolland in *St. Louis No. 4.*

Despite the problems with the grasshoppers, *No. 4* had performed flawlessly for the first twelve hours, crossing Lake Michigan at the cost of only seven of their thirty-one bags of ballast. But once over Michigan, things had started to go wrong; it became a constant struggle for Honeywell to keep the balloon in equilibrium, and at times it felt as if they were in a small craft on a rough sea, riding the crest of white-tipped waves. By midday they were down to their last ten bags of ballast, and by four thirty P.M. they had just six remaining. They had done what *Million Population Club* hadn't and defied Lake Michigan, but it would be folly to chance their arm again and attempt to cross Lake Huron a few miles to their northeast. They put down in a green wheat field near Hillman, 550 miles northeast of St. Louis, and a score of wide-eyed locals helped pack up the balloon, though not before Honeywell had "examined it and found that some patches I had pasted on before the start to cover up some [grasshopper] holes had peeled off, and I suppose that's what caused the trouble."

Of the third U.S. entry, *America II*, the *New York Times* had no news and was only able to advise readers in its Wednesday edition that no news must be good news. It added that of the seven balloons still up "the *Germania* is thought to be ahead," its distinctive aluminum covering the first to be reported crossing Lake Michigan the previous day.

The *New York Times* was way off the pace on Wednesday morning. By the time it was being read by New Yorkers on their way to work, only four balloons, not seven, were airborne, and of those one, the *Harburg II*, containing William Assmann and Lieutenant Leopold Vogt, was in desperate straits.

It had been a breeze at first for the German pair, literally and metaphorically, as they crossed Lakes Michigan and Huron without incident. At six o'clock on Tuesday evening they were over the eastern end of Georgian Bay in Ontario at a debilitating altitude of eighteen thousand feet. Vogt could see for miles, but all he saw in the dregs of daylight was a great expanse of water pockmarked with bays, inlets, and islands. They were both fearfully cold in their basket, fighting the desire to lie down and sleep; perhaps it was another effect of altitude that rendered Vogt insensate, for suddenly he decided "to take a chance . . . I pulled the valve and we descended with terrific force." It was an extraordinary gamble, a crazy one considering they had only two bags of ballast left with which to allay their drop. They were, in effect, in free fall. As they plummeted through the black sky, the pressure on their eardrums made the inside of their heads feel as if they were filled with cotton.

As Gull Island rushed up toward them, it appeared Vogt had been prodigiously foolhardy, but two hundred feet from the ground the tip of the drag rope hit the rocky shoreline and the distribution of weight fractionally altered so the basket spun round and the envelope folded over into the sort of parachute that had saved Augustus Post and Holland

Forbes in Berlin. Nonetheless the collision between water and basket was awesome, rendering both men unconscious.

They had come down in Lake Nipissing, a shallow, forty-mile-long stretch of water that drained into Georgian Bay. Pneumatic floats kept the basket from sinking as the breeze blew the senseless pair farther from the shore, until eventually a wave crashed over the rim of the basket and revived Vogt. He looked groggily around and saw that Assmann was in a terrible state. A bone protruded from his shattered left arm, and his right hand had been bent back at a hideous angle. The most serious injury, however, was the severed artery in his right arm, the blood of which had already turned the water in the basket red. Miraculously, Vogt had no broken bones, and for the next hour he endured the bitter temperatures of the lake as he towed the basket to an island shore with the drag rope. It was a maddening struggle, a ceaseless fight against the wind, which frequently caught the envelope of the balloon and pushed the basket back toward the middle of the lake. But Vogt finally felt pebbles beneath his feet and hauled the basket into shallow water. He carried Assmann up the rocky beach, and in that moment a gust of wind blew the basket out of Vogt's reach back into the lake. Inside was food and drink and a medicine chest, but Vogt was too exhausted to give chase.

Vogt fashioned a tourniquet out of a handkerchief to try to stem the flow of blood from Assmann's artery, applying soothing words of comfort. Don't worry, William, he said, a rescue party will be along at first light. As Assmann dipped in and out of consciousness, Vogt explored the island: it was uninhabited save for a colony of gulls.

Now, at around two A.M. on Wednesday morning, Assmann began a duet with the wind, a groaning dirge that troubled Vogt. "The lonesomeness and darkness of the place were appalling," he confessed later. "Our clothes were wet to the skin and we had nothing with which to light a fire. All the remainder of the night we remained on the island alone. I trying as best I could to attend to the injuries of my aide . . . His wounds bled awfully all night and I feared for his life."

Assmann only survived because two Indians left their village early on Wednesday morning to go hunting. At six o'clock they were paddling across Lake Nipissing when through the gray murk of dawn they saw a strange object in the water. What could it be? they asked one another, prodding the basket warily with their oars. Vogt heard the voices and leaped to his feet, screaming, "Over here! Over here!"

The other two competitors to come down early on Wednesday were the Swiss balloon *Azurea*, and the French crew of Alfred Le Blanc and Walther de Mumm in *Isle de France*. Emil Messner and Leon Givaudan landed near the small Ontarian town of Biscotasing at one A.M., and the *Isle de France* three hours later and only twenty miles to the southeast, having covered a similar distance of 725 miles. What had brought the two balloons to earth was the sighting of the Canadian Pacific Railroad, a thread of silver winding its way through the dense wilderness like the spoor of a giant slug. In the *Azurea* Givaudan clasped his pilot's shoulder in relief, "for had it not been for this lucky sighting . . . we would surely have been lost forever in the vicinity of Hudson Bay."

The *Isle de France* had crossed the northwestern corner of Lake Huron on Tuesday evening, and their arrival in Canadian territory was greeted, said Mumm, by a pack of wolves, which raced after the low-flying balloon, "growling and snapping and looking all too anxious for prey." Le Blanc growled back and told Mumm to load the revolver. No wolf was going to impede the progress of the irascible Frenchman, especially when he had to be in Belmont Park in three days' time to deal with an English lion, Claude Grahame-White, for whom Le Blanc had a visceral dislike.

At four A.M. Mumm spotted the railroad, what he called the "highway to civilization," and the basket came down with a bump among some trees and a herd of elk, which scattered. A bison* was "standing near, seemingly awestricken by the strange creature from the air." Le Blanc and the bison eyeballed each other for a few moments, then the animal turned and fled for its life.

The little Frenchman wasted no time in stuffing some essentials into a haversack and setting off along the track, leaving behind in their basket a treasure trove of champagne and spirits, and the unopened bottle of Bromo-Seltzer. A breathless Mumm stumbled behind his pilot as they

---

* In an article on October 25 the *St. Louis Republic* said it was unlikely to have been a bison, and "probably his assailant was a big bull moose."

walked and ran until, after five and a half hours, they reached a village. Le Blanc barked out orders in French to Mumm, who translated for the bewildered villagers, and soon they were sitting down to a breakfast of bread, jam, and coffee.

The reports in Wednesday morning's papers first piqued the interest of the American public. Hitherto the race had aroused only a couple of paragraphs in most cities' papers outside of St. Louis itself, a quaint sideshow to the Are-they-dead-or-alive? drama of Walter Wellman, and the daredevil antics of the aviators. But national pride was now at stake, what with two American balloons already down and deflated. Hopes rested on Hawley and Post—but where were they? None of the papers knew, although the *New York Herald* reported that a large yellow balloon had been seen over Manistee, on the eastern shore of Lake Michigan, early on Tuesday afternoon heading northeast. That was the last sighting.

If the *America II* was to pull off a surprise victory, they would have to go some to beat Hugo Von Abercron and August Blanckertz in *Germania*, the race favorites in everyone's eyes. Their aluminum-coated balloon had sped over a public school in West Branch, Michigan, on Tuesday afternoon at the moment the children were heading home, and a message dropped from the basket had caused pandemonium in the school yard. The boy quickest to grab the message—or perhaps the boy strongest to wrestle it from another's grip—proudly presented it to the teacher, who read aloud its contents: "Highest altitude, 5700 feet. Twenty-six bags left. Von Abercron and Blanckertz. *Germania*." A short message, but one that sent the boys and girls home exuberant.

As the papers explained on Wednesday morning, that meant the balloon had covered over five hundred miles in twenty-four hours, having used only fourteen bags of ballast. The German pair were on course to establish a new distance record in the International Balloon race, surpassing the existing mark of 873 miles, set by the late Oscar Erbslöh in 1907. The *Germania* might also challenge the world distance record of 1,193 miles, held by Count Henri de la Vaulx of France, who in 1906 had ballooned from Paris to Kiev.

The race was exciting the curiosity of Americans for an additional reason, one for which Abercron and his kinfolk had a word, and which had subsequently been incorporated into the English language: *Schaden-freude*. In its report on Wednesday morning the *New York Times* wrote that of the seven balloons still in the race, all were headed straight for Ontario, across the Great Lakes. Assuming that the balloons hadn't ditched in Lakes Michigan or Huron, they would be faced with hundreds and hundreds of miles of sparsely populated Canadian wilderness. The commuters reading their newspapers shivered and thanked God they weren't in one of those baskets.

Augustus Post wouldn't have wished to be anywhere else in the world as he updated his log in the sharp dawn air. The morning star was visible, and so, too, Venus in the west, "while to the south beautiful soft mists and haze gently spread over the sleeping lakes and virgin forests. There was no sound of chanticleers or of any animals that we were accustomed to hear. Their places were taken by the cries of an occasional loon or owl. No smoke from any chimney or any object of civilization modified the charm of this dawn in the wilderness."

As Hawley uncoiled himself from his brief nap at the bottom of the basket, he was informed by his copilot that they had just crossed into Quebec from Ontario. Below was Lake Témiscamingue. "Hawley," exclaimed Post excitedly, his dark musketeer eyes gleaming, "this is the chance of a lifetime. This direction and location north is what they [their rivals] have all been hoping and praying for. It is a wonderful opportunity." Hawley needed no persuading, he was as keen as his companion to win the race. Ballast was plentiful, and anyway, "the higher currents would carry us east . . . [so] we did not hesitate."

Not long after, they passed low over another lake, and in a clearing near the shore they saw a lumber camp and some woodcutters preparing for the day, who, when asked, shouted up the name of the lake through cupped hands—Kipawa. They also, said Post, "offered some advice, which we could not make out before we had drifted away."

The advice was probably to put down as soon as possible, for what lay beyond became apparent when the morning had fully broken and Post scanned the horizon for any sign of a place to land. There was none; nothing was to be seen but lakes and rivers. They had taken a terrible risk in pushing on east, embarking on a nerve-racking game of chance.

What if the gas should leak? What if the weather should break? They had no control over these factors. They tried to reassure one another by talking of the new Grand Trunk Pacific Railroad being constructed through the wilds of Quebec, but Post confided his true feelings to his logbook at ten A.M.: "Both realize that we are in bad country, and grave danger should we land, on account of the almost insurmountable difficulty of getting out and passing over lakes and rivers."

They rose as high as sixteen thousand feet and tore through the sky at speeds of 40 mph, casting anxious glances toward the armada of storm clouds massing in the distance. At midday Post noted the temperature in his log—forty-eight degrees—and his pulse rate, which was 85. Not long after, as he stood at the front of the basket peering through the field glasses, he gave a shout: there was a big lake to the south with three rivers running into it from the north. It was Lake St. John, Post told Hawley; he recalled it from the days when he had hunted moose in the region.

At three P.M. they started to descend, and as they dropped, the land below began to take shape. They could see in the distance cultivated fields, the odd building, even what looked like a mill. Post "made a mental survey of the country and mapped the route to the nearest houses in my mind while Hawley was handling the balloon." They began to pick up speed as they got lower, and the air currents closer to the ground buffeted their basket so that once or twice the pair lost their balance. Post threw out the drag rope as the wind bullied them north, over a small lake, and toward a forested mountain. Among the trees on the lower slopes were large boulders, so Hawley dumped another bag of ballast and the *America* rose, its drag rope touching the ground as the basket sped over the tops of seventy-foot trees. "Hang on," cried Hawley, "I'm going to take her down!"

He reached up and yanked the ripping cord and out rushed the gas. Hawley and Post grabbed hold of one another as the *America* crashed through the trees, splintering smaller branches, bouncing off larger ones, falling toward the rocky gorge below.

The SS *Trent* of the Royal Mail Steamship Company finally reached New York at three o'clock on Wednesday afternoon, having been held up by dense fog outside Sandy Hook for five hours. But at one thirty P.M., wrote the correspondent from the *New York Herald*, one of two dozen reporters on the deck of the tug *John A. Bouker*, "the sun broke through the thick mist and Captain Down proceeded slowly to the Narrows. The *Lusitania* of the Cunard Line, and half a score of other outgoing steamships, met the incoming *Trent*, and under their shrill whistles kept up a deafening salute for fully a quarter of an hour. Passengers rushed to the decks of the steamships and cheered for Mr. Wellman and the crew of the *America*."

Wellman stood on the bridge of the *Trent* bowing to well-wishers, and waving to his wife and daughters, whom he'd spotted on a tug, along with Melvin Vaniman's wife, Mildred, and Sarah Loud, mother of Lewis. Fred Aubert cradled the airship's cat in his arms and blew a kiss to Rebecca, his sweetheart, while Murray Simon took snapshots of the whole triumphant scene.

When they dropped anchor at quarantine, several of the *Trent*'s passengers began negotiating over the ship's rail with the newspapermen for the sale of photographs of the rescue, and Wellman, who had changed back into his khaki aviation suit, cupped his hands to his mouth and impatiently requested a newspaper.

A bundle of papers was thrown up to the *Trent* from one of the tugs, and the airmen "fairly tore them to pieces in their eagerness to see that the eyes of the world were directed toward them. Wellman was one of the most eager of the readers. He was really but a scanner, for he went over the front page with his trained newspaperman's eye, then laid them aside."

Wellman was desperate to discover how the voyage had been perceived by the American press. A heroic failure? A foolish dream? A humiliating farce? Having passed through quarantine and embraced their families, the crew posed for photographs and answered questions prior to checking in at the Waldorf-Astoria. What's the injury? they asked Wellman, pointing with their pencils to the sling that contained his right arm. He'd hurt his little finger, he responded, during the rescue. Some of the newsmen smirked at each other from under the brims of their derbies. A sling, just for a sore little pinkie.

Why the failure? someone asked. It wasn't because of leaking gas or faulty engines that they'd had to abandon ship, replied Wellman, it was the equilibrator. "Before starting out on this balloon voyage we were of the opinion that no dirigible could reach Europe without an equilibrator," he said. "Now we know that a dirigible cannot get there with an equilibrator." He described how the equilibrator had held the balloon back and at times pulled it down toward the water. But they'd learned the lesson, said Wellman, beaming, and wouldn't make the mistake again. So you intend to have another try? Wellman nodded and replied that he and Vaniman "think we know how a ship to achieve such a voyage must be built—larger than the late *America* with a greater lifting force, more powerful engines, greater resources of reserve gas and ballast, and a method of overcoming the fluctuations of buoyancy due to expansion and contraction" of gas. Tittering spread among the assembled reporters. So in short, start again from scratch? "Such a ship will come as surely as day follows night," replied Wellman testily, "and we cannot help feeling that our effort has been the means and will increasingly be the means, as we digest the hard lessons we learned, of hastening the day when aerial craft for purposes of, I do not say of peace, but of war, and more particularly of preventing war, will be part of the equipment of all the great powers." So in conclusion, Wellman was asked, you consider your foray out into the Atlantic has been worthwhile? "The experiment speaks for itself. We broke all records for dirigible airships. We traveled 1,010 miles over the sea and were actually in the air for seventy-two hours. Vaniman and myself learned invaluable lessons, which we think were worth learning."

The newspapers didn't share Wellman's upbeat assessment of his journey. He had already been denounced in the morning edition of the *New York Sun* for embarking on a harebrained enterprise that was destined to end in "inevitable defeat . . . and the risk of drowning." It did not, concluded the paper, "think compliments are in order, except for a safe issue from a foolish adventure." Its sister paper, the *Evening Sun*, was less censorious in its Wednesday editorial, but nonetheless asked, what had been the purpose of the trip? "He sailed forth into unknown perils, as a man jumps in the dark. Had he landed in Europe, it would have proved nothing except that he was a very bold and very lucky man. The way of flying across the Atlantic with some safety and certainty would still have had to be found."

The editorial of the *St. Louis Post-Dispatch* provided the most thought-ful analysis. The paper began by commending Wellman and his five com-panions on their gallantry, likening their voyage to that "of the old days of the Vikings." Then it turned its attention to what, if anything, the *America* had taught the world. The Wellman experiment, said the paper, "tends to confirm the growing conviction that conquest of the air is far from achievement by a dirigible balloon. The flying machine will probably beat it to the goal. The balloon is beautiful and the flight of it is a fine sport, but for the serious business of aerial transportation, it gives little promise of success."

The reporters who swarmed over Belmont Park on Wednesday morning were of a different kind from those waiting impatiently at the Battery for the arrival of the SS *Trent*. They neither knew nor cared of the differ-ence between a biplane and a monoplane, and they didn't recognize the small Chicagoan who glared at them with "eyes of agate" as he walked briskly toward his hangar. Instead they tutted in irritation at the mud that stuck to the soles of their polished shoes and blew into their hands, impatient for the arrival of the man whose name was the talk of New York. These were the correspondents whose preferred milieu was a charity ball or an opening night, where they inhaled the rarefied air of New York high society and waited for the city's rich and famous to sup-ply their columns with the oxygen of gossip. Few men in America were more famous at this moment than the one for whom they were waiting, the English aviator with the matinee-idol features whose engagement to Pauline Chase had been announced by her agent, Charles Frohman, the previous evening.

When Claude Grahame-White arrived in an automobile with his manager, Sydney McDonald, he must have been prepared for the furor. Most morning papers—and not just in New York—carried reports of the impending marriage. The *Post-Dispatch* had even had the temerity to make the story their front-page lead, shunting the latest update on the International Balloon race to a side column. Underneath a photo of the happy couple was the headline AVIATOR WINS PAJAMA GIRL IN AN AIR-PLANE, and a story that suggested Grahame-White had popped the ques-tion at five hundred feet. The *Post-Dispatch* said that while New Yorkers might not be surprised at the news, what with the Englishman having "occupied a front-row seat at every performance of *Our Miss Gibbs* at the Knickerbocker Theater," Bostonians would be shocked and disappointed. "They were sure there was going to be an airplane romance, with Grahame-White as one of the central figures, but they were only half right. The name which they had been whispering to each other was that of Miss Eleonora Sears . . . It was known that the English aviator was much in the company of Miss Sears and that he took her to dinners and social functions while he was the leading aerial lion of the Boston aviation season."

However, the paper attested, anxious that its readers shouldn't infer that Grahame-White's morals were anything less than scrupulous, friends of Miss Chase had informed the *Post-Dispatch* that "she was never jealous of Miss Sears . . . There was a perfect understanding between Grahame-White and the famous actress."

The *New York Herald*—much like the subject of its story—had scooped its rivals and carried a brief interview with Miss Chase, moments after she had confirmed her victory from the chaise lounge of her dressing room. "Yes, it's true," she said, flashing one of her enchanting smiles, "and I'm very happy. We will be married next spring in London." Chase then disclosed that her devotion to her betrothed was such that she intended to retire and would "say good-bye in *Peter Pan* in the Duke of York's Theater [in London]."

The flattering tone of the reportage was regrettably sullied by an ungentlemanly aside from the *Herald*, which whispered from behind its hand that "rumor has engaged the actress to various men in the past."

The paper had the decency not to list the suitors who had fallen by the wayside—not the American millionaire in 1902, nor the English motorcar manufacturer in 1907, not the purported alliance in 1908 with Captain Robert Falcon Scott, the noted polar explorer, not even J. M. Barrie, the creator of *Peter Pan*, in 1909.* And the *Herald* was far too discreet to

---

* Following Barrie's divorce in 1909, much speculation appeared in the American press that he intended to marry Chase, despite the fact that he had been Chase's godfather since 1906. Barrie eventually quashed the rumors by saying he felt only "paternal affection" for Chase.

point out that only last month a report had appeared in the *Chicago Daily Tribune* confidently asserting that Chase had agreed to marry a wealthy Londoner—"popular in the clubs and at the theaters"—called Nicholas Jarvis Wood.

Perhaps the snide reference in the *Herald* to his fiancée's history of engagements accounted for the dark frown upon Grahame-White's otherwise perfect face as he stepped out of the automobile on Wednesday morning. Referring all questions to his manager, Mr. McDonald, the Englishman marched toward the hangars, where John Moisant was already tuning up his monoplane.

As Grahame-White approached his two hangars, numbers 14 and 15, he could see Moisant and his mechanic, Albert Fileux—his passenger on the Channel flight—preparing the Blériot monoplane. The pair were dressed in blue overalls stained black with engine grease, and Moisant had on a thick sweater. Grahame-White walked over and introduced himself. As ever, he was impeccably dressed, in a dark blue three-piece suit and bow tie, and brogues that had been polished that morning by the bellboy of the Hotel Astor.

It was the first time the pair had met, though both were familiar with each other's prowess, and for that reason genuine respect was in the handshake. These were two men at the pinnacle of their profession, sharing a common danger and living life with an intensity few could match. But behind the bonhomie each was eyeing up the other, evaluating his strengths and weaknesses. Moisant had the brittle sensitivity of the small man and bridled inwardly at the disparity of physiques. What hair he had left on his head barely reached up to his rival's broad shoulders. Psychologically, however, the American considered himself superior to Grahame-White. Moisant was one of life's risk-takers, combining natural aggression with a gambler's daring, as he had first shown in Central America and then in his flight across the Channel. Grahame-White was more cautious. When he had arrived in Massachusetts and seen the proposed route of the race around Boston Light, he persuaded the organizers to reroute it over open country rather than the densely populated section of the city as had originally been planned.

A few weeks later, at the Brockton Fair show, Grahame-White had refused to fly in front of 120,000 people because of a vicious crosswind, even ignoring the impassioned pleas of the management, who feared a riot if there was no entertainment. Fortunately for the organizers, the showman in Grahame-White had come to the fore, and he'd addressed the jeering mob from the back of an automobile with a megaphone pressed to his lips: "Now listen to me. I know you're angry because you've paid to see me fly and here I am on the ground . . . [but] it would be flying in the face of Providence to fly this afternoon. I can buy a new airplane, ladies and gentlemen, but I can't buy a new life."

Moisant was less guarded in his approach to flying; after all, hadn't he told the newspapers earlier in the week that there was nothing much to the aviation game? It was as easy as riding a bicycle.

The two men shook hands and parted with a smile. Maybe Grahame-White was still on Moisant's mind as he climbed into his monoplane, or perhaps there was another reason he didn't open the cock to start the oil supply before he took off. For two circuits of the Belmont Park course the error went unnoticed by the American, but as he began his third lap, he glanced down at the oil gauge . . . Damn it! He'd forgotten to open the cock. If Grahame-White had been in Moisant's position, he would have landed at once, indifferent to the presence of a rival, but proud Moisant reckoned he could fix the problem forty feet from the ground. Eyewitnesses later described to the *New York Herald* how Moisant had passed the grandstand and was approaching the stables at the east corner when "the monoplane was seen to dip suddenly and then dart toward the ground, nose downward, and turn toward the right. The monoplane fell on the right wing, crumpling it like a Chinese lantern under a road roller. The machine almost somersaulted, crushing and breaking the other wing."

The first to reach the crash scene was Grahame-White, who had watched Moisant fall as he began his own takeoff. As he flew low through the cloud of dust rising from the shattered airplane, Grahame-White saw Moisant get to his feet and wave. Later the American told reporters of his mishap in the breathless tone of a man still high on adrenaline. "It was sheer carelessness and lack of forethought on my part," he confessed, a rueful smile lighting up his pale face. "These Gnome motors grip when the oil ceases to flow, and I realized I would have trouble unless I got my oil flowing at once. Of course, I might have come to the ground, but I thought that I could attend so simple a thing in the air. I lifted my foot to kick open the oil cock, but the moment I let go of the rudder control, my machine wobbled badly, almost turned turtle, and threw me completely out of my course."

Someone asked Moisant if he'd been hurt. He shook his head and, laughing, replied, "Why, nobody ever gets hurt flying!"

CHAPTER SIX

Progress Slow and Exhausting

Thursday, October 20, 1910

THE DESCENT OF the *America II* had stopped at exactly fifteen minutes to four on Wednesday afternoon. Post noted the time in the logbook. It was forty-six hours since they had left St. Louis, and the pair agreed that they must be in with a chance of winning the International Balloon Cup. First, however, they had to deal with the more urgent problem of extricating themselves from a precarious situation. Neither had been injured in the fall, but the basket had landed in a rocky, shallow gorge, and the yellow envelope of the balloon was draped over a tall pine tree. They hauled the basket out of the gorge, laid it on a large, flat stone, and secured it to the trunk of a tree with the drag rope. The storm clouds they had passed on their way down were now starting to leak sullen raindrops, so Post rigged up a shelter using "our light waterproof basket-cover over an open umbrella above the basket" while Hawley laid out a thick blanket on the basket floor.

Once inside, the pair ate some food and examined their map under a battery lamp, but they were unable to confidently identify their exact position. "After talking things over and discussing the ease with which we should walk back to the houses we had seen and send back for the balloon," said Post, "we lay down and fell asleep."

· · ·

The complacency of Hawley and Post was misplaced. Although they didn't know it, "they had landed in the angle formed by the Peribonka River and Lake Tchitagama, half a mile north of a pond called Lac de Sable, fifty-five miles from any habitation, and seventy-five miles northwest of a railway terminus called Chicoutimi." The few houses that Hawley had seen during their descent were in fact fur trappers' lodges, rarely occupied during the winter months when no one but the most experienced hunter penetrated the depths of the Quebec wilderness.

The region would become famous three years later with Louis Hémon's classic novel, *Maria Chapdelaine: A Tale of the Lake St. John Community*, a love story based on the author's own experiences. Hémon would write that in the early fall "the woods were putting on a dress of unearthly loveliness . . . of the birches, aspens, alders and wild cherries scattered upon the slope, October made splashes of many— tinted red and gold. Throughout these weeks the ruddy brown of mosses, the changeless green of fir and cypress, were no more than a background, a setting only for the ravishing colors of those leaves born with the spring, that perish with the autumn . . . but 'ere long there sweeps from out of the cold north a mighty wind like a final sentence of death, the cruel ending to a reprieve." Then comes the snow, warned Hémon, and God help the man "who loses his way, for a short day only, in that limitless forest."

The wind that tore through the mountain gorge on Wednesday evening was so fierce it uprooted birches, spruces, and pines. Post and Hawley were "awakened by the falling of the limb of a tree which struck the basket and gave the impression that we were slipping down the side of the rock on which the basket rested." Throughout the night they trembled in the bottom of the basket as the night sky bellowed and blazed. The storm had yet to blow itself out at first light on Thursday, but as snowflakes began to fall, they felt it prudent to get on their way.

While Hawley warmed some soup for breakfast, Post climbed farther up the mountain to survey their position. He returned with disconcerting news; there were no villages or farms; they were marooned in a sea of green. They had their soup, and as they mopped up the remains with a bread roll, Post said that their best hope was to head south.

The dynamics of the relationship between the pair had shifted since their landing. Up in the air, Hawley was the pilot, but down on the ground, Post tacitly took control. Though he made his money as a New York banker, Post was an outdoorsman at heart, a hunter and a sportsman with an instinct for survival. Hawley, on the other hand, belonged in the boardroom, not the backwoods, and he moved with the diffidence of a man who knew it.

They packed three ballast bags, one with their aeronautical instruments, another with food, such as crackers, ten boiled eggs, a cold chicken, jars of deviled ham and of tongue, twelve bars of chocolate, some fruit, their condensed-meat tablets, and the last three tins of soup. The third bag contained three knives, a handsaw, a hammer, a can opener, two balls of cord, two battery lamps, and a box of waterproof matches. Hawley loaded his .38-caliber revolver, and Post pinned a scribbled note to the basket:

> This is the balloon "America II," pilot, Alan R. Hawley; Aide, Augustus Post. Left October 17, 1910, 5:46 pm, representing America in the Gordon Bennett International Balloon Race and landed here October 19, 3:45 pm. We have gone south around big lake.

Not long after seven A.M. they set off, with Post leading the way in his suit of dark brown velvet corduroy, a small pocket compass cradled in his gloved hand, treading over ground "covered with a mass of rotten stumps, fallen tree trunks and decayed leaves, through which rock ledges penetrate at frequent intervals, making progress slow and exhausting, as well as dangerous."

They moved carefully down the mountainside, snaking their way through a forest of pine trees. Once they caught a glimpse down to their right of the small lake (Lac de Sable) that they had seen during the final moments of their descent. At two P.M. they sat down on a log, its black bark still damp from the snowflakes, and gorged on some pears and oranges, which were "very refreshing, but hardly in keeping with a forest that gave no sign of a human being ever having been there." Post pointed to the luxuriant carpet of moss that grew only on one side of the trees and explained to Hawley that in this region it was one of nature's compass points: moss formed only on the north face of the trees.

They washed the juice off their hands in a mountain river, then hoisted the ballast bags over their shoulders and set off south. Lower down the slope the pine trees petered out and the balloonists were confronted by an almost solid wall of underbrush. Brambles tore at their legs, ripping through the serge material of their pants and crisscrossing their shins and thighs with angry red scratches, while branches as thick as a man's wrist had them ducking and weaving. Sweat poured down Post's face and collected in his ragged beard as he hacked at the foliage with a hunting knife. Now and then he sank up to his knees in a morass, levering himself free with the aid of a branch.

Post stepped over a fallen log, then bobbed under a low-hanging branch. As he chopped and slashed at some brambles, he heard a cry from behind. Spinning round, he saw Hawley slumped over the log, clutching his right knee. "Damn it," he said, groaning, as Post put an arm under his shoulder and helped him up. "I thought the log was solid but it crumbled the moment I stepped on it."

Hawley flexed his right knee a few times, gave it a good rub, and waved Post on, telling him he was fine. For another hour they continued to battle the undergrowth until finally, just before four P.M., the branches became thinner and the brambles fewer. Soon they were moving freely and were rewarded with a view of a long stretch of water running east to west. Post gave a triumphant "Yes!" It was Lake Tchitagama. He hurriedly unfolded the map and found the lake with his finger. Lake St. John and its surrounding villages lay beyond and to the west, but Post knew from previous hunting trips that the western end of Tchitagama drained into the Peribonca River, which was too wide to cross. They would have to skirt round the eastern end of Tchitagama, then swing back west and tramp cross-country toward Lake St. John. Not long after, they decided to camp for the night next to a mountain stream. They constructed a bivouac from branches and leaves, with the waterproof basket-cover as a roof, but didn't have enough dry wood to build a fire. Shivering in the deepening cold, they dined on a boiled egg each and a can of consommé. Post borrowed Hawley's revolver and shot at a red squirrel foraging for food, but the bullet missed and the animal vanished into the trees.

The pair sat and talked for a while, then Post fished out his hip flask of cognac from his coat pocket and they toasted each other's health. They fell asleep to the soothing movement of the stream but before long Post was woken by the sound of stifled groans. Hawley mumbled an apology for his lack of stoicism but explained he was suffering terrible pains in his right knee. Post offered a few weary words of sympathy but was soon fast asleep under his blanket. Hawley tossed and turned in search of the most comfortable position and eventually dozed off. But not for long. He woke feeling scared and lonely, besieged by a wilderness that was closing in on a wounded man.

The whereabouts of Hawley and Post was largely overlooked in Thursday's newspapers. Instead, the extraordinary escape of Leopold Vogt and William Assmann in the *Harburg II* dominated the coverage of the International Balloon race with newspapers vying for the most dramatic headline. DROP 18,000; IN LAKE 3 HOURS was how the *Chicago Daily Tribune* reported it. The *New York Times* ran with BALLOON IN LAKE; CREW SWIM ASHORE, while the *St. Louis Globe-Democrat* headlined its front page VOGT AND ASSMANN PLUNGE INTO LAKE, adding in its subheading that they had had "a thrilling descent."

Vogt wouldn't have used that adjective; instead he told reporters that it had been "an experience which I do not care to repeat," and that if not for the appearance of the two "Cherokee Indian hunters," who had paddled them to the mainland and dropped them within walking distance of a railroad station, he didn't think Assmann would have survived much longer. Vogt's copilot was now sitting up in a hospital bed, bruised and blooded, but in remarkably good heart.

The *St. Louis Republic* also gave a full account of the *Harburg*'s terrifying ordeal and added that Alfred Le Blanc had descended in the *Isle de France* "on the edge of civilization . . . rather than attempt to go further and land in some inaccessible place, from which he could not return for the New York airplane meet next week." According to the *Republic*, five balloons were still up in the race, but that figure was amended to four in the evening edition of the *St. Louis Post-Dispatch*, which also told its readers of an unconfirmed report that the race favorite, *Germania*, had come down somewhere in Quebec.

The SS *Trent* had reached New York on Wednesday afternoon, twelve hours before the hurricane that had ripped through the Caribbean roared across the city's latitude. Though much of its energy had been dissipated since its destruction of Cuba, the driving rain that drenched Walter Wellman on Thursday morning as he left the Waldorf-Astoria bound for Atlantic City was a chilling reminder of just how close he and his crew had come to disaster.

Nearly four inches of rain poured from the skies, more than had fallen in the preceding four months of drought. Streets were flooded, sewers clogged, trolley lines stalled, and the subways received great cataracts from the stairways and through ventilator gratings. Water had to be pumped out from the Pennsylvania tubes under the East River, and in Brooklyn several buildings were evacuated when the rain began to weaken foundations. A horse was killed when it was driven through a pool of electrified water on East Twelfth Street in Flatbush, and the church of St. Thomas Aquinas at Fourth Avenue and Ninth Street in Brighton Beach was badly damaged when a fifteen-foot section of the sidewalk immediately outside subsided under the weight of floodwater.

By noon the storm had passed and New Yorkers emerged blinking into the pale sunlight. The damage wasn't as bad as they'd first feared, and the *New York Sun* reported there was "almost a spring freshness in the grass of the parks, which had been looking dingy and desolate." Some of the wild-chestnut trees in Battery Park had begun to blossom again, and the city as a whole felt revivified by the storm.

Early on Thursday afternoon the *Teutonic* docked at New York, and among the green-about-the-gills passengers who staggered down the gangplank were a trio of French aviators—Emile Aubrun, René Simon, and René Barrier—and a Swiss flier, twenty-eight-year-old Edmond Audemars. There to greet them was Cortlandt Field Bishop, who unknotted their frayed nerves with an automobile trip around the city, then a stroll through Central Park in the company of a *New York Herald* reporter. Audemars told the paper that he would be flying a Demoiselle—like his good friend

Roland Garros—and though the plane had a comic appearance, he believed it would surprise a few people at Belmont Park. "I intend to enter most of the general events," he said, "and I certainly do not intend to miss any of the regular prizes if I can help it."

Emile Aubrun cut a stylish figure as he admired Central Park. He was wearing a double-breasted, tan overcoat and derby, and he frequently rolled the ends of his waxed mustache between thumb and forefinger. The twenty-nine-year-old had learned to fly in 1909—the twenty-first Frenchman to receive his aviation license—but the first to go through his training without having once crashed his airplane, a feat his instructor attributed to his "cool head and cleverness." A month before leaving France for New York, Aubrun had flown 186 miles in three hours and thirty-three minutes in his Blériot monoplane, but his greatest exploit, in the eyes of the *New York Herald* reporter, "was that of flying second to Mons. Le Blanc in the 'Circuit de L'Est,' the recent 488 miles cross country race over half of France. They were the only aviators who finished in the contest."

Once the tour of the city was over, the four aviators were deposited at their hotel, the Knickerbocker, where they were welcomed by Hubert Latham and Bertrand de Lesseps and his sister Countess de la Bergassiere, both of whom were becoming increasingly anxious about their brother Jacques, who had gone to Canada three days earlier to call on a young woman and who had not been heard from since.

Not too far from the Knickerbocker, at the Manhattan Hotel, the fliers of the Wright Exhibition Team had also just checked in, having arrived from St. Louis. Ralph Johnstone retired to his room with his wife and young son, Walter Brookins was his usual unapproachable self, but Arch Hoxsey "was full of snap and ginger," as he often was when the stern-faced Wright brothers weren't loitering in the background. Although he didn't let on to the *New York Herald* correspondent (who had hotfooted it to the Manhattan Hotel from Central Park), Hoxsey had almost been fired from the Wright Exhibition Team the previous week after he took Theodore Roosevelt for a quick spin during the St. Louis Meet. Wilbur Wright had reportedly been "very, very angry over the incident" and warned Hoxsey that if something similar occurred in the future, he would be sacked because the Wrights "don't care for that kind of notoriety." With Wilbur Wright en route to New York from Dayton, Ohio, and Orville to follow at the weekend, Hoxsey felt less constricted and he sat in the hotel lobby chatting away to the reporter, though Hoxsey drew a veil over the Roosevelt faux pas. "Of one thing the public may be sure," he forecast, "that as long as a Wright machine is in the game, there will be some flying at Belmont Park every afternoon. It will take more than a fifty-mile zephyr to scare the operator of a Wright biplane!"

Sensing that Hoxsey was in a talkative mood, the correspondent brought up the subject of the Wrights' new plane. What was so secret about it? Hoxsey was having none of it. He'd just had one verbal warning from the brothers, and if he divulged details of their secret machine, he might well be out on his ear. He shook his head and, with a smile, apologized that "he was not at liberty to go into details." But he did confirm that a new airplane was on its way from Dayton to challenge for the international trophy, and in his opinion it was a dark horse worthy of comparison with any of the four-legged creatures that had graced Belmont Park in the past few years.

CHAPTER SEVEN

Wait Until Orville Comes

Friday, October 21, 1910

ALAN HAWLEY HAD eventually fallen into a fitful sleep in the early hours of Friday, but he had been awake for a couple of hours when dawn broke over their bivouac. He was cold and hungry and stiff all over, but the excruciating pain in his knee of a few hours earlier was now just a dull ache. He flexed the knee under his blanket and hope began to warm his body: perhaps Augustus Post wouldn't need to continue alone.

Hawley crawled out of the bivouac and hopped to his feet, putting all his weight on his uninjured left leg. He gently laid his right foot on the ground and began to walk around their camping ground, limping at first until he grew more confident as the knee bore his weight. It was sore, but tolerable.

Post joined his companion outside and they breakfasted on a bar of chocolate and a boiled egg each. Then they went through their packs, discarding those items that were essential in a balloon but superfluous on the ground: two statiscopes, a thermometer, a hydrometer, and one of the two electric lamps, which they tied to the limb of a tree. They hesitated over the barograph, discussing its merits and faults as if it were a pretty girl walking down Broadway; finally Post stowed it in the ballast bag that he slung over his shoulder.

At ten minutes to seven they set off southeast, their feet throwing up a fine spray of dew as they looked for a place to ford the mountain stream. Post soon spotted a fallen log, and once Hawley had stamped on it with his left foot to make sure it wasn't going to crumble under their weight, they crossed without trouble.

With their entire focus now on what lay immediately before them, the pair's morale fluctuated with the smallest detail. Post came across another felled log, its bark covered in a rug of moss, but this one gave evidence of having been chopped down a long time ago. It was comforting to think that another human being had once been at this spot. Not long after they encountered a river that could only be crossed by jumping from rock to rock in their hobnailed boots. Hawley slipped and "got a wetting so that we had to go out . . . and lay out the things to dry, including Hawley's clothes."

They waited an hour in the weak morning sunshine before Hawley struggled into his damp gray tweed suit and knotted his red tie, then they struck out south again. By 10 A.M. they were skirting a small lake, jostling their way through a dense thicket of alder bushes with always one eye on the ground for any of nature's hidden traps. At noon Hawley was grimacing in pain, so they rested for a few minutes and Post cut a sliver of chicken for their lunch. Hawley reluctantly agreed to discard his heavy aneroid—a gift from the Aero Club of America—and he hung the instrument from a tree with its glass face open so that perhaps a hunter might find it winking in the sun and return it.

At four P.M. they issued from the alder bushes onto a thin strip of sandy beach that ran alongside the lake. They had covered only seven miles, but Hawley was exhausted, and Post considered the beach a good spot to camp for the night. There was freshwater and plenty of dry wood. While Hawley rested, Post constructed a pyre of logs that was soon well ablaze.

Supper consisted of a piece of chicken and two eggs, and a cup of hot water, then they built a bivouac and settled down for the night. Hawley was soon asleep, shattered by the day's trek, but Post the outdoorsman went for a walk along the beach to pay homage to nature's beauty: "The northern lights lit up the horizon, revealing the silhouette of the mountains," he wrote in his log. "The lake was black and perfectly calm, and later the moon came up and added its silver light to the scene, while the red embers of the fire glowed as the weather-beaten logs burned on the beach."

The sensational headline in Friday morning's *New York Times* read HEL-VETIA LANDS; WENT 1,100 MILES. The accompanying report said that the Aero Club of St. Louis had announced the Swiss balloon crewed by Colonel Theodore Schaeck and his aide, Paul Armbruster, had landed in Quebec, thereby smashing the existing International Balloon race distance record of 873 miles. If only they'd managed another 94 miles, the pair would have surpassed Count Henri de la Vaulx's world-record distance record of 1,193 miles. However, the *New York Times* was quick to point out that this record might yet be broken because the *Helvetia* was "not thought to be the balloon sighted . . . at Kiskisink, Canada, 1,200 miles from St. Louis."

The *Times* knew not the identity of the balloon, but with the *Germania* also reported down—with only 850 miles covered—it could be one of only three: "The Swiss balloon, *Azurea*, Lieut Messner, pilot; the German balloon *Düsseldorf II*, Lieut. Hans Gericke, pilot; and the *America II*, A. R. Hawley, pilot."

A few hours later, St. Louis's only evening paper, the *Post-Dispatch*, suggested that while the *Helvetia* and *Germania* had indeed descended, reports had them confused, and in fact the German balloon had covered the greater distance, not the Swiss one.* But the main thrust of the newspaper's front-page article on Friday evening was the growing sense of dread among race organizers that one or all of the missing three balloons had met with calamity. The *Post-Dispatch* reported that the board of governors of the St. Louis Aero Club had convened a meeting on Friday morning to discuss their plan of action. The upshot of that meeting was a telegram from Albert Lambert, the president, in which he asked all steamship companies operating on the Great Lakes to be on the lookout for any trace of the balloons. Lambert then sent duplicate telegrams to

---

* This was correct; the *Germania* put down in Coocoocache, Quebec, and was later officially credited with 1,079 miles, and the *Helvetia* landed near Ville-Marie in Quebec after a journey of 850 miles.

Colonel J. M. Gibson, lieutenant governor of Ontario, to Sir Alphonse Pelletier, lieutenant governor of the province of Quebec, and to the offices of Hudson Bay Company in Montreal, in which he appealed for their help in locating three balloons "last sighted Tuesday sailing over Lake Huron and the region adjoining. Their course, east of north, would take them into the Canadian wilds. Their provisions and wearing apparel are limited. They should have landed Wednesday night."

The Hudson Bay Company replied at once to the request, informing the Aero Club that it had alerted all its trapping and hunting posts scattered throughout northern Ontario and Quebec and that within a few hours a search covering the two provinces would be instituted.

The front page of the *St. Louis Post-Dispatch* on Friday evening was a collector's item for all balloon aficionados. Not only was there the ominous news from the International Balloon race, but also what the paper justifiably called "a remarkable photo" of the death throes of the *America*. Taken by a passenger aboard the SS *Trent*, the photograph showed the airship in the early-morning sunshine with the lifeboat still attached and the malevolent shape of the equilibrator just visible under the water.

By the time the newspaper was on sale, the men of the *America* were back in Atlantic City, their low-key reception in New York just a distant memory as "two military companies and a band escorted Walter Wellman and his crew from the station to the Hotel Chalfonte," and an estimated five thousand people lined the streets to cheer them on their way. The six men had barely enough time to deposit their bags in their rooms before they were whisked off to a dinner in their honor in the banquet room of the Hotel Shelburne. Telegrams were read out from those unable to attend, including one from President Taft, and then Joseph Saius, head of the American Exhibition Company, the expedition's biggest financial backer, addressed the diners. "No name since Columbus has been regarded with such respect as that of Wellman," he exclaimed. "No names have ever been received with greater commendation than the name of Wellman and the men who with him made up the crew of the *America* . . . Since the *America* has left Atlantic City, the entire world has watched the progress of the Wellman project, and I believe tonight that the scientists of the world have secured solutions to new problems of the air through the bravery of the crew of the *America*."

When the thunderous applause had abated, Wellman rose to his feet and thanked the people of Atlantic City for their loyalty in those dragging weeks when the American press had subjected him and his men to "calumny and abuse while we were forced to await proper conditions." But that was all in the past, and Wellman let it be known that he was prepared to reach out the hand of friendship to his erstwhile traducers. "One of the things demonstrated by the *America*'s trip," he explained to the men and women seated before him, "was the possibility of offering a real conquest of the air. With all its mistakes, I believe that American journalism seeks only to do right. I, who have suffered much from its attacks, still believe that it is only mistaken, and not pessimistic."

As Wellman's chest swelled with sanctimony, the *Chicago Daily Tribune* was laying the last of its type for the Saturday edition. Among the latest reports of the International Balloon race and the imminent start of the Belmont Park Meet, the paper took time to wonder why Wellman had been so touchy ever since his return. After all, it said, "Any person that attempts the highly improbable with no convincingly good reason is a legitimate subject of banter." And that was a neat encapsulation of— the *Tribune* hesitated to use the word *adventure*—Wellman's escapade, which had proved only that "an unwieldy gas bag, a 'dirigible,' that steers like a thistle seed, will remain in the air, under favorable circumstances, a certain number of hours." The paper was quick to reassure its readers that it yielded to no one in its admiration of Wellman's daring, but then "we have long admired Mr. Empedocies, who, peradventurous [*sic*] as Mr. Wellman, dove into a volcano and presently reappeared as a cinder." The *Tribune*'s peremptory conclusion was that "the air craft has not yet been designed that will cross the Atlantic."

For the favored five hundred spectators admitted to Belmont Park on Friday, the afternoon of aviation thrills was "such has seldom been seen in this country." Most of the people admitted to the course were friends and relatives of the fliers, but a few were enthusiasts who had come on the off chance of gaining admittance a day before the start of the tournament proper. Midway through the afternoon, reported the *New York*

Herald in a breathless tone, "Arch Hoxsey in a Wright biplane, Mr. Grahame-White in a Farman biplane, and Mr. J. Armstrong Drexel, in a Blériot monoplane, were in the air at one time . . . by far the most remarkable sight those in the vicinity of New York have ever been permitted to witness."

Drexel remained in the air for three minutes, but Hoxsey and Grahame-White were up for ten, circling the five-kilometer course like a pair of boxers prowling the ring at the start of a bout. When Grahame-White touched down on the grass, still soggy after the heavy rain of the previous day, Drexel was waiting to welcome him. Drexel was in his late twenties, a "heavily-built and good-natured man," with a small mustache that looked more as if he had forgotten to shave above his lip for a few days rather than any serious attempt at facial fashion. A millionaire playboy with the common touch, he had no side and no sense of self-importance. His great-grandfather Francis Drexel had fled Austria during the Napoleonic Wars to avoid conscription and arrived in America in 1817, eventually founding the eponymous banking firm in Philadelphia twenty years later. Now the family was one of the richest in the country, and earlier in the year a union had taken place with the Goulds, the banking family whose estimated fortune of $200 million exceeded that of even the Drexels.

The engagement party for Anthony Drexel—Armstrong's younger brother—and his fiancée, Marjorie Gould, had been held in February 1910, in the Fifth Avenue mansion of her parents, and 250 of New York's "400"* attended what was as much a celebration of excess as it was of a forthcoming marriage. More than five thousand orchids, each costing $1, decorated the many rooms and halls of the house, and each guest was presented with a jeweled charm as a keepsake (rings for the ladies, scarf pins for the gentlemen) from the famous Mrs. Van Rensselaer. An orchestra, hidden behind the greenery at the foot of the staircase, entertained the lucky few, before everyone sat down to a meal that cost $100 (approximately $1,600 today) per head.

---

* This was the name given to the inner circle of New York's high society, said to number four hundred persons, with the Astor family at its heart.

Two months later Armstrong had been his brother's best man at the wedding at St. Bartholomew's Episcopal Church on Madison Avenue, and his speech at the reception was well received, though not as well received as the $2 million worth of wedding presents, or the $2,500 cake, which was decorated with jewels supplied by Tiffany and arrived under armed guard.

In June, Armstrong Drexel had seen another of his siblings married off, this time his sister, Marguerite, who had stepped out of a London church as the wife of Guy Montagu George Finch-Hatton,* better known in England as Viscount Maidstone. The alliance didn't go down well across the Atlantic, with one newspaper saying that "another cofferful of American dollars [has] found its way into the custody of the British nobility."

A fortnight after the wedding Armstrong Drexel, who had been taking flying lessons in England for several months, was awarded his aviation license by the Royal Aero Club of Great Britain, only the fourteenth issued. Having learned to fly under the instruction of Claude Grahame-White, Drexel accompanied him to various meets in England and Scotland throughout July and August.

The pair had got on famously from the start, with each man finding qualities to admire in the other that were deficient in his own character. Drexel lacked Grahame-White's physical grace, and his own amiable but rather oafish appearance made him one of those cursed men who was always considered by a woman as a friend, never a suitor. Grahame-White, for his part, enjoyed Drexel's modesty and manners, and his unwillingness to take either life or himself too seriously. In short, the American's innate security complemented the Englishman's innate insecurity. What they did share, however, was an uncommon courage. They were intelligent, imaginative men, aware of the risks of every flight, but prepared to run them nonetheless. "If you think of danger when you're flying, you're as good as killed," said Drexel once. "The aviator must act as if there were no difference between life and death." When Grahame-White taxied to a standstill at Belmont Park after his ten-minute practice spin, Drexel helped him from his Farman biplane and introduced his

---

* His younger brother, Denys, later became a big-game hunter in Africa and was immortalized in the film *Out of Africa*, in which he was portrayed by Robert Redford.

brother, Anthony, and his sister-in-law, Marjorie, both of whom were aviation enthusiasts. Soon, however, someone else arrived at Belmont Park whose interest in the machines was even more acute, but far less welcome to Grahame-White than Mr. and Mrs. Drexel's. Wilbur Wright appeared in the middle of the afternoon with a team of mechanics and a large wooden crate containing the brothers' new airplane. The indefatigable correspondent of the *New York Herald* pressed for details of the machine, "but not a man connected with the Wrights would say a word about it and not a line of the new machine will be revealed until it is uncrated the next morning." All Wilbur was prepared to say to the paper was "Wait until Orville comes."

Wilbur Wright then cast a beady eye down hangar row, counting the number of airplanes on view that, in his opinion, infringed the patent of the Wrights' original flying machine.

Their tenacity in pursuing lawsuits had made the Wrights the most despised men in the world of aviation in 1910. Louis Paulhan, the hero of Los Angeles in January, had been served with an injunction after the meet, which prevented him competing elsewhere in the United States and led him to describe Wilbur Wright as a "bird of prey." The manager of Glenn Curtiss's aircraft factory, Harry Genung, said it appeared that the Wright brothers believed "the world owed them a bounty" when Genung's boss's activities were also grounded by a legal challenge. The resentment created by the Wrights' paranoiac greed was best summed up by a newspaper cartoon that depicted the brothers furiously waving their fists at an airplane passing overhead and shouting, "Keep out of my air!"

That any French and British aviators had dared come to America to compete at Belmont Park was due to the persuasive powers of Cortlandt Field Bishop, who, as president of the Aero Club of America, had got the brothers to agree to leave their legal team at home when they came to New York. "The Wright Company has given guarantee that no obstacle will be placed in the way of foreign competitors," Bishop had written in a letter to the Royal Aero Club of Great Britain in August, "and no proceedings will be taken against them during the different events of the meeting. The Gordon Bennett Aviation Cup is included in this agreement."

The Wrights had acceded to the request from Bishop in the belief that the aviators would be in America only to compete at Belmont Park; but then they had gone to Boston and spluttered in indignation as Grahame-White humiliated their own fliers in a machine they believed—as they did all airplanes—infringed on their copyright. They had been outmaneuvered by the English matinee idol, but what could they do? They couldn't serve an injunction against Grahame-White, the most popular aviator in the world, and prevent him flying in New York because they had given their word, and to two men to whom their integrity was far more important than their popularity, their word was their bond. They could do nothing, they realized, except prevail in the International Aviation Cup with their new, very secret machine, then pounce on Grahame-White if he should so much as set foot in an airplane in America once the Belmont Park Meet was at an end.

As the shadows on the Belmont Park course lengthened in the autumnal sun of Friday afternoon, a convoy of horse-drawn trucks began to arrive at the hangars carrying the crated machines of the foreign competitors. Hubert Latham directed one of the trucks to the front of his hangar, No. 20, one along from that of Roland Garros, who had just landed after a twenty-minute flight in his Demoiselle.

Latham and his chief mechanic, a Frenchman called Weber, breathed a sigh of relief as they began to pry open the rectangular wooden crate containing the Antoinette monoplane. The machine had been held at the port for three days since its arrival in the hold of the *Niagara*, and it had taken a furious telephone call on Thursday evening before customs officials agreed to allow the airplane to be delivered to Belmont Park. Eager for his first sight of the famous Antoinette, the correspondent from the *New York Herald* looked on as the crate was opened. Weber and Latham disappeared inside the crate, and suddenly there was a curse. Then another, and another, each one more vehement than its predecessor. Latham emerged and requested that the *Herald*'s reporter inspect the plane "as a witness of the condition it was in." The correspondent peered in and "found that the wings had been severely crushed in by the timbers thrown into the inside by the truckmen, and that under the strain the frail braces of the big wings had collapsed in several places. The tail had also been crushed by some heavy weight falling on it."

Officials from the Aero Club of America were summoned so they could see for themselves the incompetence of the truckmen, and it was nearly dark when they arrived to find Latham, with a cigarette in his mouth, still trying to calm his irate mechanic. The four men who had brought the crate from the dock offered to help unload it, but their suggestion was met with a barrage of furious Gallic obscenities. The officials apologized and promised Latham every assistance in repairing the damage first thing in the morning.

Latham accepted their apology with characteristic good grace. It was, after all, his fifty-horsepower Antoinette; his hundred-horsepower machine was due to arrive aboard the steamer *Chicago* in three days, ample time to prepare for the International Aviation Cup race the following Saturday. Weber wasn't so easily placated, however, and he muttered dark oaths to the *Herald* about a deliberate American plot to wreck Monsieur Latham's chances of victory. "We have traveled with that machine crated in exactly the same manner as it now is all over Europe and have never had it injured . . . I have never seen anybody attempt to handle it in the manner that these men have gone about it."

CHAPTER EIGHT

An Epoch-Making Event

Saturday, October 22, 1910

FROM THE WEST COAST OF AMERICA to Western Europe, the fate of the three missing balloons (the *America II*, the *Azurea*, and the *Düsseldorf II*) was dissected by the Saturday newspapers. The *Times* of London ascribed a "feeling of alarm" to the race organizers in St. Louis because "it is believed that they landed on Wednesday night, and that the pilots and their assistants are in distress in the forests of Canada."

The *San Francisco Chronicle*, which had hitherto given the race only perfunctory coverage, ran a scaremongering report on its front page, saying that if the crews hadn't drowned in one of the Great Lakes, then they would most likely be "somewhere in the wilds of Canada, where they may be the victims of starvation before succor can reach them."

Randolph Hearst's *New York American* also took a perverse delight in speculating what might have happened to the men, in a front-page article that was illustrated with photographs of Alan Hawley and Augustus Post in the *America II*, and Leon Givaudan and Emil Messner in the *Azurea*. Starvation and drowning were the most probable scenarios, said the paper, though of course they might have frozen to death in "the severe snow storms that have been raging over Canada," or then again, "they may be destroyed by wild beasts."

Pessimism laced the rest of Saturday's newspaper coverage, from the front-page headline on the *Boston Daily Globe*—FEAR THAT SUCCOR MAY NOT REACH THE AERONAUTS IN TIME—to the *World*'s NEW YORK PILOTS MAY HAVE PERISHED. The exception was the *New York Herald*, which felt obliged to strike a more upbeat note as their proprietor had, after all, given his name to the race. In its front-page story the paper said that the missing six men were all "inured to such hardships and privations as may befall them in case they have landed in a wild and uninhabited region." However, what convinced the *Herald* that there would be a happy outcome was "that Captain Abercron [in the *Germania*] landed Wednesday morning but was not able to get into communication with the Aero Club before last night, fifty-seven hours later."

The confidence of the *New York Herald* was borne out a few hours later when the Aero Club of America received a telegram from Messner and Givaudan of the *Azurea*:

> Have landed thirty-two miles northeast of Biscotasing. Algoma district. Had three days and one night to work our way through woods, passing Lake swimming. Temperature at night 11 Fahrenheit. Please wire news to Biscotasing. Messner. Givaudan.

From the offices of the Aero Club the news hummed down the wires to the *St. Louis Post-Dispatch* minutes before they were due to go to press, dashing hopes of a relaxing Saturday evening for the editorial staff. As sleeves were rolled up and fresh coffee ordered, the editor struggled to find Biscotasing on the giant map of the Great Lakes region pinned to the wall of his office. Where the goddamn is it! he yelled.

Someone eventually found it, and carefully the editor measured the distance between the small Ontarian town and his own city—772 miles. Okay, he said, new headline: AZUREA IS DOWN; GERMANIA SEEMS WINNER OF RACE. Time was running out if they wanted to get to press on time, but they had still one thing to do: update the log of the finishing positions with the Swiss balloon. It was a hurried job, rejigging the template at the last minute, and it showed when the paper was bought and read by St. Louisians on Saturday evening. *Azurea* was spelled *Azuria*, and its pilot was "Meisner," not Messner. A small error, however, and one barely noticed by the men and women who were more interested to read that "officials of the Aero Club of America in New York, Saturday, declared unofficially, according to news telegrams to the *Post-Dispatch*, that they believe the balloon *Germania* is the probable winner of the race . . . [and] estimate that their distance traveled was 1,200 miles. This would give the Germans the world's record."

As for Alan Hawley and Augustus Post, the *Post-Dispatch* had no news. On a sketch of the Canadian wilderness the paper superimposed a photo of the pair along with a large question mark, as black and forboding as most people's fears.

The cold woke Augustus Post on Saturday morning, the sort of cold that pierces a man and wraps itself around his bones. He lay curled up in a ball under his blanket, listening to the wind whip the sand against the bivouac. One glance at Hawley's gaunt face told Post that it had been another wretched night for his companion. His soft jawline was covered in a tabby-colored stubble, and the gentle eyes were rimmed red with exhaustion.

He didn't lie when Post asked about his knee—it hurt like hell—but he was game to press on. It would soon improve once he'd walked out the overnight stiffness. Post prepared breakfast, a chicken roll for Hawley and a piece of chicken and an egg for himself. It was gone in seconds and neither man felt any the better for it. They set off along the beach "with the weather so cold that at times our clothing was frozen to our bodies." After a mile or so the sand ended at the foot of a jumble of smooth boulders, clustered together like giant eggs in a basket. Hawley told Post he would give it a go, but as they started to climb over the boulders, "Hawley's leg hurt him so severely that we could go no farther that day. We forced ourselves back a quarter of a mile to a protected spot we had passed under a bank overhung with balsam and sheltered by the projecting roots of a big white birch."

The sky was now pencil gray and Post knew more snow was on its way, so while Hawley made a bivouac from the balsam boughs, Post took care of the fire, and "none too soon, for it began to rain, first a drizzle, ending in light snow."

They remained in camp for the rest of the day, sleeping and sharing the odd chocolate bar as the snow fell. Now and again Post braved the elements to scour the beach for fresh supplies of driftwood with which to feed the fire, and when it was blazing to his satisfaction he and Hawley "talked over the events of the voyage and incidents in our lives." They buoyed each other with confident predictions that they must have won the race; after all, if their calculations were correct, they had traveled around twelve hundred miles, a new world's record; they talked of food and described to one another the first meal they would order when back in New York. Post pulled Hawley's leg about his promise to the Bronx Zoological Gardens to bring back a muskrat from their trip. If we do see a muskrat, Post said to his friend, laughing, we'll eat it, not carry it.

The snow had turned to sleet by the time the sky turned black, but before the pair turned in, Post fed the fire more logs and Hawley experimented with several positions before settling on the one that caused his knee the least discomfort. Hawley bade his friend good-night and closed his eyes, but long after Post had fallen asleep, he was still awake, wrestling with a dilemma he knew he could no longer postpone. Finally Hawley dozed off, having decided that in the morning if he was unable to continue, he would insist that his companion go on alone, leaving behind half their stash of food, and the revolver.

Rain was still over Belmont Park on Saturday morning, but only a persistent drizzle, not the heavy downpour of a few hours earlier. A stiff breeze carried the rain from the east, past the grandstand, past dead man's turn, until it lashed the doors of the green hangars at the western end of the track.

Sodden reporters congregated in the press box and told each other it could be worse—at least they hadn't had to fork out $450 for the privilege of a box in the covered grandstand. They looked out across the course, "at the rain-soaked stretches of the grass field [which] rapidly promised signs of being transformed into a lake," and shook their heads glumly at the sight of the muddy dirt track over which the likes of Sysonby had once galloped. The national flags that drooped from their poles above the hangars mirrored the shoulders of the few optimists who'd arrived at first light and paid $1 for the privilege of getting soaked in the field enclosure. Some of those bedraggled spectators had bought a cup of coffee for twenty-five cents from a kiosk and were now sheltering under the steel arches of the grandstand, while others huddled under umbrellas, flicking through the official program, which they'd bought for twenty-five cents. They weren't amused: 114 pages, of which 72 were advertisements. Others unfurled newspapers from inside their thick jackets and caught up with the latest news on the hunt for Hawley and Post. Then they turned their attention to the previews of today's events at Belmont Park and laughed sardonically as they read the opening sentence of the *New York Herald*'s front-page story: "At the dawn of the opening day of the great International aviation tournament at Belmont Park auspicious weather is all there is now needed to make the Meet an epoch-making event."

The *New York Sun*, promising its readers that they were about to witness the best airplane show in the short but exciting history of aviation, cautioned those intending to attend later in the day that though the meet wasn't scheduled to start until one thirty P.M., "airmen have a habit of working not only during office hours but before and after as well [so] you'll run little risk of having time hang heavy by making the early start."

Not all newspapers were so toadying in their coverage of the tournament. Those spectators who had bought their weekly copy of the *New York City Review* were surprised to read a venomous piece by Colgate Baker. All the recent aviation hullabaloo had annoyed Baker, who reckoned that the fliers would have people believe there was some great mystery to flying a plane when in fact there was none. Yet they'd fooled the public, and now they were "coining their heroic feats at our expense in greedy and almost frenzied haste." Baker excepted John Moisant from his polemic, a man he considered frank and honest, and reserved his fiercest criticism for Claude Grahame-White. Baker was sick of Americans fawning over the Englishman and found it distasteful to see him treated as a "conquering hero, followed everywhere by a crowd of adoring flying fans." Hero? hissed Baker. He was nothing of the sort; while Moisant "is painfully modest and self-deprecating in his manner, avoiding the limelight whenever possible, Mr. Grahame-White . . . delights to bask in the full glare of the calcium and wants all that there is in the game."

"Look over there!" the cry went up, and all eyes turned toward where the spectator was pointing. The doors of hangar No. 17 were being folded back by two men in damp overalls, and in the next instant the nose of a biplane appeared. "Who's seventeen?" someone shouted. People leafed through the advertisement-laden program until they found the hangar numbers. Seventeen belonged to Tod Shriver, a former printer from Manchester, Ohio, who had been one of Glenn Curtiss's mechanics when he triumphed at Rheims in 1909. Earlier in the summer Shriver had qualified as an aviator in his own right, only to break his legs in a crash two weeks later. But here he was, Slim as he was known, in leather coat and well-cut suit, gamely hobbling toward his machine on crutches. He handed the sticks to a mechanic and accepted a helping hand up into the seat. Once he'd made himself comfortable and carried out his final checks, Shriver signaled for his mechanic to start him up. The fifty-horsepower engine of his Dietz biplane hummed into life, and the spectators sheltering under the grandstand raced round to see the first flight proper of the Belmont Park Meet.

Shriver took off into the easterly wind and soon passed the grandstand at a height of one hundred feet, the engine now burring contentedly. He banked left, round one of the red-and-white pylons, and flew north for a few hundred meters before negotiating another pylon and turning west, so he was flying parallel to the back straight of the racecourse. Everyone watched as Shriver swung southwest, past hangar row, and toward dead man's turn. To the spectators standing nearest to the tight corner, the strength of the wind was the same as it had been when Shriver had wheeled out his plane, but a hundred feet in the air there were eddies and gusts, one of which caught the little biplane as it approached the dreaded turn. Shriver's plane dipped, then listed to the right. A collective gasp came from the press box; one or two of the journalists jumped to their feet, their hands covering their mouths. They could see Shriver tussling with the machine's controls. "At 50 feet the biplane appeared to have righted itself," reported the *New York Herald*, "then it suddenly turned and plunged to the earth. As it struck the machine crumpled up and it seemed that the aviator must have been killed or seriously injured."

People ducked under the white guardrail and sprinted across the grass toward the wreck. Shriver was pulled out, bleeding heavily from deep wounds to his face and to his hip, where a bolt had gouged out a lump of flesh. He promised he would be back flying by the end of the week, but his helpers knew they were the words of a man whose senses lay among the wreckage of his airplane. Shriver was put in an automobile and driven to Nassau Hospital in Mineola by Mr. Dietz, the man whose machine was now being cleared away by officials.*

Throughout the morning the other aviators began to arrive at Belmont Park. Armstrong Drexel stepped out of his chauffeur-driven automobile, along with his brother and sister-in-law, who retired to the box they had hired for the week. Jacques de Lesseps, reinvigorated after his Canadian tryst, turned up with his brother and sister, and Hubert Latham appeared with his mechanic to see to their damaged airplane. Roland Garros and Edmond Audemars journeyed out together from the Knickerbocker Hotel and tossed a coin to see if it would be the French tricolor or Swiss cross that fluttered above their hangar. Audemars guessed right and the Swiss flag was run up the pole.

John Moisant skipped onto the grounds with all the excitement of a small boy on Christmas Day, thrilled at the prospect of the challenges that lay ahead. He was greeted by his French mechanics, including the faithful Albert Fileux, who had spent the night sleeping in the hangar under the wings of Moisant's replacement Blériot.

Claude Grahame-White showed up soon after with Pauline Chase, whom he escorted to her seat in the grandstand. Having kissed her good-bye, he walked over to the hangars, stopping for a friendly word outside most, but not the four cavernous tents in which were housed the Wrights' machines.

Although the rain had started to leak through the roof of the tents, forcing the machines to be covered with tarpaulin, Wilbur Wright was surprisingly unconcerned. In fact, for a man who was usually solemnly reserved, he seemed in singularly good humor. When the correspondent from the *Washington Post* plucked up the courage to ask why, Wright explained that shortly after breakfast he had received a telegram from his

---

* Dr. John Moorhead, with a corps of assistants from Bellevue Hospital, was in charge of a "fast automobile ambulance," but this was not yet in place at the time of Shriver's accident.

legal team. "All our suits for infringement of patent rights have been decided in our favor in the German courts," he exclaimed, his hawklike eyes bright with triumph. The suits elsewhere were still pending, he continued, but Wright was clearly "confident that the courts of America and European countries would follow Germany's lead."

Word of the decision carried swiftly down the row of hangars, and, said the *Post*'s correspondent, it "concerned the foreign fliers." If other countries did indeed endorse the German ruling, then "no Blériot, Curtiss, Farman, or in fact any make of machine that has adapted the . . . vital points first worked to a practical solution by the Wrights—which includes every design of air machine in existence—henceforth can legally be flown."

It wasn't just the foreign aviators who now faced the prospect of being grounded by the Wrights' bloody-minded tenacity. Glenn Curtiss, the winner of the 1909 International Aviation Cup, was also embroiled in a bitter legal battle with the brothers, one that was being buffeted from court to court, and although for the moment he was still at liberty to fly and manufacture airplanes, the German decision had worrying implications for his company.

Curtiss and his team of fliers arrived at the racecourse from the Belvedere Hotel, bringing with them on the back of a truck their new airplane, the one that was almost as secret as the Wrights' and had so excited the *New York Herald* a few days earlier. Enmity ran deep between the two factions, and the Curtiss aviators received welcoming sneers from the Wright fliers as they approached hangars 5 and 6. Curtiss considered the brothers grasping and dogmatic, while the Wrights let it be known "that they didn't think the Curtiss planes were any good and that they were dangerous to fly." Furthermore, Walter Brookins, Arch Hoxsey, Ralph Johnstone, and Frank Coffyn (who had recently retired from flying but who was present at Belmont Park) "were taught by the Wrights that the Curtiss crowd was just no good at all." Curtiss and his quartet of fliers shut the door of hangar No. 5 and began to uncrate the airplane as the rain continued to drum on the roof. The eldest of the four aviators was James "Bud" Mars, a thirty-four-year-old from Michigan, who had changed his family name from McBride to Mars on joining a circus as a trapeze artist. Further stints followed as a high diver and fairground parachutist, before

Mars earned his aviation license in August 1910. Two months later, on October 1, he'd unsuccessfully tried to win the $1,000 on offer for the first man to fly across the Rocky Mountains. He was found by a search party sitting unharmed beside his smashed machine having crashed into a rock face.

Mars was best pals with Eugene Ely, a married man from Davenport, Iowa, who carried the nickname King of the Ozone and was famous for thrilling the crowds with the Ely Glide. Climbing to a thousand feet, he would then shut off his engine and rush down to earth at an angle sometimes as steep as thirty degrees before pulling out of the dive at the last moment.

The other two members of the team were Charles Willard, "Daredevil" to his friends, a twenty-seven-year-old Harvard graduate who seemed to eat nothing but chocolate, and a twenty-four-year-old Canadian, John Mc-Curdy, who had first flown in 1907, a year after graduating from Toronto University with an engineering degree.

As Curtiss and his men started to assemble their new airplane, Wilbur Wright was inviting members of the press into his hangar to view his latest invention. "The cup will remain in America," said Wright, patting the machine's yellow-pine propeller. Reporters gathered round the aircraft asking questions as they examined it. It was built of ash and spruce, with the wings covered with bleached cotton. Some of the taller correspondents could reach up on tiptoe and almost touch the top of the six-foot-ten-inch biplane. The *New York Herald* reporter scribbled furiously as Wright gave the visitors a tour of the machine that he and his brother had christened the Baby Grand. "The exact dimensions of the new Wright racer can now be given," he wrote. "The planes [wings] are 26 feet long and 3 feet 4 inches wide. They are set 3 feet apart, and the radiator and gasoline tank are placed directly behind the driver. There is only one seat on the racing machine."

Compare this new compact plane with the traditional Wright biplane, Wilbur said, the wingspan of which was thirty-nine feet. He invited reporters to have a look at the rudder—"hardly larger than a handkerchief"—and he also drew attention to the four-wheeled undercarriage and the antiskidding blinkers on the forward skids, which would increase the machine's keel. "The engines used are the same that have been used by the Wrights for years," added the impressed correspondent from the *New York Herald*, "but they are far more powerful than any so far set up in the Wright factory." Instead of four cylinders, the Baby Grand had twice that number. Yes, admitted Wright when asked, the sixty-horsepower engine was still inferior to the hundred-horsepower engines of the Blériot, but that wouldn't matter come the day of the big race. He paused for dramatic effect . . . before revealing that in a series of trial flights in the Baby Grand, his brother, Orville, had reached a top speed of 72 mph. There was an intake of breath from the correspondents. If that was true, then Wilbur was right, the cup would remain in America.

Later in the morning, when the rain had eased, members of the Glenn Curtiss team folded back the doors of hangar No. 5 and bade reporters inside to view their latest innovation. An awkward silence ensued as the newsmen made mental comparisons between what was now before them and what they had just seen in the Wright hangar. The *New York Herald* correspondent turned a page in his notebook and wrote, "The Curtiss racer, on the other hand, looks like a handkerchief just out of the shop."

The man from the *New York Sun* made the mistake of asking Curtiss to describe some of the features of his monoplane; he soon stood corrected. "He calls [it] a 'single surface' airplane," explained the *Sun*'s reporter, "which at first glance looks like a monoplane. In fact the secondary plane is merely a small auxiliary only 8 feet long and 2 feet wide."

Other outstanding details noted by the newsmen were the aircraft's fifty-horsepower engine, its tricycle undercarriage, its wingspan of twenty-six feet, and its size, just twenty-five feet from tip to tail. Unusually for a new monoplane, it was a *pusher*, the name given to those airplanes in which the engine was situated to the pilot's rear. Most manufacturers had stopped producing pushers after several men had been crushed to death by the engine in crashes they would otherwise have survived. Curtiss shrugged when pulled up on the point and admitted that the plane "has never been flown and is wholly an experiment." The *Sun* reporter told Curtiss that a few hangars along, Wilbur Wright was fizzing with confidence about his prospects in the International Aviation Cup, so how did he rate his own chances? Curtiss didn't want to speculate, and if anything, he sounded rather diffident about his new invention. "Whether it will fly well—or fly at all—remains to be found out at the present meet," he said.

The first "special" train, laid on solely for the benefit of the meet, arrived at the Belmont Park station at noon and the race-goers were ready with their umbrellas as they stepped onto the platform. Having seen a large white flag atop the 395-foot-high Times Tower on Forty-second Street a while earlier as they made their way to Pennsylvania Station, they were confident of seeing some flying, despite the rain. The owner of the tower, the *New York Times*, had agreed to a request from the meet organizers to communicate to New Yorkers the course conditions by way of one of three flags: blue—no flight; white—flight probable; red—flight in progress. Thousands of spectators drove from Manhattan, and the prime parking spaces were soon full of mud-spattered automobiles. Local residents were quick to spot the shortage of parking places, and soon signs appeared outside their homes offering the use of their front yards as parking spaces in return for $1.

The entrance to the course was flanked by two lines of gray-uniformed security guards, members of the Pinkerton Detective Agency, which had been hired to control a tournament that was on private land and thus outside the jurisdiction of the Nassau County police. The guards had an unsmiling swagger, an enjoyment of the power that came with the well-cut uniform, and anyone who was slow in handing over the $1 entrance fee to the turnstile operator was harshly rebuked.

Once inside Belmont Park the whole atmosphere changed, and instead of menacing stares from Pinkerton's men, the spectators were accosted by myriad "vendors who hawked programmes [*sic*], sandwiches, aviation postal cards, peanuts and candy . . . and the highest prices possible were asked of the spectators."

Children pestered their parents for a toy airplane or a souvenir pennant from one of the many kiosks, while their fathers attempted to win choice cigars by knocking down puppets with three balls. Mothers browsed the knickknack stalls for household decorations made from smoked glass before the entire family eventually hired a set of camp stools—thirty cents each—and made their way to the field enclosure on the opposite side of the course to the grandstand.

Signs guided the bewildered with arrows pointing to the "popular-priced" restaurants and those, such as the Turf and Field Club, which were affordable only to the affluent. A reporter from the *New York Sun* stopped outside one of the more affordable restaurants and examined the menu. "Popular prices, eh?" grumbled the man next to him. "Popular with the man who owns the eatables, I guess." The cheapest food joint was the kiosk under the grandstand where beef stew cost fifty cents, a plate of ham and eggs sixty cents, a roast fresh ham sandwich seventy-five cents, and an apple pie twenty-five cents.

The society correspondents of the newspapers, those same ones who had harassed Claude Grahame-White earlier in the week, had returned in force and were now either besieging the entrance to the members' clubhouse or commandeering a table in the Turf and Field Club, fork in one hand, pencil in the other, noting which members of the fashionable set were present. There was Mrs. William K. Vanderbilt (recently returned from Europe, where she'd spent $18,000 on the latest Paris fashions) looking resplendent in an "apricot-colored polo coat and bell-shaped blue hat." Was that a white muff she was carrying? wondered the correspondent from the *Sun*. No, it was her little white dog. Armstrong Drexel's willowy sister-in-law, Marjorie, "excited much admiration in a gown of black velvet and a large black picture hat." Mrs. Sidney Dillon Ripley, who wore a loose-fitting coat and black hat "with two quills jauntily fastened on the left side," was lunching with Mrs. Tyler Morse, who had come "well prepared for the weather in a white fur coat worn over a checked polo coat." The *Sun*'s society correspondent rated Mrs. James Brown's outfit "one of the most startling costumes" he'd seen in a long time. A flame-colored coat fastened at the bottom with small black buttons was topped off with a black velvet hat adorned with feathers.

The *New York Sun*'s correspondent next turned his attention to the wisteria gown worn by the wife of General Stewart Woodford. She and her husband were hosting a lunch party in the Turf and Field Club, and so engrossing was the conversation that no one noticed it was nearly one thirty P.M., the hour when the tournament officially began. Over the polite murmur of luncheon chat there came the noise of an airplane engine. On hearing the sound, reported the *Sun*, General Woodford "became so excited . . . that he ran out of the dining room and carried his napkin along."

As General Woodford hurtled out of the restaurant, a pall of yellow smoke drifted across the course from the aerial bomb that had just been exploded to signal the meet was under way. The wreckage of Tod Shriver's machine had been cleared by workmen, his blood washed away by rain, and only a few early-bird spectators were aware he had ever flown.

The engine that had so galvanized the general was Claude Grahame-White's, and as he continued to warm it up, Peter Prunty used his megaphone to inform the six-thousand-strong audience of the day's schedule. From one thirty P.M. to two thirty P.M. was the Hourly Distance event; after a break of fifteen minutes, the second Hourly Distance event and the Hourly Altitude event would commence. At four P.M. the twenty-mile cross-country flight would begin, at the same time as the Grand Altitude competition. Prunty reminded spectators that the cross-country race, to a captive balloon ten miles east over Hempstead Plains and back, was dependent on the weather not deteriorating, as otherwise it would be deemed too hazardous.

Now Grahame-White was taxiing across the grass, and Prunty fell silent and watched with the rest of the crowd. In the grandstand Pauline Chase sat with her hands clasped tightly together as her fiancée with "an ever-increasing humming roar crossed the starting line." He rose into the air as the band at the front of the grandstand struck up "Every Little Movement Has a Meaning All Its Own," and the crowd tapped their feet in time to the music. A couple of minutes later Armstrong Drexel was airborne, perched on the hollow body of his Blériot monoplane, which, to the *Washington Post*, sounded like a "mosquito," but to the *New York Herald* correspondent was more like a "bumblebee."

John Moisant, flying an identical machine to Drexel's, was next to leave the ground, and he climbed swiftly to two hundred feet, higher than both Drexel and Grahame-White, who chugged slowly round the 2.5 km course, rarely rising higher than the eaves of the grandstand. All three fliers were competing in the Hourly Distance event, the aim of which was to complete as many laps as possible within sixty minutes, but it was also the opportunity to qualify for Thursday's Statue of Liberty race, a late and controversial addition to the meet's schedule.

A fortnight earlier a New York businessman, Thomas Ryan, had offered a prize of $10,000 for the first man to fly from Belmont Park to the Statue of Liberty and back. What an idea! cried the Aero Club of America. Instead of New York City coming to Belmont Park, Belmont Park will go to New York City. What better way to spread the aviation message? Neither Ryan nor the organizers expected the fliers to take the safe route, across country to the sea and then along the coastline; that was approximately sixty-six miles, whereas the direct route was only thirty-three miles. That was, however, as the *New York Times* pointed out, "over the populous sections of South Brooklyn." The *New York City Herald* thought it a wonderful prospect, a "thrilling event," but added with a harrumph that Wilbur Wright was "strongly opposed to flying over cities . . . He says that while it is an aviator's own business whether he decides or not to risk his own neck, he has no right to endanger the lives of others."

Taking into account the concern of Wright and some other aviators, the Belmont Park organizers had imposed a stringent entry criterion for any aviator wishing to compete for Thursday's Statue of Liberty race: "The prize will be open to all competitors who shall have remained in the air in one continuous flight one hour or more during previous contests in the meet."

Thus Grahame-White, Drexel, and Moisant were competing in the Hourly Distance event not just in the hope of winning the $500 on offer, but also to qualify for the Statue of Liberty race. To Drexel, $10,000 (approximately $160,000 today) was small fry, he flew just for the sport; but the sum was large enough to tempt Grahame-White to drop his objection to flying over cities, which he had manifested at Boston. For Moisant, $10,000 would go a long way in bankrolling his next revolution.

For an hour Grahame-White flew placidly but persistently round the circuit. The crowd clapped respectfully, and the man from the *Washington*

Post praised his "workmanlike precision," but it was hardly edge-of-the-seat stuff. "Here he comes again," shouted someone in the grandstand, as Grahame-White angled into the home straight past dead man's turn, "it's Merry-go-round White."

Drexel dropped out having completed ten laps in nineteen minutes, and soon Moisant tired of the plodding procession and started to lay on a show for the masses, "rising and falling, turning and dipping, as easily and gracefully as a swallow." Suddenly he swooped down from three hundred feet and shot across the grass as if he were trying to cut it, bringing several hundred spectators to their feet in excitement. And all the while Grahame-White continued on his remorseless way, ignoring the American gadfly, and "turning the corners as closely as a trained race horse."

Moisant was down after fifty-one minutes with only eighteen laps to his name after all his showboating. He had a small problem with the engine, he explained, but would be back to try again in the second Hourly Distance events. Grahame-White remained aloft the full hour and descended only when he saw his manager, Sydney McDonald, flagging that the time was up. Grahame-White came down smiling; not only had he flown twenty circuits, he'd also qualified for the Statue of Liberty event.

Moisant took off again at two forty-five P.M. in a foul mood, having been docked four laps by the officials on his first flight, "on account of cutting slightly inside a pylon." What a surprise, muttered some of his rivals, Moisant penalized for cutting corners. His second attempt to qualify for the Statue of Liberty race again ended in failure, this time after forty minutes because of a mechnical problem. His disappointment, however, was small compared to that felt by the Curtiss team when Eugene Ely took the new single-surface machine out of the hangar. Within a few minutes Ely was down with engine trouble, and only one of the Wright fliers, Arch Hoxsey, in an old biplane, could give the crowd their money's worth. The *New York Herald* described how he went up "growing smaller and smaller, until he finally disappeared in the fog. He was completely lost to view in the clouds for about a minute. He descended as he had ascended, in great spirals, landing as gently on the turf as a leaf dropping from a tree." Belmont Park exploded in a cacophony of hollering and hurrahs as Hoxsey, in a black leather coat with fur-lined combination leggings and boots that reached to the hips, jumped down and received the congratulations of Ralph Johnstone.

The fog that had shrouded Hoxsey from view sank lower throughout the afternoon, forcing the organizers to cancel the Grand Altitude Contest. They were about to do the same to the cross-country competition when John Moisant whispered something in Peter Prunty's ear. The next minute the crowd were on their feet applauding as Prunty announced that Moisant wouldn't be deterred by a spot of fog: he intended to try for the cross-country prize.

It took him thirty-nine minutes and forty-one seconds to fly the twenty miles to the captive balloon and back. When he landed, he was so cold he had to be lifted from his seat. Later Moisant confessed to reporters that the fog hadn't troubled him, but he'd been "so blinded by rain that he couldn't make out the balloon afloat in the Hempstead Plains."

Moisant basked in the crowd's acclaim as around him the other aviators packed up for the day unnoticed. The first day of the Belmont Park Meet had ended with no doubt as to who had been its star. Playing to the press with all the adroitness of Grahame-White, Moisant donated his airplane's propeller to the *New York Herald*, the most influential newspaper in America as far as aviation was concerned. The paper blushed at such largesse and thanked Moisant, the man whose daring skill "has won for him a host of friends."

CHAPTER NINE

Tears Started to Our Eyes

Sunday, October 23, 1910

NEITHER AUGUSTUS POST nor Alan Hawley felt much like talking when they woke early on Sunday morning. It was still raining and the pair felt weak and in no condition to endure another day's trek through the tyrannical wilderness. They breakfasted on an egg and a couple of crackers as the rain beat on the canvas roof of their bivouac in a despondent symphony. Post wrote in his log, "Each of us realized without mentioning it to the other, that our lives might be drawing to a close." After they had eaten, Hawley took an envelope from the inside pocket of his shabby overcoat and told Post that it had been given to him by a friend shortly before he'd left New York; it was to be opened only if Hawley found himself in trouble. It felt an appropriate moment. He opened the envelope and removed the card. It's a prayer, Hawley told Post, and he began to read:

A PRAYER FOR MR. HAWLEY
Dear God, the best friend of all: Watch over and keep him from danger in his perilous trip and may his heart go up to Thee in tender gratefulness for all thy goodness. Grant him his ambition to win and bring him safely back.

Hawley slipped the envelope back inside his jacket as "tears started to our eyes." A short while later they noticed the rain easing, and within the hour it had stopped. "Our ambitions," Post wrote, "which had been at rather a low ebb, flowed strong again, and urged us on." They were soon striding purposefully along the damp beach with Hawley telling Post his knee felt much improved after a day's rest. They clambered up and over the boulders without impediment and saw that ahead the shoreline appeared free of obstacles, except for a series of streams that emptied into the lake. Post peered through his field glasses and told Hawley that none of them should pose a problem, even for an old cripple like him. They started to laugh as they struck out east, and by lunchtime the two men had forded the streams.

At three o'clock they agreed to pitch camp when next they came to a suitable spot, and a few minutes later they found such a place in the lee of a steep bank by the lake. "There was plenty of driftwood and birch-bark," wrote Post, "and a fire was soon crackling to cheer us up." Post informed Hawley with a melodramatic flourish that he was going to pre-pare for them both a most sumptuous supper, a surprise dish he had been planning for a couple of days. He unwrapped a dozen chicken bones from a handkerchief, and with what meat remained on the bird he cooked a de-licious broth. Afterward they lay back in their bivouac plump with satis-faction, both with a sense that they were through the worst of their ordeal.

In the early hours of Sunday, Samuel Perkins sent a message to his father in Boston: ALL SAFE. 1230 MILES. LAKE KISKISINK, QUEBEC. By the time the news was made public it was too late for many of the Sunday papers, but not the *St. Louis Republic*, which had been tipped off by a member of the St. Louis Aero Club. The editor summoned his staff and a new front page was laid in time for the distribution trucks: DÜSSELDORF II DOWN AT KISKISINK, QUEBEC; NEW WORLD'S RECORD. Having checked Kiskisink on the map, the *Republic* editor estimated the balloon had flown 1,240 miles, not the 1,230 miles given by Perkins in his telegram. But 1,240 miles or 1,230 miles, who cared. It was a new balloon record, one that beat the *Germania* into second place. The *Düsseldorf II* was the winner of the

International Balloon Cup. Yes, it was unfortunate that it bore the name of a German city and was piloted by a German, but the aide was an American boy, and for most newspapers that was reason enough to rejoice.

For the *Boston Globe* there was an additional cause for celebration: Perkins was not only an American, he was one of theirs. PERKINS OF BOSTON AND GUERICKE SAFE ran the headline, as if in misspelling the German pilot's name they were puckishly undermining his significance. The *Globe* proudly listed Perkins's aviation achievements and boasted that though he was "perhaps better known as a manipulator of kites of all descriptions than as a balloonist . . . his knowledge of the upper air currents has long been recognized."

More details emerged throughout the day as Perkins talked to re-porters either over the telephone or face-to-face with those who had al-ready been dispatched to the region to search for Hawley and Post. Perkins began with the bare bones of their story, but then, like Augustus Post and his chicken broth, he began to flesh out his tale with each sub-sequent recital. In his first interview, quoted in the Sunday edition of the *St. Louis Post-Dispatch*, Perkins described how they had descended from ten thousand feet as they approached Lake Kiskisink; not long after he told the *World* that the *Düsseldorf II* had "dropped eighteen thousand feet in nine minutes." Once on the ground he and Gericke had packed a few provisions and started to traipse "through dense undergrowth" for three days. On later reflection, the pair "literally had to cut our way through the underbrush. We crawled on our hands and knees. Our clothes were torn almost to shreds." Was that the most harrowing part of your trip? he was asked. Oh, no, said Perkins, that was when "we heard wolves and other wild animals . . . the only weapon we had was a little .22-caliber revolver." By the time the *New York Times* got hold of Perkins he "had seen tracks of very large animals, evidently bears . . . The worry was constant, especially as we had no firearms and our only weapons were jackknives."

But amid all the contradictory accounts of their adventure, which had ended when they encountered a gamekeeper on Saturday afternoon, the one unequivocal fact was that the *Düsseldorf II* had covered 1,240 miles. They had won the balloon race. And as for the whereabouts of Hawley and Post . . . ?

The Sunday papers didn't hold out much hope. The *New York American* said they probably landed in "the wild Nipigon country, inhabited only by a scattered tribe of Ojibway Indians and infested with wolves." Iowa's *Sunday Times Tribune* reported that Colonel Theodore Schaeck of the *Helvetia* had seen a balloon falling into Lake Huron, which he now took to be the *America II*. Even if they hadn't plunged into a lake, said the *St. Louis Post-Dispatch*, how could they possibly survive now that "winter has already begun in Canada and the berries and roots on which the missing aeronauts might have subsisted in another season have disappeared"?

The signal bomb exploded at one thirty P.M. on Sunday afternoon and the second day of the Belmont Park Meet began, but within seconds the yellow smoke was being whipped across the course by a violent wind from the northwest. While the sun played peekaboo through the clouds, the flags on top of the hangars were taut in the gale. A khaki-clad man scaled the ladder to the giant scoreboard and hung two big white letters, *K* and *R*—the code for a wind velocity of more than 25 mph. None of the aviators felt like venturing out; they shared Grahame-White's view that with the flimsy construction of their machines an airman "flying in a wind is rather in the position of a man who puts to sea in a small boat when waves are high. Once he can clear the shore, the boatman feels at ease; but should a breaker catch him before he reaches the smooth, rolling billows a little distance from the beach, his craft may be over-turned and dashed to pieces. So with the airman; his moments of peril, when flying in a gusty wind, come just as he is soaring from the ground, and when descending from a flight. Then an airwave, like a seawave, may lift his craft and drive it with a crash to earth."

There was no ill wind for the vendors, however, who enjoyed a roaring trade as the majority of spectators idled away the time buying things they didn't need. A photographer who had constructed a replica of a small bi-plane charged people to have their picture taken sitting at the controls wearing a tatty flying helmet he'd picked up from somewhere. Not far away two Gypsy fortune-tellers dressed in yellow-and-red kimonos pledged to disclose people's future for a quarter. Up at the very top of the grandstand, the cheap seats, a covey of impish fans decided it would be fun to play a prank on the ladies and gentlemen preening on the lawn below. Sometimes it was a whooping cheer, sometimes a burst of excited applause, but each time the youngsters made a noise "the unfortunates who were promenading, assuming that a machine was coming out of its hangar across the field, would charge in a wild rush for the railing."

Among the cream of Manhattan society, wraps and furs were much in evidence, with a veritable menagerie of animals sacrificed to keep out the cold: black beaver hats, brown beaver hats, a muff of silver-fox fur, coats of baby seal, white coney, or bearskin, one entire costume of baby lamb, and a hat bordered with Russian sable. Only one lady, according to the *New York Herald*, had bucked the trend, and that was Eleonora Sears, the Boston socialite and erstwhile passenger of Claude Grahame-White's. She was "dressed in a severely plain costume of brown tweed, made shorter than walking length."

Suddenly a message was relayed from the clubhouse to the hangars by one of the race organizers. The measurement of the wind's velocity was mistaken, the anemometer on top of the grandstand had been checked and the wind was sixteen miles an hour, not twenty-five. The implication was clear—would someone mind putting on a show for the public?

A small man with oversize ears, sallow skin, sunken eyes, and hair the color of copper wire gave a contemptuous laugh from a rickety steamer chair outside the door of hangar No. 2. Charles Keeney Hamilton might have risen from his chair to remonstrate with the official if his legs had allowed, but he'd arrived at Belmont Park on Friday "limping, scarred and speaking with an impediment." What is it this time, Charlie? the other aviators had asked, laughing. The twenty-nine-year-old from Connecticut dismissed their questions with a playful wave of his cane. Everyone knew the history of the likable Hamilton, the man the French called *trompe-la-morte* (death dodger) because of his record of fifty crashes in the past two years. "There's little left of the original Hamilton" was the joke rookie aviators all heard when first introduced to the man. He'd broken both legs, both collarbones, one ankle, several ribs, dislocated a shoulder, crushed his pelvis, and in his most recent accident, the one from which he was still suffering, he'd endured a novel agony. Flying in a meet at Sacramento, California, the previous month, Hamilton's rudder had jammed and he'd flopped from the sky in front of twenty thousand spectators. Several days later, swathed in bandages and propped up in a hospital bed, he told reporters that as he smashed into the ground "the steering wheel jammed me back against the radiator and held me fast, while the scalding water trickled over me." He was still conscious when they carried him to the ambulance, and even after being pumped full of opiates, one thing had stuck in Hamilton's memory—the looks of pitiless satisfaction on the faces of the spectators. "I really believe," he said later, "that this game has gotten to the stage where they are disappointed if someone isn't injured or killed."

No, Hamilton told the Belmont Park official, he wouldn't take to the air in such a wind just to amuse the paying public. Firm shakes of the head came from other aviators, too, many of whom shared Hamilton's views on the people who came to watch them, people who would in another time have shrieked with delight in Rome's Colosseum. A reporter who'd asked Eugene Ely for his thoughts on the average aviation spectator was told, "I see the crowd below me looking upward, and I know every man who watches me start downward half expects to see me killed. I suppose they all figure how they'll help pick up my bones someday." And Ralph Johnstone, though he might fly like a man with neither wit nor wisdom, was no fool when it came to the public. They weren't there for the "advancement of science," as one newspaper had suggested to Johnstone, that was pure bunk. The people went to see him and Arch Hoxsey because "what they want are thrills. And if we fail, do they think of us and go away weeping? Not by a long shot. They're too busy watching the next man and wondering if he will repeat the performance."

No one seemed prepared to fly. Up in the press stand the *New York Sun* correspondent noted, "When 1:30 came and went and there was no starting of the first events most folks climbed down [from their boxes] to the platform before the grandstand or to the field lawn just for the sake of keeping moving." A few lost patience and began to drift away, a terrible apparition for the Belmont Park committee, who thought of all the bills and dimes escaping their grasp.

More pressure was applied to the aviators, and this time with success. Perhaps John Moisant succumbed first to the pleading of the organizers, or maybe it was Grahame-White, ignoring his own advice about the wind. But whoever, a few minutes before two o'clock the pair had ordered their mechanics to wheel out their planes and the race was on to see who would be first to take off.

As the blue flag above the scoreboard was lowered and the white one run up, spectators thumbed through their programs searching for the page with the flag denotations, the same ones in use at the Times Tower: red—flight in progress; white—flight probable; blue—no flight. The committeemen sat back smiling.

Grahame-White fastened his fur-lined gabardine jacket as his mechanics filled the tanks of his Farman biplane with petrol and castor oil. Armstrong Drexel wandered over and asked his friend if thought it prudent to go up on such a day. Wasn't Grahame-White breaking one of his cardinal laws—never to take a risk just to please the public? But the Englishman had been upstaged by Moisant the previous day, and now was his opportunity to reclaim his mantle as the world's greatest flier. And besides, Eleonora Sears was in the audience.

Grahame-White climbed up on the seat of the Farman in front of the seven-cylinder engine and the two-bladed wooden propeller. A mechanic squirted petrol into the valves, and another started the propeller with a sharp downward tug. The engine gave a heartening roar, and the men holding on to the airplane watched for Grahame-White's signal. He pulled his goggles down over his eyes and waved a hand in the air. The mechanics released their grip, and Grahame-White worked the controls as the biplane began to move across the grass.

The spectators who had come down to gossip on the lawn in front of the grandstand hurried back to their seats, while reporters in the press stand picked up their pencils and watched the black castor-oil fumes spew from the plane's exhaust. Grahame-White rose warily, wrote the correspondent for the United Press news agency, but "he needed all his caution, for even at a height of not more than forty feet he pitched like a ship in a heavy storm." Grahame-White knew at once he was in trouble. He signaled to his mechanics that he was in distress and started to descend. But a gust of wind tilted his biplane to such an angle that the machine stopped moving forward and began to career sideways. This was what Blériot had taught him was a *side-slip*, the aviator's equivalent of skidding across the road in an automobile. The *Brooklyn Daily Eagle* described how Grahame-White was now "drifting helplessly for 800 feet" across the course at the mercy of the wind. He could do nothing to save himself because he was too low to the ground. He would just have to brace himself for the crash and put into practice Blériot's favorite maxim: "a man who keeps his head can never be injured through a fall."

Grahame-White's machine trembled in the air for a moment, then, with a slow roll, toppled out of the sky and hit the ground with a thud that reverberated around Belmont Park. A wing concertinaed and a wheel was seen to bounce across the course. The whirring propeller slashed the grass, sending up a fountain of turf and wooden splinters. Grahame-White emerged without a scratch, noted the incredulous correspondent from the *Brooklyn Daily Eagle*, and for a few moments "ruefully surveyed the wreck" before making for the hangar.

In the distance, outside hangar No. 18, Moisant's Blériot was being trundled out by six mechanics. This machine had taken the American across the Channel, its white canvas wings still tattooed with the autographs of the people who'd welcomed him in England. Moisant appeared from his hangar wearing his distinctive flying helmet with its two drooping ear protectors, but before he could climb up onto the seat of his monoplane, the wind picked up the plane, threw it high into the air, and smashed it to the ground.

The right wing was wrecked, the left one badly damaged, and the propeller reduced to kindling. Albert Fileux, Moisant's chief mechanic, had been flipped ten feet into the air as he clung faithfully to the left wing. The Frenchman was uninjured, but both Moisant's Blériots now needed repairing if he was to be ready for the International Cup.

Within minutes someone had given the order to revert the strength of wind velocity on the scoreboard to twenty-five, and the blue flag, signaling "no flight," was also hoisted. The aviators were furious and "accused the committee of attempting to deceive them to appease the waiting crowd." The wind had never dropped, they said, it was a committee ruse. Nonsense, said Allan Ryan, the general manager of the meet, for some inexplicable reason the anemometer on top of the grandstand had simply failed to register the full force of the gale.

Later, however, when the hullabaloo had died down and the aviators were welcoming friends and family into their hangars, Ryan sneaked into the Wrights' hangars and asked if someone would go up. Hoxsey and Johnstone told Ryan they'd like to fly but they couldn't; a contractual stip- ulation of the Wrights' forbid flying on a Sunday. Such were the strength of Wilbur's convictions that he hadn't even come to the ground, preferring instead to remain at his hotel. Ryan implored the fliers to try to change their boss's mind, but a twenty-minute phone call from Brookins had no effect. On no account would a Wright aviator desecrate the Sabbath.

At four thirty P.M. a glum Peter Prunty informed the crowd that the wind had put paid to the rest of the day's events, but he did have some good news. To compensate for the cancellation the aviation committee had agreed to extend the meet by an extra day, so all of Sunday's tickets would be valid the following Monday, October 31. Later in the evening several of the fliers met in the bar of the Hotel Astor. Having let off steam about the Belmont Park committee, and about the ignorance of the crowd, they finished their aperitifs and moved into the dining room. Near the end of the meal Hubert Latham asked the waiter to charge his friends' glasses. He got to his feet and announced some sad news: Cap- tain Madiot, an old friend of his, had been killed on Saturday during an air show in France. Would everyone join in toasting a brave man.

CHAPTER TEN

A Death Trap

Monday, October 24, 1910

THE OFFICIAL SEARCH for Alan Hawley and Augustus Post was launched at daybreak on Monday. The Syracuse *Post Standard* reported that on the explicit instructions of Sir Wilfrid Laurier, Canada's first French-Canadian prime minister, "the celebrated mountain police will begin ranging over the wild territory north and northwest of the Great Lakes. These men, who starve like martyrs and ride and fight like demons when it is necessary, will go over hundreds of square miles." The Royal Northwest Mounted Police also intended to interview every hunter, trapper, huntsman, and woodsman they encountered to ascertain if a large yellow balloon had been seen. In addition to the police hunt, the head of the National Transcontinental Railway said he had sent word to the "thousands of men blazing the way for the new line through the wilderness" to be on the lookout for the two balloonists.

The Aero Club of America had dispatched one of its members, Lewis Spindler, who, so it was said, knew the Great Lakes region like the back of his hand. He had left St. Louis on Sunday for Toronto. Upon his arrival he met Colonel Gibson, lieutenant governor of Canada, and listened to what information had so far come in. A hunter, Charles Treadway, said he'd seen a balloon the previous Wednesday, as he'd tracked a moose near the Kippewa River in northern Quebec. He reckoned the balloon was going fast, about forty miles an hour. Damn near startled the moose, it did. A guide, Richard Cole, was canoeing down a river in Ontario on Thursday when he saw a balloon crash into "impenetrable forest."

A telegram had also recently arrived from Sam Perkins, copilot of the *Düsseldorf II*, in response to a request for information. "We have no idea of the location of the *America II*," he said. "The only balloon we saw was a yellow one over Northern Michigan Tuesday afternoon, going south. If the *America* went north, the case is hopeless, as we are as far north as the railroad goes, and for the last 500 miles we saw no civilization."

The most substantial clue was the message dropped from the basket of *America II* over Thompsonville on Tuesday afternoon. The authorities in Michigan had already made inquiries in the state to discover if anyone had seen the balloon after it passed Thompsonville, and someone had, over the town of St. Ignace on the Upper Peninsula. It was headed northeast, on a course, as was explained to Spindler, "which would carry it east of Lake Superior, past Sault Ste. Marie and into the wilderness north of the Canadian Pacific Railroad." It was agreed that Spindler would depart in the evening for Chapleau, a remote Ontarian settlement 350 miles northwest of Toronto, from where the search would be coordinated.

The commencement of the search sent a frisson down the spines of American newspapers. LOST AERONAUTS, LIVING OR DEAD? was the headline in the *Chicago Daily Tribune* on Monday morning, which then answered the question in the first paragraph, saying they were "more probably dead from exposure or by accident." That is, if the bears and wolves hadn't polished them off first. But the *Tribune* ended with a flight of fancy: "It is within the range of possibilities that the *America II* has succeeded in traveling an even greater distance than was covered by the *Düsseldorf II* and that its crew, after enduring as great, or even greater hardships, has reached in safety some trapper's cabin too remote to permit of communication with the outside world within a week or more."

Hawley and Post awoke on Monday cold, hungry, and depressed. The contentment of the previous evening, like the broth, was gone. They had little left to eat now, just a box of biscuits, a few of their meat lozenges, and a tin of soup. The contents of their ballast bags they used as haversacks had been reduced to simple necessities, yet they seemed as heavy as ever. Four hard days had already started to emaciate Hawley's once flabby physique, and his gray tweed suit, darkened with grime, flapped about his belly. Post's brown velvet corduroy outfit had been shredded during the fight with the undergrowth, and his feet were blistered from his hobnailed boots, which had started to come apart. His goatee had grown wild across his face and itched with a week's worth of dirt. They set off along the shore at seven A.M., the water to their right and the sky above blue and black like a deep bruise. The ground was flat for the first mile, and Hawley's knee bore up well as they walked along the beach. Post fell back a little so his companion could lead for the first time. Suddenly Hawley stopped dead in his tracks and "gave an exclamation of surprise." Post quickened his step and looked to where his companion was pointing. A few yards in front was a shovel leaning against a chopped log. Hawley looked about him and spotted something through the trees on their left. "There's a tent!" he yelled.

A narrow path just wide enough for one man led through the trees to a clearing where the small white tent had been pitched. An ax was lying in the grass, near a homemade paddle, and a couple of pails containing pieces of muskrat and rabbit. Post could also see a short stick with a fish-hook and several traps, but there was no sign of recent life, no footprints in the dew or lingering whiff of breakfast. They unfastened the tent and ducked inside. Good God, they couldn't believe their eyes. In the center of the tent was a sheet-iron stove with a brown teapot underneath, and hanging from the ridgepole was a pair of round snowshoes. Two large pails were to one side. Hawley peered inside and told Post one contained lard and the other flour. What's that under the blanket? asked Post. Hawley lifted the blanket. It was a sack of flour. There was a box of home-spun clothing, a half-burned wax candle, a can of black powder, a bag of shot. Hawley uncorked a bottle of something syrupy and black and sniffed. Ugh! Post laughed and said it was probably all-purpose medicine for "what ails you."

Post clicked his tongue in satisfaction when he saw a full box of matches, then gave an admiring whistle as he held up a knife with a curved blade and curiously made handle, which, he told Hawley, "was to be used as a wedge in getting bark off a birch tree to make a canoe." In the far corner of the tent was a pot of cooked beans, a can of brown sugar, and a bar of soap.

Post went outside to collect a few pieces of wood for the stove and returned with a relieved look. It had started to snow. They put up the stovepipe, built a fire, and "as the flames crackled, we unrolled our blankets on the dry balsam floor and relaxed into a delightful state of mind." "Post," said Hawley, "if anyone asks me what heaven is like, I shall say it's a trapper's tent after four days of terrible travel."

Post rested for an hour and then, leaving his friend asleep, crawled out of the five-foot-high tent and set about exploring their surrounds. With the snow still falling, he thought it prudent to husband some firewood for their stove. Once he'd chopped some logs and stashed them in the tent, Post began to walk along the trail that led from the shore toward the higher ground. "I had not gone far when I saw a cache on a big birch tree off to one side of the trail," he wrote in his logbook. The cache was a big roll of birch bark, and inside were various articles of clothing, a tin pail, and a bag of salt. Attached to the cache was a note in French: *No admission without business. Gone down to hunt and trap in lake Suniore.* Hawley took a pencil from his jacket and added, *Oct. 24, 1910. Alan R. Hawley and Augustus Post in the Balloon "America II" landed 15 miles northeast from here, Oct. 19, 1910. Left Mo. Oct. 17, 1910.*

Post pressed on up the trail in the hope that when he reached the top of the ridge he would see further signs of habitation, or possibly find a canoe. But he saw nothing and after several minutes of fruitless halloing he returned the way he had come "as the snow was getting thick." Hawley was awake and Post described his brief exploration. Hawley told Post he had been doing some thinking. He intended to stay at the campsite "to wait for the trapper, if it took all winter."

Post didn't argue, now wasn't the time, but he knew better than his companion that unless the trapper returned before the spring, this tent would be their tomb. The snow had arrived and would remain for the next four or five months; not even the most skilled Canadian woodsman could survive such a climate, particularly if he was wearing a city suit.

Post concealed his anxiety from Hawley and instead cooked up a banquet of biscuits and hot soup. Then Post repaired his boot with a length of cord he had found in the tent and "with a smart fire burning in the stove, we rested, reviewing our hardships, speculating as to the return of the trapper, and canvassing our ability to cook the flour into cakes and biscuits."

Later in the day Post exchanged a few strong words with his partner when "Hawley thought I was stingy with the firewood, but it took strength to split it, and I had been taught prudence." Hawley also pestered for more food, confident that they were now out of danger, but Post advised caution. They replenished the stove with wood, finished off the box of biscuits, and settled down for the night, as outside the snow continued to fall.

Allan Ryan arrived at Belmont Park early on Monday morning in need of a change in fortune. Sunday had not been a good day for the general manager of the aviation tournament. No flying, a restless crowd, accusations of endangering aviators' lives, an official protest about the safety of the course from Alfred Le Blanc, and a threatening letter from a Mr. William Ellison. To cap it all off, his wife—or rather, the family chauffeur—had been caught speeding on the way home from Sunday's event. At this very moment his wife was waiting to appear at a Queens courthouse.

As if Ryan needed reminding of his trying Sunday, it was all there in the morning papers waiting for him on his desk. Even his wife's indiscretion. He picked up the *New York Herald* with its disturbing front-page headline: FRENCH AVIATORS IN REVOLT, DEMAND NEW COURSE FOR TROPHY RACE. The *New York American* carried an interview with the troublesome Monsieur Le Blanc in which he was quoted as saying, "The international course as it has been laid out by the Aero Club of America is a death trap. It goes over tall trees, stables, telegraph wires, and railroad tracks with scarcely a patch three hundred yards wide at any place where an airplane may land."

Le Blanc had outlined his dissatisfaction in a wire to the Aero Club of France and was awaiting their response, but if they advised him to withdraw from the tournament, then he would not hesitate to do so. So would Hubert Latham, said the *Herald*, who had been asked by a reporter on

Sunday what he thought of the course. "If I were to tell the truth about the track, it would be 'suicidal,' " he had replied, adding, "and after that I probably would have to leave America."

Unfortunately for Ryan, sipping his coffee as he flicked through the papers, the French aviators weren't alone in disliking the course. Armstrong Drexel had been quoted in the *New York Sun* saying that the course was "doubly dangerous," not just because of the obstacles listed by Le Blanc, but also because of the high winds. "Most emphatically do I say," concluded Drexel, "that the international course is to be protested."

What worried Charles Hamilton, according to an interview in the *New York Sun*, was that final corner before the home stretch. He didn't use the expression *dead man's turn*, but in the presence of the paper's correspondent the American had jabbed his cane in the direction of the red-and-white pylon and warned that if Le Blanc or any flier in a hundred-horsepower machine "tried to make that turn at the acute angle marked by the pylons the fore and aft ends of his airplane would come together like a jackknife while the engine broke through the center." The *Sun* asked Hamilton how, if the organizers refused to alter the course before Saturday's big race, one might successfully negotiate the corner. Well, that's just the problem, replied Hamilton: "To get around that turn at great speed, a man would have to fly so wide that he would have covered eighty miles before he could be credited with flying the sixty miles prescribed. But if you make a wide turn, you have to fly over the grandstand, and if you fly over the grandstand, you will be penalized, and there you are."

Hamilton, though, had no intention of withdrawing from the race, and neither did John Moisant, whose name brought a smile to Allan's face. Good old John, he could always be relied on to offer his support. Asked to comment on the circuit by the *New York Herald*, Moisant had replied that he found the criticism a bit puzzling; after all, "at Rheims [in the 1909 International Aviation Cup] Mr. Curtiss had to fly over houses and trees when he won the cup. There isn't a course in the world of five kilometers that is entirely free of obstructions of some sort. I certainly shall fly over the course."

Claude Grahame-White and the two other British fliers, Alec Ogilvie and James Radley, were reported to have no gripes about the course, and neither did the Wright or Curtiss teams. We'll have a race, Allan said to himself, aware that he was chairing a meeting of the committee later in the morning to discuss the French protest. Then he turned to the next problem—William Ellison, spokesman for the homeowners in the vicinity of the Belmont Park course.

The *New York Sun* carried a front-page report about the letter that Ellison had sent on Sunday to every aviator in which he expressed the anger felt by many local residents whose homes were under the flight path of the international course. What vexed them so was the erection of the giant canvas screens along the fence at the west end of the course. Not only were they an eyesore, they also blocked the residents' view of the flying. If the screens were not removed, the paper reported, then "aviators who fly above certain adjacent properties will be winged with bullets."

Ryan had already given his initial reaction to the letter—"childish"— but he couldn't risk a few hotheaded cranks taking potshots at his aviators, so the screens, or at least some of them, would have to be dismantled. First, however, he had to attend to another pressing problem. Ryan called the head of the Pinkerton security team to his office. Have you seen the morning papers? he asked. No, he hadn't. Ryan told him they were full of accounts of the heavy-handedness of his men; worse than that, it wasn't the spectators complaining, it was the aviators. Ryan picked up a copy of the *New York American* and read a paragraph describing how John Moisant— *the* John Moisant—"was obliged to pay his own way into the meet on Sunday because he had forgotten his arm brassard." Then Ryan's old friend Monsieur Le Blanc was livid because his ballooning partner and translator, Walther de Mumm, hadn't been granted access to the hangar area. The less we antagonize Le Blanc, the better, Ryan suggested. Then, pointing to the *World*, Ryan read the report about Claude Grahame-White being turned away from the entrance because he hadn't his pass. How can your men not recognize the most famous aviator in the world—particularly when he had Pauline Chase on his arm? It had taken a few choice words from Grahame-White, the *World* said—"that sounded like the roaring of the lion"—to convince the Pinkerton guards it would be wise to step aside.

And then, said Ryan, the crowning indignity, the most astonishing blunder . . . Wilbur Wright barred from entering. Wilbur Wright . . . the man who invented the airplane. If not for him, none of us would be here! Ryan dismissed the Pinkerton chief with a demand that his men show a little bit of discretion, not to mention common sense.

Ryan then walked out of the clubhouse to organize the removal of the canvas screens. He looked up at the blue sky, then across toward the hangars and the flags curled sleepily round their poles. No wind. Perhaps his fortunes were about to turn.

The noon trains that departed Pennsylvania Station on Monday were filled to standing room, and the onboard vendors selling aviation magazines had to force their way through the carriages. Some of the passengers squashed in the center of the carriages swung themselves up to the racks and looked through the ventilators as they neared the grounds in the hope of being first to spot a flying machine.

Streetcars bound for Belmont Park "looked like Broadway cars at rush hour," and by one P.M. not a parking space was to be had. Every one of the ten thousand spectators who clicked through the turnstiles glanced across at the scoreboard and smiled when they saw the flag was white, indicating "flight probable." Pinned to the bulletin board was a statement just released by the Belmont Park committee, their response to the official French protest of the previous day. The statement concluded by saying that "Mr. [Cortlandt] Bishop again went over the course and made other suggestions as to improvements. This work will be done tomorrow in order that the course may be ready . . . The small trees and signposts are to be removed and it is suggested that one of the pylons be placed more to the north in order to avoid one or two houses and sheds which are in the way. It is not expected nor is it possible to provide a billiard table for the entire five kilometer course, but every effort will be made to render the course as safe as possible."

It appeared, too, that the Pinkerton security men had heeded Ryan's censure, and smiles had replaced snarls on the faces of gray-uniformed guards who patrolled the grounds. They were even allowing friends and family members of the fliers to visit the hangars, provided they were vouched for by an aviator. One of the first to flitter over was the delectable Grace McKenzie, the Canadian girl for whom Jacques de Lesseps had fallen. A "clubhouse rumor" was that an engagement was imminent. Tongues were also wagging about Claude Grahame-White, with a battalion of binoculars in the grandstand trained on hangar No. 14 as the Englishman laughed and joked with Eleonora Sears, who after Sunday's "severely plain costume" was now wearing what the *New York Sun*'s style guru described as "a navy blue suit with the skirt at least six inches from the ground." More than one newspaper found it curious that Pauline Chase was nowhere to be seen.

Armstrong Drexel spent a long time chatting with his brother and sister-in-law and generally, as was his nature, "being courteous to all visitors and [he] even allowed his flying toggery to be inspected." He showed off his helmet to one reporter, explaining that experience had taught him it was invaluable when trying for an altitude prize. Drexel was one of the few aviators to wear a helmet, and his was "leather with several inches of padding . . . The flaps over the ears are perforated so that he can tell how his engine is working."

As the spectators shopped, lunched, and gossiped, waiting for the program to start at one thirty P.M., great interest was shown in the "moving picture people" who were at Belmont Park for the first time since the meet's inception, and not everyone approved of their presence.

Since September the *New York World* had been at the forefront of a campaign to clean up the moving-picture industry, citing as its reason a spate of juvenile crimes that had allegedly been inspired by films. A thirteen-year-old adolescent arrested for robbery had told police that he acquired the methods at a moving-picture show, while another boy had "conceived the idea of becoming a criminal and learned to go about it from a scene in a picture show." The magistrate who convicted him of theft called the picture houses "sinks of iniquity" and demanded they clean up their act before it was too late.

Carl Laemmle, president of the Independent Moving Picture Company, had responded swiftly to the demand, issuing a circular warning scriptwriters that he would refuse to consider any scripts "which are built around murders or suicide or crimes of any kind . . . His company is trying to put the moving picture business on a higher plane and what it wants is preferably good, clean, light comedy."

Aviation offered picture houses the chance to redeem themselves by showing wholesome entertainment, and one of the most popular films of the early autumn had been footage from the 1909 International Aviation Cup race in France. Now the camera operators were at Belmont Park to record the action from America's biggest-ever aviation tournament. They began by setting up outside the Wright hangar and using an entire roll of film to capture Wilbur inspecting his airplane. His brother, Orville, had arrived from Dayton late on Sunday evening, but he was busy inside the hangar making final adjustments to their new machine. Next the camera-man tried to get some footage of the crowd moving around the course. This caused a few difficulties, much to the amusement of the *New York Sun*'s correspondent. What was so funny, he wrote, "was that many seemed to think that they had to walk as fast as they had seen figures move on the screen to get the right effect."

The moving-picture people couldn't have chosen a better day to visit Belmont Park. It was, in the opinion of the *New York Herald*, the greatest flying exhibition the world had ever known. It started with Arch Hoxsey and Ralph Johnstone performing a selection of their aerial stunts for the masses, including Johnstone's heart-stopping loop-the-loop one thousand feet from the ground, during which, as he momentarily hung up-side down, he could hear "the struts straining and . . . the singing of the winds through the wires shrilling higher in key." Then came the ex-traordinary sight of "ten airplanes in simultaneous flight" competing in the day's first discipline, the Hourly Distance contests. Up went the Frenchman Emile Aubrun, then Hubert Latham in his Antoinette mono-plane; Armstrong Drexel slipped on his flying helmet, shook hands with his brother, and shot off in his Blériot. The debonair Englishman Grahame-White, reported the *World*, "with a bow and a smile, cut off an animated conversation with Miss Eleonora Sears, that dashing young sportswoman, and took to the air in his Farman biplane." Then out of the hangar came the machines of Jacques de Lesseps; Eugene Ely and John McCurdy of the Curtiss team; and finally Walter Brookins, not in the Wright racer, but in another new model that had been brought to New York from Dayton by Orville Wright. No flier remained aloft for the full hour but Drexel circled the two-and-a-half-kilometer course

Walter Wellman, captain of the *America* dirigible.

Taken from the deck of the SS *Trent* on the morning of the *America*'s rescue, this dramatic shot shows the lifeboat and the ominous trail in the water of the equilibrator.

Melvin Vaniman of the *America* and Kiddo the cat aboard the SS *Trent*.

The start of the 1910 International Balloon Cup in St. Louis. *Million Population Club*, second from left, and *St. Louis No. 4* were the two American balloons ravaged by grasshoppers on the eve of the race.

Four German balloonists on their way to America in October 1910 (l–r): Hugo Von Abercron, Hans Gericke, August Blanckertz, and Leopold Vogt.

Million Population Club narrowly misses the grandstand as it lifts off from St. Louis on October 17, 1910.

Berlin 1908: Augustus Post
and Holland Forbes rise in
the *Conqueror*. Minutes later
the balloon burst and they
plummeted from the sky.

Augustus Post the actor, in a
photo taken in early 1910.

Alan Hawley (front right) and Augustus Post (rear right) enjoy the attention lavished on them at Belmont Park, just days after they emerged from the Canadian wilderness.

Aloof, exciting, and unfortunate: Alfred Le Blanc in the cockpit of his Bleriot.

Edmond Audemars (underneath) and his comical Demoiselle, a machine that was likened to a "grasshopper in a furious rage."

Armstrong Drexel, Walter Brookins, and Charles Hamilton at Belmont Park.

The daring but doomed Arch Hoxsey.

Illinois governor Charles Deneen and Arch Hoxsey in a Wright biplane during the St. Louis Meet in October 1910.

The ever-dapper Claude
Grahame-White
charms Eleonora Sears
at Belmont Park.

Grahame-White, cap back
to front, at the controls of a
Farman biplane.

The American actress
Pauline Chase, who
found fame as Peter Pan.

Glenn Curtiss (center) greets Count Jacques de Lesseps (left) and Hubert Latham (right) in New York on October 15, 1910.

The Wright brothers' baby biplane in October 1910.

Wilbur and Orville Wright
on the steps of their back porch
in Dayton, Ohio, in 1909.

The Wright brothers on
the prowl at Belmont Park.

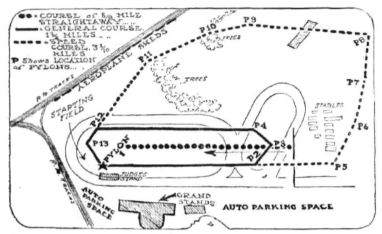

Plan of Belmont Park, New York, as arranged for the International
Aviation Meeting commencing to-day (Saturday).

The Belmont Park aviation course. The dark-edged hexagon is the 2.5km circuit and
the dotted trail represents the 5km course. Dead man's turn is around
pylon No. 1, and pylon No. 5 is where Le Blanc crashed. (FLIGHT MAGAZINE ARCHIVE)

The Belmont Park grandstand. Airplanes flew from left to right and then turned
toward the line of trees on the horizon.

The Belmont Park hangars, marked as "airplane sheds" on the course map (opposite).

Spectators demonstrate the "Airplane Stare" during the Belmont Park meet.

Hubert Latham (left) in his Antoinette races Claude Grahame-White in his Farman biplane in 1910.

Orville Wright chats to the cigarette-smoking Hubert Latham outside the Belmont Park hangars.

Hubert Latham in his Antoinette during his ill-fated attempt to cross the English Channel in 1909. (TOPICAL PRESS AGENCY/GETTY IMAGES)

Incredulous crowds in Washington, D.C., watch Claude Grahame-White descend on Executive Avenue.

John Moisant's flying career
was brilliant but brief.

The wreck of Moisant's Bleriot after the Belmont Park wind had got hold of it on Sunday, October 23

twenty-seven times in fifty-four minutes, Aubrun twenty-six times, Johnstone twenty-one, and Hoxsey and Grahame-White finished even on eighteen laps.

That was the end of the day's flying for Grahame-White, who returned his borrowed machine to Clifford Harmon. Grahame-White had no interest in the next event, the hourly altitude contest; that wasn't his forte. The Farman biplane* wasn't the right airplane in which to go climbing to the heavens, and anyway Grahame-White preferred distance to height. He alone had already qualified for Thursday's Statue of Liberty race, and with the International Aviation Cup two days later, he was loath to run any further risks similar to the one he had taken on Sunday. John Moisant, meanwhile, was grounded after the wreck of his machines, and his hopes were pinned on the Lovelace-Thompson Company, which had taken charge of his Blériot with a promise to have it repaired by Wednesday.

Walter Brookins took off and made a couple of slow laps, increasing his height as he began to deviate from the course. He was flying a Baby Wright, a machine similar in design and dimensions to the Baby Grand—the plane introduced to the press by Wilbur Wright on Saturday—although the Baby Wright had inferior power.

The spectators in the grandstand began moving down to the front lawns to get a better view as Brookins started to climb. They craned their necks, the men clamping a hand on their straw boaters and looking over their starched collars, the women using their programs to shield the sun from their eyes as he rose higher, leaving behind Emile Aubrun and James Radley, one of the British fliers, who had started out on the second Hourly Distance competition. That event had suddenly become humdrum, compared to the sight of Walter Brookins's small Wright biplane disappearing into the sky. Then someone gave a shout and pointed to the southeast. Look, over there, isn't that another machine? For several minutes the identity of the mysterious biplane was unknown. Press

---

* The Farman had been loaned to Grahame-White by his friend Clifford Harmon, as his own airplane of that make had been damaged on Sunday and he was still waiting to take delivery of a Blériot with which he planned to compete in the International Aviation Cup.

and public searched the hangars with their field glasses to see who was missing. "It was Count de Lesseps," wrote the correspondent from the *New York Sun*, "who to get room to circle wide in and also to give Brookins some air acres of his own for maneuvering had gone off toward Meadow Brook and Hempstead to take his running jump at the sky."

Higher and higher the two aircraft climbed, sometimes vanishing momentarily behind the few cotton clouds in the warm blue sky, watched all the while by ten thousand astonished people, but not by Viola Justin, the society correspondent for New York's *Evening Mail*. This was her first visit to the aviation show, though she had watched many a horse race at Belmont Park, and as she observed the wealthy onlookers standing on the tips of their patent leather shoes, a thought struck her. How best to describe it? She mused in print, "The Four Hundred had at last discovered a new sensation and a new expression . . . a human thrilled look of intense, absorbing interest . . . faces that have become so hardened from years of immobility that they look like plaster casts relaxed and wrinkled." While New York's high society scanned the sky, Justin stood on the lawn scanning them with their "straining lines of necks and double chins . . . faces so foreshortened and out of perspective that only the tips of teeth were visible to those directly under the boxes." It was, she told her readers, "a strange new angle of society." The "airplane stare" had been born. But even Miss Justin lifted her mordant eyes when the hordes began to puff and blow and point to the heavens. Brookins and de Lesseps, their aircraft resembling what the *Sun* called "elongated postage stamps," appeared to be heading directly toward each other thousands of feet above the ground. Men gave a strangled cry and women's hands went to their mouths as it seemed the inevitable was sure to occur. The correspondent from the *World* wasn't fooled, however; he knew that "the crowd watched fascinated and motionless for the meeting which might—which might, you know—mean a collision. And then the two specks merged until the specks were patterned one upon the other and had become just one speck. They separated in a moment and for minutes afterwards the discussions about the 'collision' took eyes off the specks which necessitated a refocusing of the eyes."

Now the planes were circling each other with de Lesseps's machine above the square biplane of Brookins. How close do you think they are to one another? children asked their fathers with a mix of fear and excitement. The airplanes dived and rose and drifted for what seemed like hours to the crowd. Necks began to stiffen and heads began to throb as spectators concentrated on the drama high above their heads.

Over at hangar row Orville Wright was standing with his brother and their sister, Katharine, watching the show. "Well, Brooky seems to have caught him," said Orville to Wilbur, fully aware that the two machines were hundreds of feet apart. Nearby the correspondent from the *New York Herald* laughed at a rare Orville quip, then resumed his stare. Brookins suddenly broke off and began to dive. The onlookers applauded the aviator's audacity, but the Wrights knew at once that something had gone wrong. The *New York Herald* reporter saw that "the softly moving lips of Wilbur Wright were framing a silent prayer for the boy who was taking such desperate chances."

Walter Brookins's engine had cut out without a warning, and now he sat at the controls—without a seat belt—gliding back down to earth in wide spirals. At two thousand feet he knew the wind wasn't going to take him close to Belmont Park, so he singled out some fields two miles to the north as the best chance for a safe landing.

Brookins had previously suffered engine failure thousands of feet up in the air. During an air show in Indianapolis the previous June, he had reached forty-two hundred feet when he heard a tearing noise from the engine behind him and the motor died. Unable to turn around to investigate the cause of the sound, Brookins started to drop out of the sky. At least he had broken the world's altitude record, he told reporters later, "and if my luck held, I'd break the gliding record, too. If it didn't, I'd probably break my neck."

He had landed without trouble on that occasion, and now as he glimpsed Belmont Park away to his left, the twenty-two-year-old calmly slid out of the sky. Passengers waiting for a train at the station one stop before Belmont Park jumped down onto the line and tracked the machine's descent. The Wright brothers commandeered an automobile and told the driver to "follow that airplane."

They found Brookins in a field. The biplane had its nose in the mud, like a pig with its snout in a trough, but the aviator was unharmed.

Dressed in a two-piece, green tweed suit and brown boots, he might have passed for one of the bystanders who had reached the downed machine from the railroad station, were it not for the patina of black grease on his young face.

Upon landing, Count de Lesseps unfastened the small aneroid barometer from his wrist and handed it to an officer from the Signal Corps. Its reading of 5,615 feet was impressive, provided it was corroborated by the official barograph now being removed from the Frenchman's plane. A corpsman passed both instruments to an official, who handed them to the judges' box. The glass lid on the barograph was lifted and a strip of paper peeled from the cylinder on which was a frenetic scribble of red lines, each one indicating approximately 165 feet in height. It took the official several minutes to count and recount the lines, but at the end he was satisfied that Count de Lesseps had climbed to 5,615 feet.

Brookins reappeared with the Wrights a little later, and his barograph indicated that he'd reached 4,882 feet, way inferior to his personal best of 6,175 feet, established at Atlantic City three months earlier.

At four o'clock Peter Prunty roared through his megaphone that it was time for the second hourly altitude contest, but only Armstrong Drexel signaled his desire to try to outdo de Lesseps. Having watched the earlier aerial duel as he lunched from a picnic hamper on the grass in front of his hangar, Drexel now fancied going up in the air. Dressed in black oilskins, and with his queer-looking helmet, he rose at a rapid rate until once more the spectators' heads and necks began to feel the strain. Then the black dot to the northeast became slowly bigger as he descended. He had none of the problems that had afflicted Brookins; it appeared to the press and the public that Drexel had climbed and dropped in thirty-two effortless minutes. His brother outsprinted the French mechanics in a race across the grass to congratulate Drexel on what Peter Prunty told the crowd (subject to official confirmation) was an altitude of 7,105 feet, a height only ever bettered by two men.* Anthony Drexel reached the machine, expecting his brother to jump into his arms in tri-

---

* The world's record was 9,186 feet, attained by Holland's Henry Wynmalen on October 1, 1910.

umph, but Armstrong remained in his seat, literally frozen to it. Eventually, said the *World*, Drexel was assisted down by his brother and mechanics, and he "plodded unsteadily over the field to his hangar. His face was marked with oil that had flowed from his motor. His teeth were chattering." Someone suggested a swig of brandy, but Armstrong shook his head, saying he wanted only water. He gulped down two large goblets while a lady's fur coat was wrapped around his shoulders and reporters gathered around for a quote from the normally garrulous aviator. Confirmation came through the megaphone that Armstrong Drexel had indeed reached a height of 7,105 feet.

Prunty built to a crescendo as he screamed into his megaphone. Or put it another way, folks, that's "more than a mile and a third up in the air." To think, aviation fans told each other, that this time last year the altitude record had been a puny 508 feet.

The house saluted a new American altitude record, but the millionaire flier's arms were too stiff to acknowledge the applause. How cold was it up there? he was asked. "It was beastly cold," he replied. "Hell was high."

One more event was scheduled for Monday—the grand speed contest. But after the drama of the altitude competitions, the organizers thought it best to first lay on a comic interlude for the crowd, the equivalent of the aviation clown entering the big top in his spluttering automobile to hoots of laughter. Roland Garros and his mechanics wheeled his Demoiselle from its hangar and the Frenchman jumped up onto what the correspondent from the *New York Sun* likened to a good-size umbrella. The propeller was engaged, and a ripple of giggles swept the grandstand as the engine started up with a *pfut, pfut*. He's not really going to go up in that, is he? people asked one another as Garros began to hop across the grass. "When she first leaves the ground one is minded of a rubber ball," wrote the *Sun*. "She bounces back to brush the grass blades for just a moment and then she is off for good." But once up in the air Garros picked up speed, and he was soon zipping around the course, taking the corners with far more ease than the big biplanes, then ripping along the homestretch at a pace that startled the spectators. He returned to earth after a few minutes, his machine wreathed in its exhaust fumes. "No policeman in Central Park would stand for the way a Demoiselle smokes for a minute," wrote the *Sun*, as Garros touched down with a bump and a bounce, waving to the crowd, who stood and cheered and roared with laughter.

For the final event of the day, the crowd pushed and shoved for the best view of the three machines that were being shouldered one by one across the wide infield from the hangars to the sandy racetrack in front of the grandstand. Peter Prunty announced the names of the three entrants in a speed race open only for biplanes: John McCurdy and James Mars in their Curtiss machines, and the little-known American John Frisbie in an invention of his own. Then Prunty explained the rules of the contest: the race would be over ten laps of the two-and-a-half-kilometer inner course, but each airplane was obliged to cover the twenty-five kilometers in under forty minutes or their time would be annulled. The three machines would take off one after another, from a standing position at the starting post used in horse races. At a shot from the timekeeper's pistol the engine would be engaged while mechanics held the machine in place; a second shot fired from the timekeeper's pistol sixty seconds later would be the signal for the plane to start moving. The second machine would start to run its engine only when the first was safely in the air, and likewise the third craft.

Hundreds of spectators pressed against the white rail in front of the grandstand as John McCurdy's aircraft was placed on the sandy track, its nose just nudging the white canvas strip that was the starting line. McCurdy settled back into the seat and bent down to hear a final set of instructions from Glenn Curtiss as the first pistol shot rang out. A mechanic spun the propeller but the engine didn't catch. There was a groan from the crowd. Someone yelled out words of encouragement. The mechanic tried again, and this time the engine started. McCurdy shouted something to Curtiss, who fumbled around in the pockets of his jacket and handed the flier his goggles. The timekeeper was staring intently at his watch, shouting down the seconds as the machine coughed out black smoke. The mechanics began to edge themselves into positions from where they could safely let go of the machine. Five . . . four . . . three . . . two . . . one . . . bang! The reporter from the *New York Sun* was up out of his seat as McCurdy pushed down the throttle and the "plane was dancing right down the middle of the track as clean away as a thorough-bred and then up, to a path it liked better." Frisbie was up next, and then Mars, who rose into the air just as McCurdy negotiated dead man's turn for the first time and tore down the home straight. The timekeeper told Peter Prunty the time for McCurdy's opening lap—two minutes and 14⅕ seconds. The crowd roared its approval, and they did so with even more gusto when the same aviator dipped under two minutes on his second lap.

Frisbie wasn't as quick but he seemed to be picking up speed as he scooted down the back straight toward the western end of the field, then past the high fence along which the contentious canvas screens had been erected. A few of them had been dismantled earlier in the day on the orders of Allan Ryan, but not all. As Frisbie passed the fence, a gust of wind rushed through "and sent the airplane crashing to the grass on its beam ends, smashing a wing and rolling Frisbie along the sod for yards." The aviator staggered to his feet mouthing obscenities at the fence and kicking great lumps out of the grass. "He's up!" Prunty cheerfully informed the crowd, whose eyes reverted to the two remaining contestants, both of whom took note of Frisbie's fate and increased their height.

The crowd reluctantly began to take their leave of Belmont Park once McCurdy had beaten Mars to win the speed race. Ten laps, twenty-five kilometers, in nineteen minutes—the feat sent the ten thousand spectators home in high spirits. One of them, Mrs. Florence Langworthy Richmond, wrote next day to a friend in Warren, Pennsylvania, describing her emotions at what she'd witnessed: "Aviation is so contrary to all our hitherto conceived ideas of the boundaries of man's power and endeavors. I understand the sensations of the Indians when they first saw steamboats . . . I cannot begin to tell you of the fascination which these new air creatures have for us poor earth-bound things . . . I felt that we were looking upon the dawn of a new era of which I could not live to see the full light. The airplanes were apparently perfectly guided and controlled; they rose, they dipped, they held a straight course, they turned with no visible effort. They stand for much done, but they are only pioneer craft after all."

Those durable enthusiasts who dallied over their picnic hampers under a saffron sky had the unexpected pleasure of seeing Charles Hamilton try out his formidable Hamilton racer, with its 110-horsepower engine. To the reporter from the *Evening Sun* still filing his copy in the press stand, the airplane "roared around the course twice like an eighteen hour train to Chicago hitting a wagonload of loose rails at 2 o'clock in the morning." Pleased with her? he asked Hamilton later. Not too bad, replied the flier, "but I didn't dare let her out." That would happen only on the day of the International Aviation Cup race.

As Hamilton limped toward his automobile, he passed one of the Wrights' hangars, its canvas walls illuminated by the lanterns that were still burning inside. All the other aviators had retired for the night; Claude Grahame-White was in the front row of the audience watching Pauline Chase in *Our Miss Gibbs*, John Moisant was dining with his brother, Alfred, in the Hotel Astor, and in the private banquet room of the Knickerbocker Hotel, Hubert Latham, Alfred Le Blanc, and two balloonists, Jacques Faure and Walther de Mumm, were enjoying the hospitality of James Regan, the hotel's proprietor, at an extravagant party to celebrate his establishment's fourth birthday. But Orville and Wilbur planned to burn the midnight oil this evening, tuning up their Baby Grand racer. On Tuesday, Orville intended to stun Belmont Park, and the world, with the first public demonstration of his new machine.

CHAPTER ELEVEN

Here Are Two Men in a Boat

Tuesday, October 25, 1910

THE SEARCH FOR Alan Hawley and Augustus Post had intensified by Tuesday morning and now included a reward of $200 for any trapper "supplying information leading to the finding of the balloonists."* The money came from Mr. H. Diamant, president of the Commission Company, a fur-dealing business with ten thousand correspondents among the trappers and runners in the semicircular district extending from Montreal to James Bay and south to the western extremity of Ontario.

The papers also carried news from a Monday-evening meeting of the board of directors of the Aero Club of America. If no word of Hawley or Post had been received by Wednesday, October 26, then Louis Von Phul and Joseph O'Reilly—the first crew to have descended in the balloon race—would ascend at Sault Ste. Marie, Michigan, and attempt to find the same air currents that took the *America II* north. Wisely, added the *Chicago Daily Tribune*, the pair would not be piloting the balloon that had been ravaged by grasshoppers.

---

* The *New York American* reported on October 29, 1910, that according to Edward Stratton of the Aero Club of America, "not less than 50,000 men were engaged in the search for Hawley and Post."

It was a fanciful plan, but as the Aero Club's spokesman, Edward Stratton, admitted in an interview with the *Albany Evening Journal*, the formulation of any coherent search plan was proving problematic because of the lack of definite information. "I concede that as the situation now stands, it would be ridiculous to send out relief expeditions," he said. "But with the cooperation of the press of Canada and the reports from all sources, I believe we can figure with a fair amount of accuracy the course of the *America II*, provided she got safely across Lake Huron and the Georgian Bay."

While Stratton called on the Canadian press to alert their readers to the missing men, the rest of the world's press spent Tuesday hypothesizing on the fate of Hawley and Post. A headline in the *New York Evening Sun* screamed WAS POINTED FOR POLE, and the front page of the *Boston Daily Globe* used an interview with Samuel Perkins as the inspiration for its headline: HAWLEY AND POST, HE FEARS, LOST FOREVER. Perkins expressed his opinion to the paper as he waited at Montreal Station to board the Central Vermont train to New York, where he and Hans Gericke, the pilot of *Düsseldorf II*, hoped to be crowned the winners of the International Balloon race. That they would be hailed triumphant had been unofficially confirmed to the London *Times* by a telegram it received from New York. Under the heading GERMAN BALLOON'S SUCCESS, the British newspaper said the *Düsseldorf II* was the winner of the tournament with another German crew, *Germania*, the runner-up.

It was inconceivable to most Americans that two people—their people—could simply vanish off the face of the earth. This was the twentieth century, after all, an age of unprecedented scientific and technological expansion. Already the world had witnessed the birth of Marconi wireless telegraphy, the invention of the airplane, the extraordinary sight of moving pictures, and the completion of the largest ever ocean liner, the forty-five-thousand-ton *Olympic*. The vessel had been launched five days earlier in Belfast, with the directors of the White Star Line telling reporters that the *Olympic*'s sister, the *Titanic*, would be even more impressive when it was finished. With the sea conquered, the air invaded, the north pole reached (by Robert Peary in 1909), Americans wondered how it was possible that two balloonists couldn't be found.

· · ·

Joseph Pedneaud and Joseph Simard had never heard of wireless telegraphy or airplanes or moving pictures. They lived off the land, without recourse to electricity or machines, making their own clothes and gathering their own food. Their interest in the world was confined to the province of Quebec and all that lay in it. Pedneaud had, for a brief while, worked in a mill in Potsdam, New York, but he'd pined for the Canadian wilderness and returned home. Now he farmed the land, and his friend Simard scratched a living as a shoemaker. The pair lived near Saint-Ambroise, a settlement approximately fifteen miles northwest of Chicoutimi, but since the weekend they had been on a hunting expedition, and now, at eight o'clock on Tuesday morning, they were "in a bark canoe, on the south side of Sotogama [Tchitagama] Lake, about two miles from the place where the River Blanche pours its water into the lake."

The snow of the previous day had ceased, but the trees on the north shore of the lake were powdered white, and the cheerless sky above suggested a fresh layer would soon arrive. Suddenly they spotted a thin trail of smoke coiling above the trees, close to where they knew a trapper called Jacques Maltais often camped.

Simard, kneeling Indian-style in the bow of the canoe, turned to Pedneaud at the stern and suggested that they paddle across to say hello to Maltais. As they moved swiftly through the water toward the shore, they caught sight of a white tent through the trees, and in the next instant a man in a gray suit emerged on his hand and knees. He stood up, stretched, and halloed loudly. "He was facing the mountain north of the lake," Simard recalled later, "and did not see us . . . Joseph Pedneaud answered by a loud hallo."

Augustus Post and Alan Hawley had enjoyed the luxury of a hot mug of water for breakfast on Tuesday morning along with a couple of crackers each.* Now the flap of their tent was open and an inquisitive squirrel snuck in to see what crumbs he could find. Hawley told Post he

---

* In the accounts given by Hawley and Post to newspapers in the immediate aftermath of their rescue, they confused their time line, presumably because of their exhausted mental state, telling reporters that they had come across the tent on Sunday morning. However, in an extensive article written by Augustus Post, published in the December 1910 edition of *Century Magazine*, he states that it was Monday morning. This is corroborated in written statements provided by Pedneaud and Simard.

was going to go for a wash in the lake, just as soon as he found that bar of soap they had seen the previous day. As his friend searched for the soap, Post opened his logbook and began to write:

> Another night has passed with no sign of life, but God provided tent, stove, and eatables, which we dare not touch. Mr. Squirrel has come to bid us good-morning, and eat our shoes, and bite Hawley. He is smelling him just now. He has two black stripes down his back. Looks like the inside of my "Micmac" coat. Mr. Jean Jacques Rousseau* has not yet returned to welcome his anxious guest of whom he is unaware. The custom of staying out all night is not confined to any particular locality.

Hawley and the squirrel departed the tent as Post closed his logbook and began to put on his boots. He heard his companion's morning greeting, and a few seconds later he heard it answered. Was it an echo? Then Hawley screamed, "Come out, Post! Here are two men in a boat."

Post was out of the tent in a flash, and together he and Hawley—even with his bad knee—ran down to the water's edge to welcome the canoe. "We dropped here in a balloon," said Hawley, pointing to the sky and making a circle with his hands, "and have found this camp. Will you help us get out to the nearest habitation?" Pedneaud smiled and replied in English that all the hand gestures were unnecessary.

As Hawley and Post helped drag the canoe up onto the beach, the French Canadians regarded them with a quizzical eye. Clearly "they had suffered much misery, and had had little to eat for several days." After they had all retired to the warmth of the tent, Post replenished the stove as Hawley gave a vivid account of the last five days. Then he asked where exactly they were. Pedneaud told them that the nearest habitation was nearly twenty miles to the south, nothing more than a small settlement called Rivière à l'Ours (Bear River). What about the houses they had seen from the balloon during their descent? Hawley inquired. The two hunters listened to a description of the *America*'s final resting place

---

* A tongue-in-cheek reference to the French philosopher whose work during the Age of Enlightenment in the eighteenth century brought him enduring fame.

and agreed that the buildings Hawley and Post saw "were near where the Peribonka River empties into Lake St. John, fifteen miles to the west, over an almost impassable country." Had you not found Maltais's camp, Pedneaud told the balloonists, your chances of survival would have been slim, very slim. Did Pedneaud know Maltais? Post asked. He did, he was a trapper, but he had no idea when he would return. They hadn't touched any of his belongings, stressed Post, not even his food.

Simard and Pedneaud exchanged a few words in French, then the latter turned to Post and said, "We will take you up the river in our canoe to the nearest habitation." Post grabbed the Canadian's hand and thanked him, saying, "We will pay you." The two accepted the offer, explaining that they were at the start of a three-week trapping expedition and would expect to be paid only for the hours they lost in paddling them to safety.

With everyone satisfied, Hawley asked if either man possessed some tea. "We have not had anything hot for a week, and we are almost starved." Pedneaud said, yes, they did have some tea. Then he turned to Simard and said something in French. They both laughed. Pedneaud explained that his friend, who knew no English, was the expedition cook, and if they liked, he would prepare the greatest breakfast of their lives. Hawley and Post stared in joyful disbelief as Simard dipped into his haversack and removed "some big slices of bread and pork, which he soon had frying in the pan, sending out an odor that nearly drove us crazy with anticipation."

The bread was a big loaf not long out of its outdoor clay oven, and soon the beards of the two Americans were glistening with hot pork fat. They swirled each mouthful of sweet, hot tea around their mouths and told Pedneaud he was right, it was a meal they would never forget. "It is remarkable how different one's feelings can become in about ten minutes," wrote Post in his log. "The world had changed to a most delightful place, and these men, who were only two good-hearted fellows out for a vacation trapping muskrats, seemed to us to be emissaries of all our friends and of the whole universe."

As a reward for cooking such a delicious breakfast, Hawley gave Simaud his pistol and a box of cartridges, then they packed their meager belongings into their ballast bags and departed the camp. Post and Hawley sat back-to-back in the center of the canoe, the latter facing Pedneaud in the stern and

Post looking at the back of Simaud kneeling in the bow. They headed south toward the settlement of Rivière à l'Ours with the balloonists marveling at the way the thin bark of the canoe glided through the water. At one moment Simaud "whipped out the pistol and pointed it at the head of a muskrat swimming away." He blazed away unsuccessfully at the animal without upsetting the delicate equilibrium of the canoe. A poor shot, but a skilled canoeist, thought Post.

A series of rapids at the head of the lake required a portage. Pedneaud shouldered the canoe, and Simaud carried their provisions as Hawley and Post trotted obediently behind like two puppies trailing their masters. For the next couple of hours they paddled up a narrow river, "with bushes and trees on each side almost shutting us in, and no sound but the drip of the paddle." To break the silence, Post sometimes broke into a rendition of "Sing Hosanna," but for most of the trip the balloonists leaned back against one another and savored the experience.

They came to another set of rapids and another portage, and as Post followed the trail through the undergrowth alongside the river, he saw the recent camping place of an Indian family. Over lunch Pedneaud told him that the Indians were headed deep into the wilderness to spend the winter hunting so they could return in the spring and sell the pelts.

They made camp in the late afternoon, not long after they had passed the southern end of Lake à l'Ours. Post asked Simaud if he could borrow his hook and line, then spent a happy hour before supper fishing for trout in the lake. He caught several and brought them back to the tent, proud that he had proved himself of some value in the wild. Simaud put aside the fish for breakfast and served up some fried pork and bread. Then Post and Hawley began to chat to Pedneaud about their voyage, explaining that in a balloon such as theirs it was possible to rise to twenty thousand feet. At first Pedneaud refused to believe it possible, but when Post dug out his barograph charts, Pedneaud accepted that the feat was not impossible. Next, the two balloonists spread out on the floor of the tent a map of their route from St. Louis to where they believed they had descended. Did Pedneaud agree they were correct in their landing place? He studied the map and after a few moments said, yes, he believed they were "substantially correct." In which case, Post and Hawley told one another, they had traveled more than twelve hundred miles in their balloon. The International Balloon Cup must surely belong to them.

The International Aviation Cup was foremost in Orville Wright's mind as he arrived at Belmont Park on Tuesday morning. The breeze from the southwest was a little stiffer than on Monday, perhaps ten or twelve miles an hour, but no sign of rain clouds was in the blue-gray sky. Orville joined his brother in a hangar and prepared to take out the Baby Grand racer.

A couple of thousand spectators were already on the grounds, many of whom had bought an official tournament flag—a gilt-edged airplane on a red-and-blue background—from one of the Boy Scout vendors on their way from the railroad station. Now they were waving them as Count de Lesseps took Grace McKenzie for a spin in his Blériot monoplane. Those already ensconced in the corporate boxes peered haughtily through their field glasses and wondered aloud when the engagement would be announced. The correspondent of the *New York Sun* noted that many in the grandstand had foot rugs, to protect against the wind, while a number of ladies complained that all that craning of the neck the previous day had played havoc with their hairpins. Some of the more hardy members of New York's high society had installed themselves on thick woolen rugs on the lawn and were discussing what would be best to ease the strain of the aero stare. A barber's chair, proposed someone, which raised a chorus of titters. Another suggested that a fortune was "waiting for the genius who can construct a neat, serviceable check rein . . . a strong strap which can pull the head back to any given angle and hold fast in that position. Such a strap could be fastened to a belt worn around the waist."

De Lesseps returned to earth with Miss McKenzie and helped her down from his airplane. Did that hand linger a fraction too long on her waist? asked the snoopers in the grandstand. As the young Canadian woman moved elegantly toward the grandstand, she was intercepted by a patrol of reporters. How was the flight? they inquired. Wonderful, replied Miss McKenzie. "Count de Lesseps handles his machine with such confidence and with such skill that one would have to be a coward indeed to doubt his ability to take care of things." Will you be going up again? "I shall certainly fly again." Has he asked you to marry him? McKenzie gave a smile, a coy smile, but fluttered up to her box without saying another word.

Just before noon a mechanic pulled back the two large flaps of the Wrights' canvas hangar, and a few moments later the Baby Grand racer was wheeled out to cries of delight from the crowd.

Reporters lounging in the press stand jumped to their feet when they saw the Wrights' great secret out in the open. When they picked up their field glasses and recognized Orville as the man in the flying clothes, they could barely contain their exhilaration. The younger of the two brothers had never before flown in the East—discounting the brief exhibition he had performed for the military at Fort Myer, Virginia, in 1908*—but here he was about to take the controls of what, in the eyes of the *New York Sun*'s reporter, resembled a "boy's sized edition of the Wright biplane of familiar model." He noticed that as the Baby Grand was shouldered onto the infield, "the foreign birds and their mechanics dropped everything else to see what the new type of racer would do."

Wearing a leather coat, Orville Wright climbed up into the seat, "placed to the left of the center of the lower plane so that the driver's weight will help in the stabilization of the airplane by making up for increased weight of heavier engine at his right." Wilbur exchanged a few words with his brother, then, with a confident smile, he retreated to the grass in front of the hangar, where he squatted, the position he always adopted when watching his machines at work.

The propeller was engaged, the engine started, and off went Orville Wright, bouncing across the grass and rising into the air. He circled the course, then, after he cornered dead man's turn with ease, he let out the engine and shot past the grandstand at a speed that left the reporters flabbergasted. Sixty miles an hour? No, sixty-five. More like seventy-five, said the

---

* On September 17, 1908, Orville Wright and Thomas Selfridge crashed during a trial flight for the U.S. military as a result of a broken propeller blade. Wright spent seven weeks recovering in hospital, but Selfridge was killed—the powered airplane's first fatality.

man from the *New York Sun*. The correspondent from the *New York Herald* had a stopwatch on the Baby Grand as it streaked around the two-and-a-half-kilometer course. Wright turned into the home straight as all around the grounds "men, women and children jumped up on camp chairs, on seats and on railings, and yelled themselves hoarse."

The *Herald*'s man stopped the timer as the Baby Grand crossed the strip of white canvas running across the sandy track. He puffed out his cheeks in astonishment: one minute and twenty-six seconds—more than half a minute faster than John McCurdy's best lap in Monday's speed race. Watching from his rickety steamer chair outside his hangar, Charles Hamilton was equally impressed. The Baby Grand was half the size of his monstrous 110-horsepower Hamilton, but its agility was awesome. The most worrying thing, however, he told the *Sun*'s correspondent, was that "you can't tell whether Orville is letting her out or not. The chain gear makes so much noise that down here I can't tell exactly how hard and fast the engines are going."

When the demonstration had finished, several reporters hurried over to hangar row to discover if the Wrights were happy with how the machine had performed. On his way past some of the other hangars the *New York Herald* correspondent couldn't help but notice the "intense discouragement in the camps of the foreign competitors" in the light of the Baby Grand's display. The normally taciturn Orville Wright was "communicative to a slight extent," and for several minutes he talked about his latest invention, explaining first that he and his brother had had no time to make anything especially for the machine because they wanted to have it ready for the Belmont Park Meet. For example, the gearing, the sprocket wheels, and the propellers came from existing stock in their Dayton factory. "When I have time, I will turn out propellers especially for these machines," he continued, "and these will give a much higher rate of speed than we will get from these stock parts." The *Herald*'s correspondent noted how Orville was like a man on his honeymoon, "gazing lovingly" at the airplane as he spoke, oblivious of the presence of others. The *Herald* asked why it was that while other inventors, particularly the French, were increasingly putting their faith in the monoplane, he and Wilbur believed in the superiority of the biplane. Wright admitted that the monoplane was a thing of beauty but, he added, "The innate fault of the single-plane machine is its weakness. It can never be made as strong as the biplane. The single plane always will be a weakness that will make advances beyond a certain point impossible."

Then the *New York Sun* correspondent asked Orville what were the chances of England or France lifting the International Cup now that everyone had seen the power of the Baby Grand? "Well," Wright answered with a wry smile, "I don't know. I can't tell yet whether Hamilton will keep the cup here or not!"

Tuesday at Belmont Park turned out to be what the *New York Herald* called "Wright Day."* Orville had opened proceedings with his startling flight in the Baby Grand, and Ralph Johnstone wrapped up events by climbing to 7,303 feet, two hundred feet higher than Armstrong Drexel's mark of the previous day. Earlier in the afternoon Johnstone and another of the Wright fliers, Arch Hoxsey—the "Stardust Twins"—had set off together in the altitude contest. Hoxsey had returned first, with his barograph indicating a height of 5,791 feet. Johnstone came down a while later and was met by Wilbur Wright, who was sure his boy had gone higher than Drexel. He looked for the barograph on his machine. Where was it? Wright asked. Johnstone blanched. He'd forgotten to attach it. The reporter from the *New York Sun* couldn't see through his field glasses exactly what was being said in the center of the infield, but Wilbur Wright "conversed gently but earnestly with his pupil for a few minutes and as a punishment Mr. Johnstone was told that just for that he must go right out and break the American record before dinner."

First Johnstone returned to the hangar to unknot his nerves before his second flight. He spent an hour or so making fun of his absentmindedness with his mechanics and Arch Hoxsey. He watched as de Lesseps and Hubert Latham tried unsuccessfully for the altitude record, then, a little after three o'clock, Johnstone quit his bantering and fell into a silent fidget; his mechanics knew it was time to prepare his plane. Johnstone buttoned up his leather coat over his thick sweater and pulled on his

---

* The following day Katharine Wright sent a postcard to her father saying, "Yesterday was Wright Day all right. Johnstone holds the American record for height. Orv [Orville] took our big [or little] racer and made almost seventy miles an hour."

woolen cap, then he checked that he had his barograph, and at three thirty P.M. he and Hoxsey took off together.

Some greasy-looking clouds had started to roll in from the Jersey factories as the pair headed southeast, and by the time they were ascending in long spirals, a light drizzle was falling on Belmont Park. The crowd watched as "round and round they circled like hawks looking for prey." One of the hawks was seen to descend, but the other grew smaller and smaller, then disappeared into a dark cloud. Johnstone's leather gloves and boots were inadequate against the cold as he climbed higher, and he felt a chilling numbness. The rain had turned to a sleet that lashed and cut his face, and now the cloud brought with it a white, feathery snow. In a moment Johnstone was through the snowstorm and he glanced down at the barograph on his wrist. He could see nothing. He whipped off his goggles and banged them against his thigh, trying to break off the thin sheen of opaque ice that had formed. He thought he saw that the barograph read over seven thousand feet, but he couldn't be sure. He felt desperately tired as he fumbled his goggles back over his weeping eyes.

Down on the ground the drizzle had stopped, and "anticipating accidents the crowd deserted the grandstand seats and crowded along the rail." They watched as the speck flitted in and out of clouds, descending in great swoops, and then at a "height of about 4,000 feet and to the east of the aviation field, Johnstone dived out of a mist bank with his engine throttled down, and he finished his flight with a long volplane." He landed his airplane on the far side of the aviation field and was collected by one of the tournament's green automobiles, in which sat a race official and Wilbur Wright. Wright "delightedly held up the barograph," and it was confirmed a little later that Ralph Johnstone had set a new American altitude record of 7,303 feet. When he arrived back at hangar row, Johnstone's clothes were dripping wet and his "knees shook and his face was swollen and red." "Wow, that was cold," he told a reporter from the *New York American*. "It was snowing furiously and sleeting up there . . . If I'd been able to see, I would have gone on and smashed the world's record. That was my purpose. I'll do it yet before I leave this place."

The other achievements at Belmont Park on Tuesday were prosaic in comparison to Johnstone's towering feat. The British flier James Radley won the twenty-mile cross-country event, beating John Moisant, John McCurdy, and Armstrong Drexel, and in the gathering gloom Charles Hamilton and the Curtiss fliers took their machines for a short spin ahead of Wednesday's qualification race to decide which three American fliers would represent their country in Saturday's International Cup race. Moisant's repaired Blériot had stood up well to the rigors of the cross-country flight, and he was his normal confident self, and Hamilton had no complaints either about his machine. But as if to reassert the Wrights' preeminence, Orville Wright reappeared at the end of the day in the Baby Grand and knocked three seconds off his morning lap time by sailing round in one minute and twenty-three seconds.

It had been an unforgettable day, and an illuminating one, too, for the representatives of the American military on official assignment at Belmont Park. General James Bell, chief of staff under President Theodore Roosevelt, walked over to the Wrights' hangar to offer his congratulations, accompanied by Commander John Barry Ryan of the U.S. Aeronautic Reserve, General James Allen, chief officer of the Signal Corps, and Lieutenant Benjamin Fulois, whose task it was to write the official report about the tournament for the War Department. While Bell chatted with the Wrights—they had first met during the brothers' military trials at Fort Myer two years earlier—General Allen answered a couple of questions from the *New York Herald*. He had been mightily impressed by what he had seen, he said, stressing that "with a fleet of biplanes and monoplanes as large as that which flew here today, an army could do immeasurable damage in time of war." Would he thus be advising President Taft to increase spending on aviation? "I am encouraging the War Department to take a deeper interest in aviation all the time," he replied, adding, "We have good aviators in this country, and they prove this themselves when compared to the foreigners who are here now."

In the press stand the correspondent of the *New York Evening Sun* had also been seduced by what he had seen throughout the day, and as he watched a long line of automobiles queuing to leave Belmont Park, he wrote, "The sight of the auto chugging over the hillocks brought up a sense of ancient days and one, to be up to the minute, had only to glance to the heavens and see the graceful flights, the swift swoops, the searing aloft to dizzy altitudes, and then put off that resolution to buy an auto and determine to wait for an airplane."

The only unsavory incident of the stupendous day was the contretemps between Count de Lesseps and Cortlandt Field Bishop, president of the Aero Club of America. Admittedly discontent had been growing in the French camp for many days, said the *Evening Sun*, with "the rivalry between the English-speaking and French aviators intense and bitter in some respects," but that was no excuse for the "ugly moment" that occurred shortly before the close of the day's program. The trouble arose when Bishop told a group of reporters that de Lesseps had charged Mrs. Eustis—a friend of his sister's, the Countess de la Bergassiere—$2,000 for a brief flight. When the reporters relayed the story to de Lesseps, his face darkened, and with a Gallic roar he went "running out of hangar in his grotesque air-riding costume and dashed around until he found Bishop." With the grinning reporters ringing the two protagonists like spectators at a cockfight, de Lesseps began "shaking his fists up and down nervously" as he asked Bishop if what he had been told was true. The *New York Sun* described what followed:

"I did not," stammered Bishop. "That is, I merely—"

"You did. You told me, Mr. Bishop," said a young man hotly, who had edged through the crowd.

Mr. Bishop whirled around. "Can't you take a joke?" Mr. Bishop demanded of the indignant one. "I was only joking when I told you that."

The young man—unidentified by the newspapers—turned on his heel, but not before he had jabbed a finger at the president of the Aero Club, warning him that he was "through with you, Bishop, for good."

Bishop held out a hand to de Lesseps and swore blind that it had been a joke, albeit an ill-judged one. "I have never accepted money for taking passengers up and I never will," said the Frenchman, his gun-barrel eyes trained on Bishop. "I am a gentleman sportsman, not an aerial chauffeur." The count stepped back and allowed the American safe passage from the ring. Then he turned to the reporters and told them if any more calumnies came from Bishop, he "would smash his face."

Later that evening de Lesseps had forgotten all about the distasteful incident when his engagement to Grace McKenzie was officially announced at a discreet party at the Knickerbocker Hotel. With Bishop's apology common knowledge among the guests, de Lesseps was satisfied that his fiancée's wealthy family knew him to be a man of impeccable conduct.

CHAPTER TWELVE

Are You These Gentlemen?

Wednesday, October 26, 1910

O N   W E D N E S D A Y   M O R N I N G it appeared that everyone who was anyone in America had something to say on the likely fate of Alan Hawley and Augustus Post. The *New York Times* reported that Professor R. W. Bock, director of the Geological Survey, thought that "the aeronauts will surely perish if they sailed into the far northern sections" of Canada, while in the *World*, Wilfrid Laurier, prime minister of Canada, believed the missing pair "would come out all right." The *World* also carried an interview with Clifford Harmon, conducted from his hangar at Belmont Park, in which the former balloonist offered $1,000 "to any person who will discover them, living or dead." Harmon, however, was gloomy as to the chances of the former. "I sailed with Post and found him an excellent balloonist. He is cool, clearheaded, and has wonderful endurance, but I believe it will be impossible for him to come out of the wilderness alive."

In the *New York Herald* an old friend of Post's, Mr. R. H. Johnston, was in no doubt that there would be a happy ending to the story that was gripping America. Post, he said, was capable of enduring any amount of fatigue and hardship and also had great ingenuity. Johnston regaled the newspaper with the time his friend had used a lady's hairpin to replace the needle on his automobile's speedometer. In Johnston's view, Post "will come back all right, with new laurels for courage and endurance." On the same page of the *Herald*, Captain John Berry, who had helped inflate the *America II* on the St. Louis aero grounds, made wild and inaccurate claims that the balloonists were splendidly well equipped to survive the Canadian wilderness because they had with them "rifles and ammunition, fur-lined coats and boots . . . fishing tackle, half a dozen cold chicken, a case of crackers, several gallons of water, whiskey, brandy, and a case of medicine."

The *St. Louis Post-Dispatch* had sought the opinion of forecaster Devereux of the Weather Bureau, who, having pored over his charts from the previous week, asserted, "The balloonists were drowned in Lake Superior."

Reporting sightings continued to be received by Lewis Spindler at his headquarters in Chapleau. A Dr. D. C. Meyers, who had been on a hunting trip in Ontario, said he'd seen a balloon descending in the distance. A Constable McCurdy, a Canadian policeman, had described a balloon falling into Georgian Bay on Thursday, October 20. A railroad clerk, Guerrard, swore he'd seen the lights of a balloon headed north near Fort William in Ontario. In Quebec, a Peter Brown was adamant he had glimpsed a balloon passing over Lake Kipawa, and rumors were that an empty balloon basket had been spotted drifting on Lake Superior.

The *New York Herald* was as baffled as the rest to the whereabouts of the missing pair, particularly as every lumber company in Ontario and Quebec had alerted its men by stage and canoe. Baffled, maybe, but the newspaper still held out a glimmer of hope: "The big yellow gas bag is down somewhere in the Canadian wilds, but as yet there is no proof and scarcely any collateral evidence that the valiant aeronauts, Mr. Alan Hawley and Mr. Augustus Post, are forever lost."

It hadn't been the most comfortable of nights for the four men squeezed into the two-man tent. They had piled their boots into one corner and hung their coats from the ridgepole. Post woke to find Joseph Simard playing with his new toy, the pistol, "pointing it at imaginary game and carefully counting the cartridges." Simard blushed when he realized he'd been caught in the act and stashed the weapon in his haversack. He began to prepare Post's trout for breakfast, and once they had eaten and washed, they continued on their journey with the wind at their backs and a weak sun rising in the east. A while later Simard and Pedneaud paddled the canoe toward a high bank at the summit of which was a rough track. "Now all you have to do is follow this trail," Pedneaud told the two Americans, "and it will bring you to the nearest house." Hawley proposed that the hunters accompany them, but Pedneaud said he was keen to start on his expedition. Don't worry, he reassured Hawley, "You will have no further trouble."

Pedneaud and Simard steadied the canoe as first Hawley and then Post eased himself onto the bank. The four men shook hands, and Post asked how much the two were owed. "It will be three days' work for us," said Pedneaud, "coming and going back. Would two dollars a day be too much?" Hawley and Post doubled it and threw in their blankets and most of what remained of their equipment. Post then took from his pocket his flask of cognac and proposed they drink "a health to cement a friendship timely and strong." Pedneaud had the first swig—a long, deep mouthful, which Post thought might leave none for them—before handing the flask to Simard. There was enough for all, however, and having waved farewell, the two Americans scrambled up the bank. "With light hearts we hastened forward," said Post, "thinking only of reaching Belmont Park before Saturday, which we knew would be the great day of the aviation meet."

From where they had been dropped it was several miles to the village of St. Ambroise, but after half an hour the pair came across a frame house in a clearing. Post knocked on the door, and a voice said in French, "*Entrez.*" Inside was a young woman at a spinning wheel in a sparsely furnished room. A large crucifix was on one wall, and the room was bathed in sunlight. She didn't flinch at the sight of two ragged figures before her, but when Post began to speak in English, the woman smiled and shook her head. Post dusted off his schoolboy French and asked if they were headed toward St. Ambroise. The woman nodded and suggested they try another house, just up the track, where she knew there to be a horse and cart.

They found the next house heaving with people; a man sat outside on a rocking chair with two children on his knee, while an older girl hung out the washing. Inside, the man's wife was preparing lunch and more children darted from room to room. The two men were invited inside, and in between mouthfuls of a hot meal they told their story. Post was "sure we were thought to be visitors from the celestial regions," and none of the children seemed able to comprehend that they had fallen from the sky. After lunch the man hitched up his cart to his horse and drove the pair along a dirt track toward the church spire of St. Ambroise, depositing them outside the telegraph office. Hawley banged on the door, which was opened by a tall man who spoke excellent English. He introduced himself as Abel Simaud, the village priest, and he wasted no time in ushering them into his untidy office. Books and papers were lying everywhere, and several plants in the window needed water. He offered them a glass of wine, but Hawley impatiently pointed at the instrument with its "reels of paper, clockwork and brass keys" and said it was imperative they send a message. They stood over the priest as he began to tap the keys of the telegraph, but several minutes later he gave a shrug of his shoulders and said, "The wire is broken, probably due to a fallen tree."

The pair said they would have that glass of wine after all, and as they rued their misfortune, Post spotted a newspaper on a table. May I? he asked the priest. Of course. Post picked up the paper and his jaw dropped. There on the front page "was a big headline about Hawley and Post lost in the wilderness and all the powers of the Canadian government being rallied to their rescue." Post showed it to Hawley, and the priest jumped to his feet, exclaiming, "This is you! Are you these gentlemen?" Before Post could answer, sounds came from the telegraph, followed by squeals of excitement from the priest. Communication had been reestablished. He took his seat in front of the telegraph as Hawley asked if he would send the first message to Charles H. Heitman in New York City, a good friend but also a member of the Aero Club of America: LANDED PERIBONKA RIVER. LAKE CHILAGOMA [this was Hawley's best attempt to spell Tchitagama], NINETEENTH. ALL WELL. HAWLEY.

Hawley then instructed a telegram be sent to his brother, William, in New York, only this time he didn't attempt to wrestle with the lake:

LANDED IN WILDERNESS WEEK AGO. FIFTY MILES NORTH OF CHICOUTIMI.
BOTH WELL. ALAN

My turn, said Post, stepping forward, and asking the priest to send a
message . . . to whom? His estranged wife, Emma? No. He would prefer
to let his sister, Mrs. Clapp-Ward, in Long Island, know he was okay:
LANDED SAFELY NEAR LAKE ST. JOHN. JUST OUT OF WOODS. ALL WELL. RE-
TURNING. AUGUSTUS.

That was it, no one else needed to be notified for the time being. But
then they saw the French newspaper on the table, with news of their disappearance and the prediction that the *Düsseldorf II* had won the International Balloon Cup. Perhaps, too, there was also that quote from Sam
Perkins, about his belief that Hawley and Post were "lost forever." They
asked Abel Simaud to send one final message, to Perkins: LANDED PERI-
BONKA RIVER, NORTH LAKE CHILAGOMA. 19TH. ALL WELL, RETURNING.
HAWLEY-POST.

They didn't care that they'd butchered the name of the lake; they just
wanted Perkins to know the trophy wasn't his. The French newspaper
had printed a map of the *Düsseldorf*'s position, and Hawley and Post
knew they had landed farther north; not just farther north than the *Düsseldorf*, but farther north than every other balloon in the competition.

From St. Ambroise, Hawley and Post rode in a buckboard to Chicoutimi
along the potholed dirt track. Several times they had to jump down and
walk up the steep hills alongside the exhausted pony. They arrived at the
town's only hotel, the Château Saguenay, at ten o'clock in the evening
after a five-hour journey and thanked the priest for all his help. Please
accept this donation for the parish poor, they said, slipping several dollar
bills into the priest's hand.

No one was at the front desk when Hawley and Post entered the hotel.
They rang the bell and waited. After a few seconds the manager, Mr.
Joseph Guay, appeared from a back office. Used to welcoming city folk
on hunting trips, he wasn't perturbed by the sight of the disheveled pair.
"Back from the bush?" he said with a smile. "Well, I hope you had the
same good luck as the three gentlemen from Boston who were on my
hunting ground last week."

Post laughed. "We had good luck, but not the one you speak of."

Within minutes they were sitting down to a plate of oysters, fried fish, and steak. Quite a crowd had gathered around their table, including the third-luckiest man in Quebec—an Associated Press reporter. From the outset he had followed the drama, and a journalistic hunch that the missing balloon had come down somewhere near Lake St. John had led him to the remote hotel. A couple of days earlier he had taken a train from Quebec City—227 miles south—to Chicoutimi, the last stop on the Quebec and Lake St. John railroad before the wilderness. Now the biggest story in North America was right in front of him, chewing on a moose steak.

Guay listened to the account of the men's trek and verified their landing place. He had hunted for years in that area and was familiar with the mountainside and the gorge in which they had come down. After supper, Guay took Hawley and Post into his office and they sent a couple more telegrams; then Guay explained that as a commissioner of the Superior Court of the District of Chicoutimi, he had the power to authenticate their point of descent. He signed a statement to that effect and handed it to them. It was nearly midnight now, and Hawley tucked the statement into his pocket and with a weary "Good night" climbed the stairs to his room. Post agreed to speak to the reporter from the Associated Press, if a cognac could first be produced. The reporter yelled for a bottle of the hotel's finest, then sat down with his notepad and pencil. In his opinion the two Americans had arrived in Chicoutimi looking like "half wild men" with their clothes torn and muddy, and he was eager to hear all about it. Post narrated their trek without resorting to melodrama or mock heroics. He made no mention of his companion's injured knee nor of the bitter temperatures, saying only that the terrain had been "extremely rough and our travel was necessarily slow and arduous in the extreme, as there were no trails we could follow. The bush was dense and we had a hard time fighting our way through." Warmed by the hotel and relaxed by his drink, Post was incapable of summoning the words to adequately describe the nights they had spent in the open. It had been a strenuous trip, he told the reporter, "but we didn't suffer any really severe handicaps." Post drained his glass and got to his feet. But before he retired for the night, a thought struck him—what had happened to Walter Wellman. Did the reporter know? He told Post the outcome, and the balloonist "was disappointed but not surprised that the attempt had proven a failure."

A gale was blowing on Wednesday morning at Belmont Park, and Allan Ryan scowled as he watched the flags above the hangars dancing in the wind. The prospects of a full day's flying seemed slim. Perhaps it had been a mistake to stage America's first international aviation competition at Belmont Park, he mused. Hadn't the *New York Times* called the ground not so long ago the "breeziest race track now in use . . . a veritable cave of the winds"?

Look on the bright side, Ryan murmured: the sun was shining, his wife's speeding fine had been small, and his appendix, which had been grumbling for the past week, was dormant. Then Ryan grimaced as he remembered that later in the morning he had to tour the course with Monsieur Pierre Gasnier, a representative of the Aero Club of France, so that the Frenchman could decide whether he would advise his compatriots to compete in Saturday's big race. It was going to be another long day, Ryan told himself, treasuring the early-morning solitude of the clubhouse.

One of the first aviators to arrive at Belmont Park was Claude Grahame-White, who, along with his manager, Sydney McDonald, rode from New York City in a fancy carriage belonging to the Hotel Astor. A few reporters were already hanging around the entrance hoping for a few words from the competitors, but having read the morning papers, the Englishman was in no mood for conversation. The papers had lampooned his timidity and contrasted it with the nerve of Johnstone and Hoxsey, soaring to the heavens, and the dash of Moisant's and de Lesseps's cross-country flights. Grahame-White had done nothing more than go "for a daily promenade around the track." Perhaps, sneered the *New York Sun*, it would be best if he "substituted an aerial taximeter for his barograph," such was his penchant for charging people for a short flight. The paper then insulted Grahame-White by calling him an "air chauffeur," on the very page in which it recounted Count de Lesseps's reaction to the same description by Cortlandt Bishop.

Why had they turned against me? Grahame-White asked his manager. A fortnight earlier he'd been the darling of America, yet now he was being cruelly mocked. Some sections of the crowd had even started to sing a rhyme as he flew remorselessly round the track:

> Aviation is vexation,
> Postponement is as bad;
> They call me rash, but I get the cash
> As fast as I can add.

But Grahame-White was merely flying to his strengths. His Farman biplane was reliable but slow, ill equipped to challenge for any speed prizes or altitude contests. The Blériot racer that he'd ordered from France had yet to arrive, so all Grahame-White could do was enter the hourly distance events and use his exceptional physical stamina to good effect.* All the laps he clocked had another purpose, of course, one that hadn't occurred to the public or the press; that was to familiarize himself with every nuance of the course, so that on the day of the International Aviation Cup race he would know when best to throttle, when to bank, where the wind swirled, and, most crucially, how best to take dead man's turn. As for the charge of his being a harpy, that was nonsense. So far at Belmont Park he'd earned $1,700 in prize money, more than anyone else, but not by much. Arch Hoxsey had $1,575 and John Moisant had $1,300. As for the accusation of his being an air chauffeur, Grahame-White had taken up only one passenger at Belmont Park, and that was Eleonora Sears. It wasn't as if he'd instructed spectators to form an orderly queue outside his hangar.

But Grahame-White guessed the real reason for the hostility, and it had nothing to do with aviation. The evidence was right there in front of him, in the photographs in the *World* and the *New York Herald*, which depicted him at the controls of his grounded biplane, while snuggled up

---

* Was his stamina innate or induced? Throughout his flying career, Grahame-White was a regular user of Phosferine, an opiate marketed as a liquid "tonic." Along with stars of cricket and soccer, Grahame-White appeared in a Phosferine advertising campaign in 1910, saying that it was "most effective in preventing and overcoming the effects of nerve strain and exposure. Phosferine braces and tones the system until one is capable of exceptional endurance." Phosferine was later banned in the UK.

behind was a laughing Eleonora Sears, wearing very much the look of a young woman in love. Inside the papers were sly references to the pair's having lunched together at the Turf and Field Club. How romantic, was the intimation, were it not that Grahame-White was engaged to Pauline Chase. What sort of man would treat his fiancée with such contempt? Not a gentleman.

Now, as Grahame-White arrived at Belmont Park, he bridled with indignation at his treatment. Jumping down from the carriage, he glowered at the reporters and handed the driver a tip. The watching reporter from the *New York Sun* noticed that the "person on the box did not lose himself in transports of enthusiasm" at the size of Grahame-White's largesse.

Eleonora Sears arrived not long after her alleged beau with her brother, Frederick, who was fresh off the midnight express from Boston. He had been dispatched by his parents with implicit instructions to prevent his sister from riding the sky with Grahame-White, and a telegram had also been sent to Miss Sears. Was it because they feared for their daughter's safety, or her reputation? Eleonora didn't know, but she told the reporters at the front gate of Belmont Park that she was "disgusted" at the order. "I love it," she said of flying. "I'm crazy about it and I came down here to learn to fly."

Sears and her brother showed their passes to the Pinkerton security men and headed toward hangar row. She had braided her long brown hair before leaving the family apartment, but she had to hold on tight to her sailor's hat as the wind blew hard from the northwest.

Quite a throng had already formed in and around the aviators' hangars, and it continued to swell throughout the morning. Katharine Wright appeared, having refused to say anything to the press about her brothers' latest machine—reticence was obviously a family trait, said the reporters, laughing, after she'd gone—and the wives of Glenn Curtiss, Eugene Ely, and James Mars arrived laden with picnic hampers for a hangar lunch. Clifford Harmon escorted his wife through the gate, expressing his concern for Messrs Hawley and Post, and confirming he had indeed offered a reward of $1,000 for news of their fate.

The McKenzie sisters, Ethel and Grace, wafted through the entrance, with Grace blushing as she accepted the congratulations of everyone on her engagement to Jacques de Lesseps. Colonel John Jacob Astor emerged from his limousine with his eighteen-year-old son, Vincent, and Mrs. William H. Force and her two daughters, Katharine and seventeen-year-old Madeline, the latter trying her darnedest to look like an adult in a brown walking costume and a black felt hat topped with coque plume. Astor's look of contentment was similar to Grace McKenzie's, thought the reporters. Was he simply enjoying his newfound freedom after his recent divorce, or did it have more to do with the presence of Madeline Force, the teenage girl nearly thirty years his junior who was rumored to be his companion?* Then the reporters began to nudge each other and point toward an automobile that had just arrived. A dainty black boot emerged, then a small but perfectly formed leg . . . and out stepped Pauline Chase, looking like a million dollars in a navy blue suit with mink collar and cuffs. This should be interesting, the reporters said with a wink. The reporter from the *World* trailed Chase toward hangar row, willing Eleonora Sears to appear. And suddenly he saw her, just at the moment Chase did. "Hardly had the two conspicuous young women spied each other," he wrote, "than they promptly proceeded to pass in opposite directions without recognizing. To the spectators standing near, the incident was immediately understood."

Everyone who visited hangar row was asked to make a contribution to the reward on offer to find Alan Hawley and Augustus Post (on top of the $1,000 offered by Clifford Harmon). Aviators, their friends, and their families opened their wallets, and $2,000 was collected in little more than an hour. Glenn Curtiss and his team of fliers pledged $1,000 among them, Charles Hamilton and Ralph Johnstone threw in $100 apiece, and even Grahame-White was rumored to have dipped into his deep pockets for something. The Wright brothers were generous, too, remembering well the help Augustus Post had given them during their aeroplane trials at Fort Myer two years earlier.

The benevolence seemed to be infectious at Belmont Park this day,

---

* Astor married Madeline in September 1911, and to escape the disapproval of New York society they fled to Europe on tour. In April 1912 they returned, on board the *Titanic*. The pregnant Madeline survived, but her husband went down with the ship.

penetrating even the aloof exterior of Monsieur Pierre Gasnier, representative of the Aero Club of France. He, Allan Ryan, and Cortlandt Bishop had spent the greater part of the morning touring the course and discussing the French objections. Gasnier suggested that certain trees be cut down, that depressions be filled, and that half a dozen telegraph poles be removed. He laughed off Le Blanc's suggestion to demolish a row of houses; that was just Alfred's inimitable sense of mischief. After the trio had returned to the clubhouse Gasnier announced with a smile that, provided the changes were made before Saturday's race, "there is no further cause for controversy."

At one thirty P.M. a member of the Signal Corps knelt beside a hole in the ground at the back of the scoreboard and lit the fuse of a signal bomb. As its yellow smoke scooted across the course, the hangar doors remained firmly shut: after Sunday's debacle, no one would risk taking off in such a wind. The *Evening Sun* reporter noted that the inactivity on hangar row "brought disappointment to the calamity howlers who looked . . . for tumbles if the airmen should decide to risk their necks." The crowd had come expecting to see a battle royal—eight Americans in four types of planes flying twenty laps to decide the three places in the Stars and Stripes' team for Saturday's grand race. The fans had talked of nothing else on the trains out from New York (except whether Hawley and Post had been eaten by wolves or bears, or frozen to death, or perhaps starved), and they wanted action, but the committee had no intention of endangering America's top fliers three days before the biggest competition in international aviation. Cortlandt Bishop and Allan Ryan called a meeting of the eight competitors, and the elimination race was postponed to Thursday, with the aviators free to begin the twenty-lap course anytime between nine A.M. and five thirty P.M.

The crowd was becoming restless as the hands of the clock on the scoreboard neared four. The wind had eased since Peter Prunty's announcement two hours earlier that the International Aviation Cup elimination race had been postponed to Thursday, and the spectators wanted some action. Suddenly, over on hangar row "they saw the long shape of Hubert Latham's Antoinette being coaxed out of its lair by the diligent hostlers."

With Latham in the air, others followed, and soon a swarm of airplanes were in the sky: Emile Aubrun in his Blériot, then Count de Lesseps, René Simon, and Roland Garros. Out came the Americans, headed by Armstrong Drexel, with Arch Hoxsey and Ralph Johnstone in close attendance, and the newest of the Wright fliers, Phil Parmalee, also up. Good grief, exclaimed the reporter from the *New York Sun*, was that Grahame-White? It was, and he "was spurning his old stone sled of a Farman . . . [and] cutting aerial didoes in a Blériot."

Latham, Aubrun, and Drexel headed east, toward the captive balloon over Hempstead Plains, racing each other the twenty miles there and back in the cross-country event. Hoxsey and Johnstone laid on a few of their favorite aerial cowboy stunts before the gallery, and Parmalee and Brookins circled the course in the hourly distance event.

Brookins was flying one of the Wrights' new machines; it wasn't the Baby Grand, but it was a similar design and Orville had given him instructions to put the wind up Grahame-White. Show him what it can do, Orville told Brookins. Grahame-White had swapped his Farman for his Blériot as a defiant response to his knockers, but it was his old fifty-horsepower Blériot and not the hundred-horsepower racer that was scheduled to arrive in New York in twenty-four hours. Orville Wright didn't care. He kept a stopwatch on the pair for several laps, jotting down their times in a notepad. The reporter from the *New York Sun* watched as Brookins gained on Grahame-White until they were virtually nose to tail. The American drew level, then eased ahead, to the evident delight of his compatriots. In the grandstand a man in a leather coat leaped to his feet and screamed, "There goes the winner of the big race!" Orville Wright shared the man's confidence. He snapped shut his stopwatch and turned triumphantly to the correspondent of the *New York Herald* standing alongside him. "Seven seconds better in each lap than Grahame-White in his Blériot," Orville said with just the faintest of smiles.

In all the excitement caused by Brookins's humiliation of Grahame-White—and the return of the three machines in the cross-country race—many people had failed to spot Arch Hoxsey and Ralph Johnstone climbing off southeast into the slate-colored sky. But now, nearly an hour later, neither man had reappeared out of the night sky. Hundreds of spectators loyally waited for their return, and though the correspondent from the *New York Sun* could no longer see those people around him, he heard how they "raised their voices in excited arguments as one assured his neighbor that he could see the stars blotted out where the airplanes were coursing aloft in the blackness."

At the entrance to one of their hangars Wilbur and Orville Wright were becoming increasingly concerned. "Where are they?" fretted Wilbur, looking to the heavens. "Where are they?" The brothers ordered their mechanics to pour the contents of two five-gallon drums of gasoline onto the grass, and with a great whoosh the markers were ignited. A few minutes later people heard the "whir and thudding of propellers," then someone gave a yell "and a black form was seen flitting across a star lighted space." Then a second shape became discernible, and within sixty seconds both airplanes were safely back on the ground. Their barographs when compared showed that Hoxsey had climbed to 6,183 feet, three hundred feet higher than his friend. Not that Johnstone cared, for it took several minutes to pry his gloves from his frozen fingers, and "it was only after an hour of brisk rubbing with alcohol that he was able to dress in his street clothes and leave the tent."

The many aviation parties in Manhattan were already in full swing by the time Ralph Johnstone got back to the Hotel Manhattan and the warming embrace of his wife and son. Armstrong Drexel and Claude Grahame-White were guests of Jay Gould and his wife at their Fifth Avenue mansion, and Count de Lesseps was the host of a sumptuous banquet at the St. Regis Hotel for the French aviators. Red roses adorned each table—a celebration of his love for Grace McKenzie. Colonel John Jacob Astor had commandeered another of the St. Regis's private dining rooms, and he and his guests—including members of the Guinness family—were discussing the day's events at Belmont Park. The dining room of the Hotel Astor had been decorated to reflect New York's modish mania for all things aeronautical, with souvenir pennants from Belmont Park, model balloons and biplanes, and even airplane-shaped ices for dessert.

Amid the festivities only a spoilsport would have drawn attention to the evening papers and the news that another aviator—the third in as many days—had been killed.* The unfortunate man, Fernard Blanchard, had dropped to his death from one hundred feet during a Paris air show.

---

* A German called Monte had been killed on a Wright biplane during a meet in Germany on Tuesday.

CHAPTER THIRTEEN

There's Always a Chimney for a Man to Hang On To

Thursday, October 27, 1910

CHARLES HEITMAN HAD BEEN PACKING a few essentials into his valise on Wednesday afternoon when he heard a knock on the front door of his Manhattan home. He presumed it was his chauffeur, come to drive him to Grand Central Station so he could take a train to Canada to help in the search for his missing friends. But it wasn't his chauffeur, it was a messenger boy, and he handed the maid who answered the door a telegram for her master. When Heitman opened the message, he cried out in astonishment.

LANDED PERIBONKA RIVER. LAKE CHILAGOMA, NINETEENTH. ALL WELL. HAWLEY.

Within minutes Heitman's chauffeur had arrived, but instead of driving his master to the station, he was ordered to deposit him at the headquarters of the Aero Club of America in the Engineering Society's Building at 29 West Thirty-ninth Street. Once there Heitman "began sending messages to all points where searchers were busy, advising them of the safety of the men they sought."

Edward Stratton of the Aero Club received the news in Ottawa, where he had established a control room to liaise between the club's New York HQ and Lewis Spindler, who was in the isolated Ontarian town of Chapleau, 350 miles northwest of Toronto. Stratton gave a joyful shout, then rushed over to the "huge map of Ontario and Quebec" in his office on which were plotted the routes of the other nine balloons. The *Düsseldorf II* was represented by a circled 9 on the map; it lay east of Kiskisink, and south of Lake St. John. Stratton checked the telegram in his hand. He hadn't been mistaken, the *America II* had landed north of the lake. He banged the map in delight and hollered, "He wins the cup!"

William Hawley had been so overwrought when Heitman broke the news over the telephone, all he could muster in response was "My God." A few minutes later, however, his own telegram arrived, and he stared in mute wonder at the piece of paper that proved his brother's survival. Later, speaking from the doorstep of the apartment he shared with Alan, William described how his brother had conditioned himself prior to the contest. "For two weeks before leaving for St. Louis he planned his days with reference to the strain that would be placed upon him during the race," William said. "He retired early, almost at sundown, and gave himself time for all of the sleep which nature would accept. He was under a rather nervous tension for a few days preceding the race, but physically was in superb condition."

"Overjoyed" was the reaction of Samuel Perkins to the news, at least according to the *New York Herald*, when it called on him in New York. By then he'd had time to compose himself after the shock of receiving Hawley and Post's teasingly terse message. Perkins showed the *Herald* a facsimile of the telegram he had sent to St. Ambroise (with forwarding instructions):

> Indications are that you have beaten the world's record for sustained flight in a balloon. Please accept my sincerest congratulations on your success. You are the only ones I would be glad to see win outside myself. I know from my own experiences what you must have risked to make such a trip.

Charles Heitman had telephoned the news to Belmont Park, and the message was taken by the committee's treasurer, Charles Edwards, who "immediately dropped the telephone receiver" and rushed into the office of J. C. McCoy, chairman of the Belmont Park committee. McCoy was deep in discussion with Cortlandt Bishop and Allan Ryan about what to do if the blessed wind didn't die down, but Edwards didn't care. He threw his hat to the ceiling and shouted, "Hurrah, Hawley and Post are safe and are returning." After a round of hearty rejoicing, Bishop addressed the assembled reporters outside the clubhouse and explained that Hawley and Post's disappearance had "cast a gloom over the international meet, which will now be removed." A few minutes later Peter Prunty broke the news to the crowd, and for the next hour everyone forgot about the wind as Hawley and Post "became the sole topic of conversation" in Belmont Park.

The cartography skills of the American press left a lot to be desired when Thursday's newspapers were published. Or perhaps something had been lost in communication with all the telegrams buzzing between Canada and the United States. But no two publications could seem to agree on exactly how far the *America II* had traveled. The *New York Herald* credited Hawley and Post with 1,460 miles, but the *New York Times* was sure it was 1,450 miles. The *Daily Picayune* of New Orleans considered it more like 1,350 miles, while the *New York Sun*'s distance of 1,300 miles was the most conservative. Newspapers in Britain, such as the *Pall Mall Gazette* and the *Daily Mirror*, alighted on 1,355 miles, the number supplied to them by the *Post-Dispatch*.

Yet despite all the discrepancies in distance, Thursday's newspapers were as one in making the "back from the dead" heroics of Post and Hawley their headline story. Everything else was reduced to a few paltry paragraphs at the foot of the front page—the eruption of Mount Vesuvius and the subsequent death of two hundred Italians in the Bay of Naples; the confirmation that Dr. Hawley Crippen intended to appeal his death sentence passed by a London court earlier in the week; the escalating violence in Jersey City between police and several hundred striking express workers.

One notable feature of all the hyperbolic newspaper coverage was the ignorance displayed of the region from which Hawley and Post had emerged. The *New York Herald* described it as a "jungle"; the *New Orleans Daily Picayune* said the two balloonists were on their "way back to civilization"; and the *New York Times* commented how fortunate it was that the two trappers (few papers bothered to mention Joseph Pedneaud and

Joseph Simard by name) had been "friendly." To city-dwelling Americans in the early twentieth century, any area without stores, bars, and picture houses was wild and uncivilized, inhabited by grunting Stone Age creatures. For them the way of life of Simard and Pedneaud was as inconceivable as the Sioux's had been to Lewis and Clark a century earlier.

Of course, what most aroused the newspapers was that the *America II* had broken all existing balloon distance records, further proof of man's advancement. Maps showing the balloon's route proliferated on the pages, and from coast to coast people read the interview with Augustus Post that had been telegraphed late on Wednesday night by the lucky reporter from the Associated Press.

The *World* newspaper described how its representative had spent Wednesday evening at the headquarters of the Aero Club of America with "an excited group" that included Colonel Theodore Schaeck and Paul Armbruster of the *Helvetia*. When Clifford Harmon arrived from Belmont Park, he had been only too happy to tell the paper how glad he was that his pessimism had proved groundless. "I am frank in saying that I never expected to see either Post or Hawley again," he said. "It took men of the greatest courage to do what they have done, and ordinary courage is not enough. I know the character of that country well and I would not venture into it . . . I am mighty glad they are safe and they deserve all of the glory."

The joy of sleeping in a warm bed was short-lived for Augustus Post. At six o'clock on Thursday morning, six hours after he had bidden the reporter good-night at the Château Saguenay hotel, Post was woken by Joseph Guay, the hotel manager, who reminded him that the train for Quebec City left in an hour. Post had to summon all his willpower to slip out of his bed and into the clothes loaned him by Guay. He shaved and tidied up his goatee, then descended into the dining room, where he and Hawley breakfasted on trout and another moose steak. There was plenty of hot coffee, too, the surest sign that they were back in the benign embrace of civilization.

They boarded the train at seven o'clock with their dirty clothes folded into their ballast bags and with a small brown leather valise given them as a farewell gift by Guay. The train stopped for lunch at Kiskisink, and

Hawley and Post were wined and dined by the division superintendent at the station restaurant. It escaped neither of the balloonists' attention that Kiskisink was close to where Samuel Perkins had come down, "believing that he had won the race."

Post and Hawley slept off their lunch on Thursday afternoon as the train puffed south toward Quebec. Fifty miles outside the city they pulled into a station, where waiting on the platform was Lewis Spindler, who had dashed east from Ontario the moment he heard the news. He found the pair "well but somewhat fatigued but [they] have one predominant joy—we hold the cup." Spindler accompanied Post and Hawley on the final leg of their journey, explaining on the way that they would have four hours in Quebec City before catching a sleeper to Montreal at eleven P.M. In the intervening hours an informal dinner had been organized at a nearby hotel by the American counsel, Mr. Gebhard Willrich. Spindler also laughingly warned them to expect a monumental reception when their train arrived because Canada had gone "balloon crazy."

Police had thrown a cordon around the platform by the time the train carrying Post and Hawley reached Quebec at six forty P.M. They were greeted by Willrich and "several prominent men of the city," but the hoi polloi were held back, and reporters could only stretch up on tiptoe over the policemen's heads in a vain attempt to have their questions answered. The two men were escorted to the Château Frontenac hotel and "made comfortable in a room, the luxurious arrangement of which must have furnished a striking contrast to the wilderness of the Canadian bush." At dinner they were presented with a tottering pile of telegrams, among which were messages from Count Zeppelin, Cortlandt Bishop, the Campfire Club of America, and Walter Wellman. August Belmont, owner of the eponymous racecourse, extended his heartiest congratulations and hoped the pair "may join in the last days of our meeting and receive the homage of your expectant associates of the air and of a proud and admiring community."

After supper Post and Hawley sat before the newsmen and gave them the story of their adventure. The dozen or so reporters may have been scooped by their colleague from the Associated Press, but that made them no less attentive as Hawley spoke: "There was never a time when I considered that our lives were actually in danger, but our food supply was very short, and I consider that we were very fortunate in reaching

Jacques Maltais's cabin [*sic*] in the woods when we did." Nonetheless, butted in a reporter, it must have been a harrowing ordeal. Hawley shook his head. "Taken altogether it was not a disagreeable experience."

Post took the newsmen back to the beginning, that long-ago afternoon when they had departed. With his logbook on his lap for reference, Post described their forty-six hours in the air and summed up their descent in a single sentence: "We made a good landing in the trees and had no difficulty in getting to the ground." Post then elaborated on their plight through the wilderness—"the baffling thicket of brambles . . . branches standing out at every angle and interlacing." Hawley interjected only when his companion told of his fall. "I can stand a good deal of pain," said Hawley, looking around at the faces of the reporters, "but I never had anything take hold of me like that."

What about the *America II*? one of the correspondents asked when they had finished their tale. Post said that the owner of the hotel in Chicoutimi had promised to try to retrieve the balloon, but if he didn't, they wanted it known that they would pay $300 to any person or persons who brought it back. However, added Hawley, if it was lost, then "it's lost in a good cause. We have without doubt beaten the world's record by more than two hundred miles."

The euphoria that had greeted the news of Hawley and Post's reappearance on Wednesday afternoon had vanished, blasted miles across the Hempstead Plains by the keen southwest wind that violated through every nook and cranny of Belmont Park on Thursday morning. What do you reckon it is? the reporters sheltering in the press stand asked one another: 30 mph? 35 mph? maybe even 40? No one wished to hazard a guess, but with the flags atop the hangars "bent before it like reeds," the wind was considerably more than a zephyr and likely to scupper both the Statue of Liberty race and the elimination trial for the U.S. team.

The meet's nine A.M. start was too early for the special aviation trains laid on by the Pennsylvania Railroad, which didn't start running for another two hours, so instead the die-hard fans bought tickets for Jamaica Station, the main hub of the Long Island Rail Road, and completed their journey in trolley cars and hacks. Elsewhere the "roads swarmed with automobiles, a long motor caravan threading across the bridges."

The signal bomb was exploded, but the doors of the hangars remained resolutely closed. Men and women sat in their seats, grappling with the pages of their newspapers as they tried to read of Hawley and Post's miraculous resurrection. The band played, but no one listened; it was too cold, too windy, too depressing. The aviators refused to budge from their hangars, except one or two who, "heartbroken at the gale, took trains into town."

At least it was a bumper day for the society correspondents, all of whom were kept busy by a steady stream of illustrious arrivals. Baron von Hengelmuller, the Austrian ambassador, was a guest in the box of Mr. and Mrs. August Belmont, and the novelist Rex Beach "attracted much attention in a sort of Richard Harding war correspondent's suit." The sister of Count de Lesseps, the Countess de la Bergassiere, was wrapped up warm against the elements in a full-length sealskin coat and large beaver hat, while nearby the wife of Cortlandt Bishop amused herself with some crochet work. Vincent Astor returned for another day's aviation, minus his father, and Mr. and Mrs. Morris Kellogg made their first appearance of the week, having just returned from their wedding trip. Mrs. William K. Vanderbilt swanned into her box in a tailored suit of London smoke frieze and large velvet hat of the same color, but Eleonora Sears was conspicuous by her absence. Perhaps she had been grounded, so to speak, speculated the correspondents, by her concerned parents. But she soon arrived, and what a sensation when she did. It wasn't what she wore that sent a hurricane of gossip ripping through the Turf and Field Club—although the skirt of the blue serge suit was considered a fraction short by some—it was that, as the *New York Evening Mail* reported, "she reached Belmont Park with Claude Grahame-White in the latter's limousine."

Reporters and spectators alike watched in astonishment as the brazen pair collected Grahame-White's fan mail and "sat on the clubhouse steps reading it." Several of the more senior members of the New York Four Hundred shook their heads and muttered that in all their years they had never seen such behavior. It looked for all the world as if the couple didn't have a care in the world, until the moment Sears glanced up and saw a "few photographers pointing cameras at her." Jumping to her feet, she shooed them away, crying, "You newspapermen are a nuisance!" Moments later she and Grahame-White beat a retreat to the haven of his hangar, although not before the Englishman had jabbed a finger in the general direction of the reporters and accused them of being "prevaricators."

Grahame-White might well have leveled the accusation at the Belmont Park committee when he read their morning bulletin regarding the Statue of Liberty race. Without warning the organizers had "revoked its rule that all aviators taking part in the race . . . for the prize of $10,000, offered by Mr. Thomas Fortune Ryan, must qualify by an hour's flight at this meeting." Grahame-White could not believe it. He looked down at bulletin No. 11 and read clause one again, just to make sure he hadn't been mistaken. But, no, he hadn't, it was there in black and white. Grahame-White stormed into the clubhouse and, waving the piece of paper in the face of the unfortunate receptionist, demanded to see J. C. McCoy, the committee chairman, and Allan Ryan, the general manager. Outside the clubhouse entrance, the reporters pressed their ears to the door to see if they could hear what was being shouted. A few minutes later Grahame-White emerged and launched into a tirade against the committee: "I took out my Farman biplane on Sunday in very bad weather in order to qualify for the Liberty flight and smashed my machine," he said, his brown eyes full of anger. "This put my airplane out of business for two days and prevented my going after several prizes. Now at the last moment the committee is going to allow anybody to fly for Mr. Ryan's ten-thousand-dollar prize whether they have shown that they can keep up in the air for an hour or not."

A principle was at stake, asserted Grahame-White, an inviolable law of aviation, which said that rules were not to be changed willy-nilly at the whim of the management. Yes, he said, it was unprecedented as far as he was aware. He had never heard of a meet altering the rules of entry halfway through. Grahame-White was at a loss to think why the committee had acted in so arbitrary a fashion. Apart from himself, Armstrong Drexel, Phil Parmalee, and Ralph Johnstone were the only fliers who had legitimately qualified; but then, as a reporter pointed out, Parmalee and Johnstone were Wright fliers, and the brothers had made it clear they would not permit any of their men to enter the race because in their view it would result in "certain death." So there was your answer, they explained to the Englishman, it wouldn't be much of a contest, just you and Drexel.

Still incandescent with rage, Grahame-White left behind one of set of "prevaricators" to confront another and disappeared back inside the clubhouse to make an official protest. It was only, reported the *New York Herald*, "after considerable dipping and diving and veering around in its course [that] the committee succeeded in getting Mr. Grahame-White to return to his hangar, and when assured that he was safely on the other side of the field determined that the new rule would be adhered to, and unanimously overruled the protest."

Grahame-White took Eleonora Sears for lunch at the Turf and Field Club, but it wasn't the most congenial meal of her life. The aviator sat brooding over the morning's events, heartened only by the knowledge that "he had the moral support in his protest of most of the other aviators, among them Mr. Wilbur Wright."

Most of the aviators, but not all, and definitely not John Moisant. The American had tried and failed to qualify for the Statue of Liberty race on Saturday, going up twice in the Hourly Distance event. The best he had managed was fifty-one minutes and eleven seconds, commendable but not good enough. Yet on Wednesday evening Moisant had told a reporter from the *New York Sun* that he was "planning to set his course to the Statue of Liberty straight over Brooklyn," adding with his usual dash of bravado that he didn't "see that there's any more danger in alighting on a city than there is on water. There's always a chimney for a man to hang on to."

From the moment John Moisant had heard about the $10,000 on offer for the victor of the Statue of Liberty race, it had been his intention to win, and he was never going to allow the race small print to stand in his way. A quiet word in the committee's ear, a reminder that he was one hell of a crowd-puller, that was all it had taken; and once again Moisant had set the revolutionary wheels in motion.

As Grahame-White sulked over lunch, the wind abated and rumors began to swirl around the Turf and Field Club that it was blowing no more than fifteen miles an hour. At one thirty P.M. the bomb was detonated to signal the start of the afternoon's program, and the spectators' tenacity was rewarded with the sight of Hubert Latham puffing on a cigarette as his mechanics wheeled out his Antoinette. He took off and began to edge tentatively round the course. Meanwhile, in the Wrights' hangars, Arch Hoxsey finished a lunch of powdered sugar and tomato puree, then buttoned up his leather jacket, and Ralph Johnstone sat silently in the corner preparing himself for another ascent. This time the pair headed over the trees to the northeast and were soon out of range of even the most powerful field glasses.

No other aviator ventured from his hangar, so the crowd of twelve thousand lavished their attention on Latham's lapping of the course in the Hourly Distance event, which once had been the preserve of Grahame-White. The spectacle was riveting, wrote the correspondent from the *San Francisco Chronicle*, as the Frenchman "journeyed his way around the curves by sheer resourcefulness and nerve. The gale was so obstinate that he had to point head into it and steer due north in order to edge sideways, like a ferryboat in a tide, and make distance to the west." At one moment, as he rounded dead man's turn, Latham didn't even attempt to maneuver but instead let the wind blow him sideways across the home straight and over the top of the grandstand. Soon the wind had increased again to close on thirty miles per hour, and Latham judged it too risky to remain aloft. He descended slowly and cautiously—what was known as terracing—motoring horizontally for a hundred feet, then dropping vertically a hundred feet, then advancing again, and so on, until finally he landed without misfortune. A little later, with no sign of Johnstone and Hoxsey, and no other aviator willing to confront the wind, Latham "had an offer of $750 by the management to fly around for the benefit of the crowd," but he declined; his life was worth more than that.

An hour or so later the telephone rang in the office of the clubhouse; it was Arch Hoxsey explaining that he wouldn't be back until the morning. He had been blown a little off course. How little? asked Charles Edwards. Well, he'd landed in a field in Brentwood, twenty-five miles east of Belmont Park. No, no, he was fine, he declared, "he hadn't even soiled his collar," and a couple of bemused farmers had fetched some rope and secured his biplane to a tree. What about Johnstone, asked Hoxsey, any news? None yet, replied Edwards with a tinge of anxiety in his voice. Half an hour later, the telephone rang again. It was Johnstone. He was in a place called—What was it? he was heard to ask someone in the background—in a place called Middle Island, approximately fifty-five miles east of Belmont Park. He'd already booked in for the night at the Green View Hotel, and the proprietor, Mr. Helbeck, was busy preparing a plate of ham and eggs, and a can of gasoline was also on its way. Johnstone asked Edwards to make sure a message was passed to his wife, then he hung up and tucked into his food.

In the late afternoon a howling wester descended and "flitted the air with whirling autumn leaves, slammed down the benches in the grandstand, ripped out the canvas screens that bar the view of those who have not paid . . . and sent such a skirmish line of dust dancing around the track that the lamps had to be lighted outside the hangars for the mechanics to find their way about." John Baldwin, a journalist for the *Scientific American* journal, broke a leg when the wind blew a hangar door into his path as he inspected the machines.

With no chance of any further flying, the spectators began to depart, although a few of the more well-heeled headed to the Turf and Field for a stiff drink. Claude Grahame-White was already there, not with Eleonora Sears, whose slot had expired, but with Pauline Chase, "to whom he is supposed to be engaged," hissed the *New York Sun*.

Ralph Johnstone had unwittingly made the right decision in checking into the Green View Hotel. As he was waited on hand and foot, his fellow American aviators spent Thursday evening at the offices of the Aero Club of America in Manhattan's Engineering Society's Building in what the *New York Times* described as "a long session, productive of several heated arguments."

The problem facing all those present was to agree on which three men should be selected for Saturday's race, the blue-ribbon event of international aviation. The weather had twice forced the cancellation of the elimination trial, and with more wind forecast for Friday the Aero Club was obliged to find another way of selecting its trio of aviators. The rules stated that each nation's team had to be publicly announced twenty-four hours before the race began, so the Aero Club had only a few more hours in which to reach a decision.*

With Cortlandt Bishop in the chair, the committee of the Aero Club invited one by one Glenn Curtiss, Wilbur Wright, Armstrong Drexel, John Moisant, and Charles Hamilton to present his case in the club's assembly room. Why, the Aero Club asked, should we select you? "For nearly three hours," wrote the correspondent from the *New York Times*, "these representatives advanced their claims before the board and submitted to a series of questions. It was at this point that the conversation became heated." Just how heated, the paper didn't elaborate, but the face of Glenn Curtiss as he stormed out of the building a little after midnight suggested tempers had been at boiling point. Then Cortlandt Bishop appeared on the steps of the Engineering Society's Building to formally announce the American team for the race: Walter Brookins, Armstrong Drexel, and Charles Hamilton. First reserve, said Bishop, would be James Mars, second reserve John Moisant, and third reserve Arch Hoxsey. The reporters clamored to know by what means the committee had reached their decision, but "no explanation was offered by the Board of Governors why the men named were selected," and the papers were left to draw their own conclusions. "The failure to select a representative from the Curtiss fliers provoked considerable comment," according to the *New York Times* correspondent, who wrote the Aero Club's choice was "certain to breed considerable dissatisfaction especially among those who failed to get a place on the team."

---

* Britain's team of Grahame-White, Alec Ogilvie, and James Radley had been selected by the Royal Aero Club at the start of October. The selection of the French team had become another bone of contention for the Aero Club of France with the Americans. Originally the team comprised Léon Morane, Le Blanc, and Latham, but on the eve of their voyage to America, Morane was injured in a crash. The French assumed it would be no problem to select a third aviator once in New York, but the Aero Club of America refused to allow this on the grounds that Aubrun, Garros, and Simon had been paid to attend the meet, whereas Latham and Le Blanc had not because they had come to contest the Aviation Cup. The French, needless to say, were angered by this ruling but had to enter the race with just two fliers.

CHAPTER FOURTEEN

I'll Be Able to Give the Wrights a Good Race

Friday, October 28, 1910

ALAN HAWLEY AND Augustus Post had with great relief boarded the Canadian Pacific sleeper at Quebec City on Thursday evening. The dinner at the Château Frontenac hotel had been pleasant enough, but not so the persistence of the vaudeville impresario who had "asked how four figures would look" in return for a three-week tour of North America. "Nothing doing," Hawley had replied through gritted teeth. As the train had pulled away from Quebec City at eleven P.M. bound for Montreal, the pair nodded approvingly at the grandiloquence of their sleeping car. They had been given the stateroom, the "Fujiyama" carriage, with what they were sure were the softest beds in which they had ever slept. And as for the pillows . . . sheer bliss.

The sleeper arrived at Montreal at seven thirty on Friday morning, and the reception committee was primed to pounce. Two dozen officers and members of the Aero Club of America charged down the platform to see who could be first to shake the men's hands. In the opinion of the correspondent from the *Boston Daily Globe*—one of many at the station— Hawley and Post "reluctantly left their beds in the stateroom" to accept the greetings bestowed upon them. Hawley had a noticeable limp, and for some reason the pair had changed back into their original balloon clothes. Their spirits were revived by a substantial breakfast in the Place Viger, a château-style hotel built twelve years earlier above the station. One of the Aero Club members persuaded Hawley to part with his pants for a few minutes so they could be "patched and pressed" by a member of the laundry staff. After breakfast Post and Hawley, proudly wearing his nearly good-as-new pants, posed for photographs and answered a few questions from the Canadian press. They were bored with retelling the same old story so they became anecdotal, coloring in the outline of their story with asides that had the Montreal newsmen beaming. What items of equipment did you take with you for your wilderness trek? someone asked. Let's see, said Post: blankets, soup, a pistol, biscuits, bottle of peroxide. "Peroxide!" exclaimed the reporter. "For what?" Post looked at Hawley and began to laugh. "Well, it's a secret, but . . . Hawley is very keen on natural history and is always on the lookout for freaks for the Bronx zoo. He thought that if we could catch a muskrat, dark in color, what we had in the bottle might help it to be a freak of nature from the Canadian wilds." "Nature fakirs!" someone shouted, and the room collapsed in a fit of giggles. Later Hawley told of the time in Canada when they saw from the *America II* a "quiet-looking old gentleman who, after we had crossed his property of forest, let fly two charges of shot at us."

The double act was worthy of the vaudeville stage, and murmurings of disappointment came when Hawley and Post were informed that it was time to leave. Their "sportsmanlike demeanor [had] captivated" the Canadian press, and praise for their modesty was also universal. Before they left the hotel to catch the one fifty-five P.M. Delaware and Hudson railroad train to New York, the two Americans sent a telegram to Sir Wilfrid Laurier, Canada's prime minister: PLEASE ACCEPT THE ASSURANCES OF OUR PROFOUND GRATITUDE FOR THE GENEROUS EFFORTS OF YOURSELF AND YOUR GOVERNMENT FOR OUR ASSISTANCE.

As the two said their good-byes at the station, the correspondent from the *Montreal Star* asked Hawley if he planned to continue ballooning after his experiences. Probably, he replied, "but I shall also have a look around in the aeroplaning game." So was that where he saw the future of aeronautics? "Much has been done with airplanes, but the game is still young," said Hawley, who added that he was "anxious to see the flights at Belmont Park tomorrow."

Home, so nearly home, thought Hawley and Post as they settled back into their carriage, but not quite. First they had to endure an eight-hour journey during which they were objects of curiosity to all the other passengers. If that wasn't bad enough, the correspondent from the *Boston Daily Globe* had booked himself on the train, and nothing was going to prevent him from getting a story, particularly not the door to the balloonists' private compartment. But for the first hour of the voyage south not even the reporter could get a word in edgeways as "people learned who was present on the train and kept coming along to introduce themselves and congratulate the airmen." Even the normally impassive U.S. customs officer who boarded the train at St. John came over all misty-eyed when he spotted the pair. He pumped their hands and told them that "he shared the pride of all Americans in their great achievement." Oh, by the way, he added, had they made any purchases while they were in Canada? Hawley and Post looked at one another, suppressed a smile, and replied in unison, "A clean shirt each."

The man from the *Globe* saw clearly that Hawley and Post would have "preferred to spend the day in sleep," but that was just too bad, he needed his story. Eventually Post could take it no longer and moved to another compartment, leaving Hawley at the mercy of the reporter. For a while Hawley retold the standard story of their trip, but later he began to open up as the reporter won his confidence with his gently probing line of inquiry. Hawley said that, yes, if his knee had become so bad that he couldn't have continued, he would have been "justified in shooting himself rather than to die of cold or starvation alone in the deep forest." Fortunately, he said with a short laugh of relief, it never came to that. But there must have been a time when you despaired of salvation? the reporter asked. Hawley pursed his lips in contemplation. "There was one incident about our trip that I haven't mentioned in any of the interviews," he said hesitantly. The reporter's ears pricked up. Yes? "It was something which touched me very deeply and made a lasting impression on my mind." Yes? The reporter's pulse quickened. It was the prayer, given to Hawley by a friend before he left New York. The reporter asked to see it, but Hawley refused. The *Globe*'s correspondent persisted until he "finally won his consent."

Hawley took the envelope from the pocket of his torn overcoat and read the prayer aloud, just as he had done five days earlier on the shore of the lake when his morale had been at its lowest ebb. The reporter scribbled the words of the prayer in his notebook, then added a note at the bottom: "Mr. Hawley is not a man of emotional nature, but he was plainly impressed, if not affected, as he folded the precious bit of card back into its envelope and returned it to his pocket."

At Albany, Hawley and Post transferred to the Empire State Express for the final leg of their voyage to New York. Waiting to welcome them on board were Edward Stratton of the Aero Club of America, William Hawley, and a reporter from New York's *World*, whose eyes narrowed like a jealous suitor's when he saw the contented face of the *Boston Daily Globe*'s correspondent. No words were spoken when the brothers were reunited; there was "just a strong gripping of hands and a look that meant a great deal."

The *World* had been trumped by its rival, and neither Hawley nor Post were in the mood to recite their story for the umpteenth time. All that Hawley would give the *World*'s reporter by way of a quote was his belief that if his experience had taught him anything, it was of the urgent need for the U.S. government "to equip its [coastal] life saving stations with airplanes." For the price of one battleship, he continued, the "government could build one hundred airplanes and they would save hundreds of lives."

The *World*'s reporter in exchange gave the two men a copy of his newspaper, which featured a substantive front-page spread about their adventure and also an editorial praising "their contribution to the romance of adventure." William Hawley and Stratton produced a bundle of other clippings, including the glowing editorial in Friday's edition of the *New York Herald*. Having congratulated them on their "record breaking aerial voyage," the paper wagged a figurative finger at its readers and reminded them, "It must not be supposed that the balloon races are mere useless 'drifting matches' . . . It has trained and is training a great number of men—and women, too, for that matter—to feel at home in the upper air, and thus preparing them to use the dirigible flying machines of the present types and of the more highly perfected ones of the future. The plucky exploit of Messers. Hawley and Post adds to the luster of their country's flag and will make their names famous in aeronautic annals."

"Mere useless drifting matches"! Hawley and Post were aghast at the very suggestion. To what, or to whom, was the *New York Herald* referring when it challenged the accusation? they wanted to know. The offending article wasn't to hand; it had tactfully been omitted from the bundle of newspaper clippings, but the city's balloon fraternity was still seething over the editorial in Thursday's *New York Globe*. The *Globe* for its part was indignant that the International Balloon Cup race had the nerve to call itself such. Fiddlesticks! It wasn't a race, it was just an "aerial drifting competition . . . a manifest anachronism in these days of dirigibles and airplanes. A dozen oarless row boats 'liberated' in mid-Atlantic, each manned by a helpless crew whose only occupation was sitting still or bailing, would furnish an equally up-to-date sporting event."

The Empire State Express arrived at Grand Central Station at ten minutes past ten on Friday evening, and a delegation from the Aero Club, who had come straight from Belmont Park, were there to greet them. The more self-important the person, the louder the greeting, and Post had to push aside one or two braying oafs so he could embrace his sister. Someone called for "Three cheers," and the cry was taken up by the commuters headed home and a throng of students decked in Dartmouth colors who were in town for a Saturday football match. There was a battery of flashlights and a barrage of questions from reporters. The *New York Times* said Post "seemed nervous when he was welcomed by his friends, but it was not quite certain whether it was due to his experiences in the *America II* or the wild way in which he was rushed through the gates from the platform and snapshotted [*sic*] by the small army of photographers."

By the time the two men had arrived at the Hotel St. Regis for a celebratory dinner, Post had recovered his poise. It had all been a bit too much, he told the *New York Times*, and he apologized for his scowling demeanor at Grand Central. "You cannot imagine how it feels," he said with a smile, "to emerge suddenly from the solitude and rocks and pine trees of the Canadian wilds to meet crowds of people in this cheerful way."

After the meal came the telegrams and the toasts. Of the former, none received a bigger cheer than the one from Sir Wilfrid Laurier, prime minister of Canada. It had arrived at the Aero Club of America offices during the afternoon, sent in response to the telegram wired him by Post and Hawley in Montreal: YOU OWE ME NO THANKS FOR THE ASSISTANCE WE ENDEAVORED TO RENDER YOU. PLEASE ACCEPT MY HEARTIEST CONGRATULATIONS ON YOUR SAFE RETURN FROM A REMARKABLE TRIP.

Cortlandt Bishop laid the telegram on the table and picked up his glass. Gentlemen, he said, please be upstanding for "our heroes." The room rose as one and saluted the embarrassed pair. Neither Post nor Hawley displayed any desire to respond, observed the man from the *Boston Daily Globe*, who had stuck limpetlike to the pair since their arrival in New York, so Bishop gave a knowing nod and said, "Keep your seats. You are men of action, not words."*

A little over twelve hours earlier Cortlandt Bishop had been in a far less good humor. He'd arrived at Belmont Park at seven o'clock on Friday morning to find the course enveloped in a heavy mist and a light drizzle watering the grass. The wind was at least behaving itself, thought Bishop as he walked toward hangar row, and so it seemed was the equally capricious Alfred Le Blanc.

Marguerite Martyn, the reporter for the *St. Louis Post-Dispatch* who had spent a day touring the hangars during St. Louis's recent meet, had found Le Blanc the most intriguing aeronaut of all, a man who "would make a chapter in himself." Most of the time in St. Louis, said Martyn, Le Blanc had been aloof both figuratively and literally. Yet "when he does come to our level he is most agreeable and charming."

---

* In late November the War Department released the official distances for the race. *America II*'s mileage was reduced to 1,171, thus depriving Hawley and Post of a world record. *Düsseldorf II*'s distance had also been pared, from 1,240 to 1,131 miles, with *Germania* third with 1,079 miles.

This morning Le Blanc was at peace with the world as he waited for his mechanics to finish tuning up his Blériot monoplane. He inspected his machine, giving the rudder and rear planes one or two turns, and examining the hundred-horsepower engine with due diligence. He had on a tight-fitting helmet that covered his forehead, leaving visible two dark eyebrows that began on the bridge of his nose and climbed steeply away from his eyes, like Ralph Johnstone and Arch Hoxsey leaving Belmont Park. His mustache was long and curved, and his lower lip was unmistakably Gallic in its ability to express disdain with the slightest movement.

Up in the press stand the only reporter who had arrived early enough to witness Le Blanc's inaugural flight at Belmont Park was the correspondent from the *New York Evening Sun*. As his peers rode the railroad or drove out from New York City for the nine o'clock start, the newsman watched intently as Le Blanc ordered his men to crank up his machine. As the motor sounded, the Frenchman climbed into his seat and a few seconds later "raised his hand for the helpers behind to let go of the tugging flyer and [he] shot off like an arrow from a bow." The reporter's heart thumped as the Blériot's hundred-horsepower engine warmed to its task; he couldn't believe no one else was here to see this, the first flight of "the most formidable foreign antagonist" in the competition, as one of his colleagues had earlier described Le Blanc. He was now sweeping down the back straight of the smaller course, past the hangars—where Grahame-White stood watching his foe—and approaching dead man's turn. How would he cope with the notorious corner first time round? wondered the journalist. With ease. "His monoplane banked gracefully at the turn," wrote the *Evening Sun*'s reporter, "[and] coming into the straight the Frenchman evidently gave his motor a little more gas for the monoplane seemed to suddenly leap forward and shot past the grandstand at terrific speed." Le Blanc flew six laps, then landed close to his hangar, satisfied that he and his machine had the measure of the course. When the reporter reached him a few minutes later, Le Blanc's face was streaked with oil but the Frenchman was in an ebullient mood. "Oh, I think I'll be able to give the Wrights a good race," he told a reporter.

Now it was Grahame-White's turn to try out his new Blériot monoplane, the one that had finally arrived from France the day before. He had ordered it built to the exact specifications as Le Blanc's racer: the same steering column, the same dimensions, the same wheels, the same fourteen-cylinder, hundred-horsepower Gnome engine. But as Grahame-White's mechanics trundled out the Blériot, he noticed a difference between the two: Le Blanc's machine had a propeller manufactured by Regy Frères, while his was a Chauviere. The former was considered to be the best in the business, of a finer pitch than the Chauviere propeller. Curious, thought Grahame-White.

Once he was airborne, the English aviator handled his new machine with far less precision than Le Blanc. By now one or two of the other correspondents had appeared in the press stand, and so slow was Grahame-White in circling the two-and-a-half-kilometer course that the *New York Herald* presumed he was flying a fifty-horsepower machine. The *Evening Sun* reporter timed Grahame-White for a lap and recorded one minute and forty seconds. He flicked back through his notes to find Orville Wright's best lap time in the Baby Grand from a couple of days ago—one minute and twenty-three seconds.

After three laps Grahame-White had had enough and descended, making "rather a bad landing" on one wheel and nearly turning turtle. As he slid down from the seat, the Englishman seemed preoccupied. He said a few words to his manager, Sydney McDonald, and the two of them disappeared inside Grahame-White's hangar.

Two issues weighed heavily on the broad shoulders of Grahame-White on Friday morning. The first required a firm and forceful approach, a *letting out* of the engine, to use an aviator's vernacular. He and McDonald sat down at the table in his hanger and began to compose a letter, his response to the committee's decision to overrule his protest regarding the Statue of Liberty race. Grahame-White considered that even though he knew the committee well, the letter should contain no chummy informality. Addressing it to the Aero Club, he began:

> I must again on principle respectfully request you to reconsider your decision as I feel that it will be useless for me to take part in any further competition at the Belmont Park Meeting if the basic rules governing the competition are to be altered at the pleasure of

your committee, in this case, ostensibly, so as to be able to draw a large entry for a competition for which only a few of the hardworking aviators, with great risk to themselves and their machines, have qualified.

In a subsequent paragraph Grahame-White accused J. C. McCoy, the committee chairman, of sophistry. Yes, the pair had discussed the Statue of Liberty race on Wednesday evening, and, yes, Grahame-White had replied to a casual inquiry from McCoy that he had yet to decide whether he would enter the race.

> . . . But whatever influence [*sic*] your chairman drew from this reply it can in no way be construed into a legitimate excuse for so drastic an alteration of the rules. I cannot find that I am under any obligation to communicate my intentions with reference to contests to your committee until a few minutes before the starting of such contests.

Grahame-White read the letter through, nodded with satisfaction, and signed it. He asked McDonald to release its contents to the press. Then he turned to his second problem, one that required a gentler touch, as if he were negotiating dead man's turn in a stiff breeze. What to do about Pauline Chase?

It was a most unfortunate situation, he and McDonald agreed, and one that was not of Grahame-White's making, even though he was being cast as the villain. A week earlier Pauline Chase's widowed mother, Mrs. Ellis Bliss, had died, and he'd been present in her final hours. Shortly before she'd slipped away, old Mrs. Bliss had asked a favor of Grahame-White: look after Polly. Of course, he had replied, he would support her during the difficult days and weeks ahead. But marriage? He hadn't understood that to be part of his promise. Perhaps he had misconstrued the old girl's dying words, or perhaps it was Pauline, grief-stricken, who assumed they were engaged and informed the world after another poorly attended performance of *Our Miss Gibbs*.

Once the communiqué was finished, McDonald walked over to the press stand, where the correspondents were waiting for a flier to ginger up their morning. Gentlemen, he said, I would like to read a statement on behalf of my client. Mr Grahame-White and Miss Pauline Chase are not engaged, he began. "The engagement was not announced by either Miss Chase or Mr. Grahame-White, but was given to the public by the manager of the theater where she was playing at that time in New York. As the announcement has been spread broadcast [sic], Mr. Grahame-White, taking the stand any gentleman would in an affair of this kind, thought that silence in the matter was the best policy. He has at no time ever said he and Miss Chase were engaged." But, continued McDonald, looking up fiercely at the faces before him, "when Mr. Grahame-White was criticized for being seen so much in the company of Miss Eleonora Sears of Boston, the matter had gone far enough . . . There is no reason why he should not pay attention to her as he owes no allegiance to Miss Chase."

The proclamation was finished, but McDonald wasn't getting away that easily. If not Miss Chase, shouted the reporters, then what about Miss Sears? Rumor had it that young Harry Vanderbilt had cut short his European tour in light of what he had heard about Miss Sears and the Englishman, and was "hurrying to the scene of action at the Belmont Park aviation field." McDonald knew nothing about the movements of Mr. Vanderbilt. But might not he return to find the woman he had "tacitly" asked to marry him engaged to another? "I am in no position to say anything about it," replied McDonald. "It is not likely Mr. Grahame-White would take me into his confidence anyway, but I can say I do not believe there is any engagement at present." Rubbish, someone cried, the rumor is they're already engaged. "If that's the case," retorted McDonald, "it's only one of the many injustices that has been done Mr. Grahame-White by bally fabrications."

With the nature of his relationship with Miss Chase straightened out, Grahame-White went to lunch at the Turf and Field Club in a more relaxed frame of mind. Accompanied by McDonald and Miss Sears, he stopped outside the restaurant entrance and, in reply to a question from a waiting reporter, said he'd released the statement because he could "not allow it to be said that he had no right to pay attention to whom he pleased." What about the letter to the committee? Was it true he wouldn't fly again at the meet? Grahame-White laughed. Not at all. In fact, "he would probably make the trip to the Statue of Liberty in the afternoon in his 100-horsepower Blériot, just to show the other fellows that he really meant business."

Not a table was to be had in the sheltered sumptuousness of the Turf and Field Club at one o'clock. As Grahame-White and Sears flirted over the starters, the Duke of Richelieu, son of the prince of Monaco, was being entertained at another table by Cortlandt Bishop. Baron von Hengel-muller, the Austrian ambassador, was dining with Mr. and Mrs. August Belmont; and the dean of Columbia University, Frederick A. Goetza, lunched with a colleague, Professor Arthur Walker. Elsewhere, the table of Mr. George Huhn Jr., head of the Broadway banking firm Huhn, Edey & Co., was in an uproar after one of their guests, a woman from Philadelphia, had discovered several items of precious jewelry missing from her handbag. As the Pinkerton guards took down a description of the stolen gems, they sighed and shook their heads: Belmont Park's notorious handbag crook had struck again.

A similarly agitated atmosphere prevailed outside the Turf and Field Club as the hour of the afternoon program approached. The wind had begun to flex its muscles, slapping the flags on top of the hangars and throwing particles of dirt from the track into the faces of the mechanics who were working on the airplanes on the grass. When the signal bomb exploded at one thirty P.M., the *New York Times* correspondent estimated that over twenty thousand spectators were on the grounds, "but the prospect of seeing any immediate flying seemed remote because of the proximity of the big [International Aviation] race." Instead those fliers selected to represent their countries spent the afternoon giving their airplanes a thorough overhaul, all except Hubert Latham, who took off in his Antoinette into a wind that was now as belligerent as it had been on Thursday. Going down the back straight on his fifth lap, "he encountered an unusually strong head wind . . . and was carried over the hangars and turned completely around."

Latham landed but was soon up again, this time taking his hundred-horsepower machine around the five-kilometer course so he could famil-

iarize himself with its features. The *New York Herald* was impressed with
the way Latham handled the corners in such a high wind and regarded
him as "one of the strongest contenders" in the big race.

Where was Ralph Johnstone? That's what Belmont Park wanted to
know on Friday afternoon. Arch Hoxsey had returned from Brentwood
at noon, pausing just long enough to shake hands with the Wrights before he was up again, this time rising to 6,705 feet, two thousand feet
higher than Phil Parmalee, who deputized for the absent Johnstone.

By ten to four there was still no sign of Johnstone, and people were beginning to worry. The wind was blowing hard, and even Charles Hamilton and Walter Brookins lasted only a couple of laps before beating a
retreat to their hangars. Suddenly those spectators on the grass on the opposite side of the course to the grandstand jumped to their feet and began
pointing toward the southeast. The reporters twisted in their seats and
looked up under the eaves of the press stand to see what the fuss was about.
The *New York Times* correspondent saw "just a spot against a sky that near
the horizon was pink with the reflection of the setting sun." It was Johnstone, no doubt about it, but it took him nearly twenty minutes to battle the
headwinds toward Belmont Park. He was flying at about three thousand
feet as he approached the course, reckoned the *New York Herald*, and "as
he neared the enclosure he dropped three or four hundred feet at a time,
'terracing' downward, and at last he drove his machine over the field,
hardly fifty feet above the turf." Every man, woman, and child at Belmont
Park stood and cheered Johnstone as he touched down in front of the
grandstand. Unbelievable, people said, laughing, pointing at the flier, he's
even smoking a cigar!

He was greeted by Cortlandt Bishop and Major Reber of the Signal
Corps, and for several minutes Johnstone "stood enjoying the applause
of the spectators as a schoolboy would the applause of admiring friends
and relatives at a school entertainment."

While Johnstone savored his cigar, his barographs from Thursday's
flight were taken to the judges' box. A couple of minutes later an excited
Peter Prunty picked up his megaphone and asked the crowd to show
their appreciation for a new American altitude record—8,471 feet. Reporters ran from the press stand to grab a few words with happy-go-

lucky Johnstone. "Tell you what, boys," he said, hoping they wouldn't notice how the hand that held his cigar trembled, "it was just the mercy of Providence that I saved my neck when I thought I was within touching distance of the new world's record. I kind of forget all about the wind and began to reach out for more height. Then I suddenly said to myself, 'Young man, you better see how much gas you have got.' It's the truth, I had just enough to turn over the two propellers. When I kept her nose up, the juice ran down into the engine and she coughed. The minute I pointed down, I lost my fuel and she began to miss."

Sounds a thrill, a reporter said, laughing. "It was just like shooting the chutes," said Johnstone. "First I'd take a header, with the power off, and when the wind began to carry me out of control, I'd point up a bit, get a little headway, run level for a hundred yards, then dip again." He described how he had come down in a field, not much larger than the span of his wings, probably the best landing he'd ever made. Had he been afraid? they asked, thinking he'd laugh off the question. His face hardened. "Deathly afraid," he replied.

With the crowd still agog at the return of Johnstone, Peter Prunty announced that the wind had put paid to the Statue of Liberty race. It was now blowing at thirty miles per hour, too strong to risk a flight over Manhattan. However, he boomed, he was delighted to reveal that the twenty-mile cross-country passenger-carrying flight had three entrants.

The first to ascend was Count de Lesseps, accompanied in his Blériot by his brother. Together they disappeared toward the captive balloon ten miles east, and a short while later Claude Grahame-White prepared to take off in his Farman biplane, with Sydney McDonald as his passenger. Unfortunately, a week of lavish lunches in the Turf and Field Club had added a few pounds to the waistlines of both men, and no sooner had the Farman got off the ground than, like a father buckling under the weight of his son in a piggyback race, the machine flopped down a few feet past the start line.

John Moisant was the third entrant in the race, and with him was an employee of the Lovelace-Thompson Company; the pair cleared the perimeter fence, but the Blériot gave out a couple of minutes later and came down in a cabbage field three miles west of Belmont Park. At five P.M. Count de

Lesseps telephoned to say he and his brother had been forced down by the wind and were taking tea in a delightful place called Garden City; please send an automobile at the earliest convenience. The crowd had one last quiver of excitement before the day was out. Edmond Audemars went up in a Demoiselle, only for it to come down a few minutes later on its back. "He's walking away," shrieked Peter Prunty as Audemars lurched across the grass like a punch-drunk boxer. "He's not hurt, and the Demoiselle is unhurt as well!"

Another extraordinary escape, the spectators said to one another, as they queued to ride the railroad back into Manhattan. Perhaps John Moisant is right, aviation isn't as lethal as some would have us believe. Others referred to the small paragraph in their newspapers that described the death of Saglietti, an Italian, during an exhibition on Thursday. That made four deaths in four days, what with Madiot, Monte, and Blanchard as well. Only luck had prevented a similar tragedy at Belmont Park.

As the members of the Aero Club of America took the train to Grand Central Station to welcome Alan Hawley and Augustus Post, the aviators competing in Saturday's International Aviation Cup remained at the grounds making their final preparations.

Among the items on their checklists was the latest weather forecast, which, as with every such report, was pinned to the bulletin board outside the clubhouse. The weather bureau predicted for Saturday "moderate to brisk westerly winds."

CHAPTER FIFTEEN

I'm Not Hurt Much but I Want a Long Rest

Saturday, October 29, 1910

CLAUDE GRAHAME-WHITE WOKE early on Saturday morning, not to the sweet smell of clean sheets at the Hotel Astor, but to the pungent odor of engine grease in hangar No. 14. He'd slept the night in his hangar because he wanted to be ready to get into the air the moment the race started at eight thirty A.M. Grahame-White hadn't been the only flier to remain at the grounds, although the incessant "clatter of preparation" from Charlie Hamilton's hangar suggested the American hadn't had much chance to rest his weary head. Now, as a cold dawn broke over Belmont Park, tinkering sounds were also coming from the direction of John Moisant's hangar. One of Grahame-White's mechanics brought him a mug of coffee and a bowl of hot water so he could shave. With that done he put on a pair of black-and-white-checked knickerbockers, pulled a thick sweater over his head, and wrapped a white silk scarf around his neck.

In the press stand a smattering of reporters were already at their desks, their legs encased in woolen blankets. The correspondent from the *New York Globe* sipped his coffee and took in the scene before him. "There were almost 1,000 determined aero fans shivering in front of the grandstand," he wrote, "and vainly seeking to place themselves in the way of some vagrant ray of sun. The wind blew at ten miles an hour from the west, not enough to interfere with flying, but a rate that added to the zest of danger to the competition."

Some of the spectators had on a heavy black coat of the sort sold by Macy's for $18, one of several items featured in the store's "Aeronautic Age" promotion. With the coats came wool-lined, tan gauntlet gloves, just like those favored by the aviators, and several of the men wore under their coats one of the latest styles of starched collar—"monoplane" or "biplane"—but both guaranteed to be "strain-resisting" when it came to scanning the sky. Children waiting impatiently for eight thirty A.M. to roll around played with one of their Macy's toy airplanes, either an aluminum Blériot monoplane or a wooden Yankee Flier.

The wealthy enthusiasts who arrived by car opened their trunks and removed one of Macy's leather aviation-luncheon baskets, while others took snapshots of Belmont Park with a Macy's camera (because, as the store's ad declared, "You want more than a blur as a souvenir of your day at the Aviation Field"). Eleonora Sears had her camera with her, according to the *New York Sun*'s correspondent, who spied her wandering along hangar row "taking snapshots of the aviators."

The stalwart one thousand already on the grounds by eight A.M. were the vanguard of a great exodus from Manhattan. The four guards whose job it was to direct the crowds onto the trains at Pennsylvania Station at Thirty-fourth Street established a relay system from the stairs down to the platform in order to best preserve their voices. "Room!" shouted the first guard. "Up forward!" cried the next, ten yards farther on. "Two rear!" hollered the third, glancing toward the guard nearest the train for Belmont Park. "Car smokers!"

The newspapers read by the passengers on the trains out to the grounds were full of race information. The *New York Times* reminded its readers, "Under the rules, the Gordon Bennett Cup race must be flown over a course of not less than five kilometers (3.1 miles)—the exact size of the Belmont Park course—and the distance to be covered may not be less than 100 kilometers (sixty-two miles). Contestants may start at any time within a period of seven hours on the day fixed for the race, and there is no minimum time in which the course must be covered. Landings will be allowed, but each contestant must cross the starting line at least one and a half hours before sunset. The time at which the race may be begun will be 8:30 A.M., giving the aviators until 3:30 P.M. to make their start. A purse of $5,000 accompanies the prize."

The *New York Times* was one of the few papers to offer a balanced assessment of the likely outcome of the race, estimating that "America's chances are good." The *New York Herald* was feeling more bullish, splashing its front page with the titanic headline WRIGHT "BABY GRAND" DRIVEN BY MR. BROOKINS, PICKED TO WIN THE GREAT FLIGHT TO-DAY FOR THE INTERNATIONAL TROPHY. The *New York Sun*, meanwhile, reported "an air of quiet confidence in the hangars of the American aviators," with John Moisant offering a different view to the *Herald*, saying, "Hamilton is the man who will keep the trophy here."

Those passengers whose trains approached Belmont Park at eight A.M. stopped reading their papers, stopped talking about Hawley and Post, and looked out of the windows to their left. An airplane was in the air, a biplane, small and compact; could it be the Wrights' Baby Grand? Then the train curved right and the biplane vanished behind the enormous grandstand. A minute late the train arrived at the Belmont Park station and the doors released a torrent of humanity. Passengers ran down the steps and through the funnel-like passageway that led to the grounds, hoping to catch another glimpse of the biplane, but they were too late.

Walter Brookins's first flight in the Baby Grand had lasted just three minutes. He went up, flew a lap of the course, and came down ecstatic. "There's nothing she can't do," he said with a whoop. "The Blériots aren't in it with her!"

At the foot of each of the thirteen pylons staked out around the course were a table and two chairs, which now accommodated two members of the Signal Corps. Telephones connected ten of the pylons to the judges' box, and each pair of corpsmen had a set of powerful field glasses. The observer's job was to ensure every airplane passed on the outside of his particular pylon, as well as noting the number of the machine on the underside of the left wing. He was to then communicate the information to his assistant, who was to note the number of the plane and the exact time at which it passed the pylon, and if it was a good passage, he was to write a *G* in the margin of the form in front of him. If the aviator made a bad passage, however, he was to wave a red flag and wait for an acknowledgment from the judges' box.

With only a few minutes now until the official start of the race, inside hangar No. 14 Grahame-White was in earnest conversation with his teammates, Alec Ogilvie and James Radley. Although neither Ogilvie, who had learned to fly under the Wrights' tuition, nor Radley had much time for their leader's showmanship, they respected his judgment. They listened as Grahame-White explained their strategy for the day.

Farther along hangar row Cortlandt Bishop was introducing Augustus Post and Alan Hawley to some of the American aviators. The pair hadn't stumbled out of the Hotel St. Regis until the wee small hours of Saturday morning, but they had about them the exhilaration of men whose dream had really come true. Now and again they whispered to each other, "Think of where we were this time last week!"

Everywhere Hawley and Post went at Belmont Park people wanted to shake their hands and tell them how proud they were. The two had been invited to watch the action from the judges' box, and as they climbed the short flight of steps, they were given a standing ovation by the spectators in the grandstand.

The signal bomb detonated as Cortlandt Bishop was walking back from hangar row toward the clubhouse in the company of a reporter from the *New York Evening Sun*. Bishop twirled the ends of his mustache as he predicted, "The race will probably be over by noon." Really? said the reporter, raising his eyebrows in surprise. Oh, yes, replied Bishop, with his customary know-all air. "Curtiss got away with the cup at Rheims while the Frenchmen were wrangling about who should go up first. Curtiss made his flight early, when there was little wind. Later in the day it commenced to blow hard and the Frenchmen had no chance to better the American's time."

Grahame-White was buttoning his brown flying overalls when he heard the boom of the signal bomb. He glanced at his watch, eight thirty-two A.M., they were a couple of minutes behind schedule. He put on his cap— back to front, of course—and drank a glass of water. Then he strode outside to where his Blériot had been for the last hour. Fastened to the wing was the sprig of lucky white heather given him by a female admirer in

England. The mechanics had already given the machine a thorough maintenance, oiling and greasing the rocker arms and pushrods, checking that the u-bolts that held the bracing wires in the fuselage were tight, and ensuring the rudders at the rear of the airplane functioned properly. Now Grahame-White made a final inspection, circling the machine, once or twice dropping down on his haunches to test a bolt or a wire. He stopped at the nose of the Blériot—nicknamed the bedstead because of its resemblance to the head of a bed—and examined the fourteen-cylinder Gnome engine that was fastened to, and revolved with, the propeller. This was a stunning innovation by Blériot, a rotating engine that was also an automatic air-cooling device, thereby removing the need for a flywheel. The engine looked good to Grahame-White; so did the dipstick when he checked the plane had a full tank of gasoline. He was ready. Nodding to his mechanics, Grahame-White climbed into the monoplane as his men held the tips of the wings. The machine wobbled slightly under his weight when he slid onto the wooden seat. In front was the the control stick, which enabled him to control the lateral movement of the aircraft by warping the wings,* as well as the up-and-down movement of the elevators (tailplane). When Grahame-White pulled back on the stick, the Blériot's bedstead nose rose, and when he pushed forward, the nose dipped. Moving the stick sideways banked the aircraft, although he often needed to tilt his body in the same direction to assist. A small wooden wheel was bolted to the top of the control stick of every Blériot to make the stick easier to grip.

On a panel to the left of the control stick was the throttle switch and gas cock, and at Grahame-White's feet the wooden rudder bar, which controlled the four-and-a-half-foot-square rudder at the rear of the Blériot.

He flipped the gas and oil on, and off, and closed the throttle. As he went through his final set of checks, none of Grahame-White's mechanics wished him luck; an aviation superstition was that such a gesture portended misfortune. He gave a thumbs-up to the mechanic gripping the

---

* Wing warping was the key to the Wrights' initial success as it gave the aviator roll control, in other words control of the airplane's lateral movement. Wires connected from the control stick to the wingtips allowed the aviator to twist or "warp" the tips of the wings in flight.

propeller, who, with one mighty twist, fired the engine. The little plane began to tremble with the power of the hundred-horsepower engine, and the mechanics put a hand over their mouths as smoke swirled around them. Grahame-White pulled down his goggles, checked his watch—eight forty A.M.—and applied a little bit of throttle. He began to roll forward across the grass, his mechanics jogging alongside still holding the wings and fuselage as he picked up speed. Then he removed a gloved hand from the control stick and signaled to his mechanics to jump back.

Grahame-White's rapid departure caught people unawares. The reporter for the *New York Evening Sun* described how most of the crowd in the grandstand were blathering or reading their programs when someone shouted, "Here's Grahame-White!" "There was an instant turning of faces to the Englishman's green shed," the reporter wrote. "They saw the 100 horsepower Blériot rise with a rush from the ground and chase through the air channels in the long pylon path. With a deep-throated roar that bespoke power the dragon-winged thing raced over the white canvas band marking the start and dashed through space."

Grahame-White kept low as, with the wind at his back, he flew east, past the press stand and the ranks of automobiles parked on the grass, many with their wealthy owners watching from the backseat with a rug thrown over their lap. He banked left, and the observer standing at the foot of pylon No. 5 signaled that machine No. 10 had taken the corner without default. Now the aviator headed north for nearly half a mile, away from the stables and over some scrubland. At pylon No. 8 Grahame-White turned ninety degrees west, straight into the freshening breeze, forcing him to grip the wheel ever tighter as he struggled up the lengthy back straight. In the grandstand a mile south, only those spectators with field glasses could see Grahame-White vanish behind some trees and then reappear just in front of pylon No. 11. He cornered it to perfection and flew southwest past the hangars, where his rivals "were clocking him carefully watching every shift of the wind and every drift of the machine as the airplane rounded the pylons." Now he was coming up to dead man's turn. Inside the judges' box just behind the turn, Augustus Post and Alan Hawley looked up as the Blériot came toward them, its body shaking with the power from its engine. In the press stand the reporter from the *New York Herald* had the machine in the lenses of his field glasses when he saw it start to slide sideways with Grahame-White "trying to counteract the effect of the heavy gust of wind that caught him." For a few moments Grahame-White skidded toward the grandstand, then he brought the machine under control and throttled down the home straight to complete the first of his twenty laps. All eyes turned toward the scoreboard. People who'd clocked him with their own watches proudly shouted out their estimations. But the rest of the spectators demanded official confirmation. Then it appeared: 3 minutes 15.64 seconds. One of the sharper press boys yelled, "He's doing better than sixty miles an hour but less than sixty-five."

Grahame-White felt good as he started his second lap. It wasn't as cold as he'd feared and the Blériot was handling well. Just have to be careful going into dead man's turn, he told himself. Second time round he took the corner with more finesse, and his lap time set the crowd buzzing: 3 minutes 9.14 seconds—he'd sheared a full six seconds from his first circuit. Lap three was faster still: 3 minutes 8.07 seconds. The time for lap four was 3 minutes 12.11 seconds, but lap five was special: 3 minutes 1.06 seconds. Five laps—over fifteen miles—in 15 minutes and 46 seconds: it was impressive, even to his detractors in the press box. "There was no one who watched Mr. Grahame-White," said the correspondent from the *New York Herald*, "who did not concede that he was handling his machine in a masterly manner."

But where were the Americans? In the grandstand and on the field enclosures spectators alternated their gaze between Grahame-White and hangar row. No movement came from the Wrights' hangar; Orville seemed more concerned with timing each of Grahame-White's laps, and now and again Walter Brookins emerged from the hangar to look over his boss's shoulder and find out how the Englishman was faring. A similar lack of urgency marked the hangars of Armstrong Drexel and Charles Hamilton, the latter of whom appeared troubled by the state of his machine. Suddenly the crowd heard the starting crack of a Blériot engine outside hangar No. 8. Smoke billowed into the air, then the machine began to slowly taxi across the grass. At nine A.M. Peter Prunty shouted into his megaphone that Monsieur "Lee Blank" in his "Blearyrot" had started his first lap. Up in his box, August Belmont turned to two of his guests— Monsieur Jules Jusserand, the French ambassador to the United States, and

Count Benoit D'Azy, the French naval attaché—and apologized for the butchering of their language.

Grahame-White was halfway through his sixth lap when Le Blanc set off in pursuit in his yellow monoplane. The Frenchman's leather helmet was the only part of him visible to the crowd as they watched him negotiate the first corner with ease. Now the two machines were opposite one another, Le Blanc hurtling up the back straight and Grahame-White entering the home stretch. Spectators tried to gauge their respective speeds. It was hard to tell, but Le Blanc seemed to be fairly whizzing round the course. The scoreboard showed Grahame-White's time for his sixth lap: 3 minutes 3.76 seconds. Another quick one. Now Le Blanc was coming into dead man's turn. People jumped up from their seats, their eyes riveted on the machine as it deftly rounded the pylon at a height of one hundred feet, then shot forward, "its motor humming a fierce, defiant song of speed and power."

The amateur timekeepers looked at their watches in astonishment. That couldn't be right, could it? A deafening roar from the crowd confirmed it was. The official lap time had flashed up on the scoreboard—2 minutes 45.63 seconds. Half a minute quicker than Grahame-White's first lap. People tried to take it in, that a flying machine could travel at such speed. It was too fantastic for words.

Le Blanc's second lap was just as fast, and in the press box and around the grounds people's excitement grew as they realized that they were witnessing the quickest-ever flight in an airplane. Those spectators who'd arrived early took pleasure in "explaining to the constant stream of newcomers the race that was then on in the air."

As Le Blanc neared the end of his third lap, a second British competitor, Alec Ogilvie, took off in his Wright biplane. At least the crowd had something American to cheer now, even if it was a machine and not a man. It took just a lap from Ogilvie, however, for everyone to see "that his feeble 30-horsepower motor was outclassed by the great 100-horsepower motors in the Blériot monoplanes."

The thirty thousand people now on the grounds ignored the small biplane beetling around the course and watched transfixed as Le Blanc tore after Grahame-White "as a hound would chase a fox. It was an agile fox, a fast fox, but the hound was relentless." The spectators in the seats high up on the grandstand ran down to the grass in front so they could get a better view of the hunt. The reporter from the *World* continued his analogy as the "fox disappeared behind the clump of trees on the northern side . . . but almost before it had done so the hound had plunged in after it. Then the sky-fox took to the air running high. But the hound was on him now in the full cry of the metal voice of the humming motor. For a breathless moment it really looked as if, hound-like, Le Blanc's Blériot was about to plunge crashingly upon the fleeing monoplane of Grahame-White."

Bored with the chase, Le Blanc left behind his rival and careered round the course while the "crowd was shouting mad with the excitement of the spectacle." Straw boaters littered the infield where they had been thrown by men unable to control their emotions, and people stood on the backseats of their parked automobiles waving their arms aloft as the machines scorched overhead.

Le Blanc completed the first five laps in 13 minutes 50 seconds, nearly two minutes quicker than Grahame-White. The sixth lap he circled in 2 minutes 48 seconds, the seventh in 2 minutes 47 seconds, and the eighth also in 2 minutes 47 seconds. Le Blanc had found his rhythm and was averaging seventy miles an hour compared to Grahame-White's sixty. Nonetheless, wrote the reporter from the *World*, one couldn't but admire the Englishman "as he went persistently on, demanding from his machine all that it could give, drawing it out by skillful manipulation. Down on the scoreboard he could have seen as the laps rolled by that the Frenchman's slowest record in any of them was faster than his . . . but if he realized it, he didn't show it. He kept doggedly on his course—the conditions reversed, Le Blanc the fox, himself the dog."

By the time he had completed lap fifteen Grahame-White was in trouble. For the last few minutes his motor had been spraying oil over the fuselage, and now smoke wafted around his feet and he could "feel the woodwork of the monoplane heating and my coat . . . beginning to be uncomfortably warm. I could feel it almost parching on my back and I was stricken with the horrible feeling that I might have to make a quick dash to the ground with the wings and framework of my machine blazing about me." Having never before flown such a powerful machine, Grahame-White had no idea the smoke and heat were normal by-products of the

Gnome engine; instead, he presumed he was on fire and "for a few moments I could not help [but] picture myself projected like a cannon ball at a speed of sixty miles an hour . . . the prospect was not very agreeable." But there were no flames and Grahame-White managed to quell the rising panic. Only five more laps, he told himself, stick it out. He reduced his height, flying as close to the ground as possible, "expecting to make a drop at any moment."

Flying in fear for his life, Grahame-White dipped under three minutes each for his final five laps, and at nine forty-three A.M. he finished his twentieth lap to an extravagant wave from the starter's black-and-white-checkered flag and a rapturous ovation from the crowd. The scoreboard displayed his overall time: 1 hour, 1 minute, 4.75 seconds. A plucky performance, wrote the reporter from the *New York Herald*, "but it was taken for granted that he was hopelessly beaten."

Attention turned to Le Blanc, who was still "distance-devouring," in the words of the pressmen. With Grahame-White finished, and Ogilvie down with engine trouble, the Frenchman had the crowd to himself. They kept their eyes trained on him "with an interest that kept the breath stilled while he was passing, and was marked by a quick relieved breath as he shot off." The mathematicians in the grandstand tediously pointed out that he was traveling at a greater speed than Harry Grant, who, three weeks earlier, had driven his automobile for 278 miles at an average speed of 65 mph to win the Vanderbilt Cup. Imagine, they said, an airplane going quicker than an automobile.

As Le Blanc started his penultimate lap, the *Herald* reporter had already left his seat in the press stand and was down at the judges' box taking advantage of his newspaper's status as the meet's official organ. Waiting for the Frenchman to finish the race, the journalist tried to convey the magnitude of Le Blanc's flight. He described the Blériot's "beautiful steadiness . . . perfect pitch," and the way the Gnome engine "thrashed ceaselessly," but he needed something more, he needed a comparison. He checked the tournament program for the world record for one hundred kilometers—1 hour and 6 minutes, set by Léon Morane of France a year earlier. Yet here was Le Blanc, flying down the home straight to complete his ninety-fifth kilometer in a shade under 53 minutes, having reached a top speed of 72.5 mph—another world's record—and having "set a pace that it was known only a phenomenon in aircraft construction could equal."

The two corpsmen at pylon No. 5 watched as Le Blanc raced toward them on his final lap. The sun glinted off the windshields of the automobiles parked to their left and the roar of the crowd thundered down the track like the hooves of a hundred Thoroughbreds. Le Blanc was a hundred feet above the ground, but as he did in the approach to every pylon, he now began to drop to a height of about fifty feet. Suddenly the airplane swerved toward the infield, almost as if it were cutting the corner, but the corpsmen saw from the way the machine swiveled in the air that Le Blanc had lost control. He was headed toward the stables. No, he seemed to have righted it. The craft jerked, once, twice, and for a moment hovered like an eagle over a lake. Then without a sound the machine fell from the sky, crashing into a fourteen-inch-thick telegraph pole with such force that the pole snapped like a toothpick. The reporter from the *Sun* stifled a cry as "Le Blanc was shot forward on his hands and knees and rolled over and over until he lay limp."

The first man to reach the wreckage was one of the Pinkerton security guards, John Ellis, who'd been patrolling the eastern end of the grounds. Le Blanc was lying on the grass, a few feet clear of the broken pole, in among the yellow rags of what had once been the covering of his machine's wings. He was still alive, but he had a cut down to the bone above his right eye and three or four other gashes to his face caused by shards of wood from his propeller. Ellis took a handkerchief from his pocket and tried to stanch the blood flowing down the aviator's face. Le Blanc pushed him away, got to his feet, threw off his shattered goggles, and tried to find a way into the mangled corpse of his machine, "apparently thinking of climbing again into the seat of his craft." But no craft was left, explained the *New York Herald* reporter, who was in one of the automobiles now racing to the scene of the crash. The nose of the Blériot had hit the center of the pole twelve feet from the ground, ripping the wings from the fuselage and leaving the chassis "crumpled up into a smashed bundle of wreckage."

One of the tournament doctors, Charles Ross, put an arm around Le Blanc and noticed the faraway look in his eyes. The Frenchman was

helped into an automobile and driven round to the back of the grandstand to the hospital tent, where a tall policeman opened the door of the
vehicle. The sight of the uniform snapped the Frenchman out of his stu-
por, and he "threw his arms around the policeman and, coursing down
across the bloodstains on his face, came Le Blanc's first tears . . . and as
he sobbed Le Blanc rattled along in French to the Irish policeman whom
he was embracing."

Dr. Ross eased the aviator out of the policeman's arms and into the
tent underneath the grandstand, where he laid him down on a bed and
began to clean and dress his wounds. Le Blanc was still gibbering when
from above came a fearful cry.

Grahame-White had arrived back at his hangar just as Le Blanc started his
last lap. He knew he'd lost, but he had no complaints. He'd given it his best
shot, and he had beaten the existing record for a hundred-kilometer flight,
and in a machine he had never before flown. He removed his flying goggles,
revealing two white-saucer eyes in a face blackened by oil, and whipped off
his gloves so he could shake hands with his mechanics. Eleonora Sears ran
over to take a snapshot, and as she did so, the Frenchman dropped out of the
sky, and the race.

In the commotion that followed, only a handful of spectators saw that
the flaps of the Wrights' tent were being folded back. Suddenly the Baby
Grand emerged into the cold sunshine. The *World*'s reporter swept the
field with his field glasses, leaving behind Le Blanc and focusing instead
on the "tall, lithe, boyish-face of Walter Brookins [who] appeared to
have no anxiety other than to begin the race." Now the biplane was on
the grass, and the mechanics were helping the aviator into his seat on the
leading edge of the lower plane. Wilbur and Orville Wright said a few
words to Brookins, who then signaled he was ready to start. A couple of
minutes later—as a bleeding Le Blanc was being driven to the hospital
tent—Brookins climbed into the air, working the two levers either side
of his seat.

The *New York Times* reporter knew something was wrong the moment Brookins left the ground. It wasn't that the wind had picked up and
was now blowing in fitful gusts at twenty miles an hour, but more that
the motor didn't sound right. The reporter knew an eight-cylinder

engine when he heard one, and that wasn't the sound coming from the Baby Grand. At most, he reckoned that four of the cylinders were firing. The machine came round dead man's turn toward the start line at a height of no more than eighty feet. It began to head toward the infield, then back out, then it started to lose height. "He's going to come about into the wind and land," someone shouted from a seat close to the press stand, but through his glasses the *Times* reporter saw Brookins pulling frantically at the levers, then the propeller stopped. What happened next took no more than thirty seconds, he wrote, "although to the spectators it seemed like minutes." The Baby Grand was only fifty yards from the lawn on which promenaded the ladies and gentlemen in their finest furs and stiffest collars. They stopped and looked up at the drama unfolding before their eyes. The machine's nose rose for a moment, then fell, and Brookins nearly went with it. He grabbed a wire and steadied himself, then pulled again at the levers. It looked as if the nose was leveling up . . . was he winning his battle? And then, just as suddenly as the propeller had stopped, it started, and the Wright Baby Grand machine arrowed toward the ground. "Women in the stands cried aloud and more than one man turned away," wrote the reporter from the *New York Sun* as Brookins, wearing his favorite two-piece green suit, made "a quick move backward from his seat as if to get as far from the first smashing point as possible." The airplane slammed nose-first into the earth, "and in a dense dust cloud it turned tail upwards and crumpled into a roll of muslin, broken wood and steel, and settled into wreckage like a crushed paper bag." Each reporter differed on the fine details of the crash, but they all agreed on the deafening silence in the seconds that followed. It was as if, said the *New York Times*, spectators and officials alike had been "dazed into a trance." Young Brookins was finished, and with him America's best hope of retaining the International Aviation Cup. It was hard to believe.

Then the spectral figure of Brookins crawled from the smash. He reached up to his helmet, said the *Times* correspondent, "and tore it from his head, and cast it from him. Then his hands pressed his temples and he reeled as he tried to stand and face the spectators. Again he clutched at his waist, while an expression of agony convulsed his face, and then he turned, staggered a step or two, and sank to the ground."

The Wright brothers, and their sister, Katharine, reached Brookins as he was being eased onto a stretcher. He was slipping in and out of consciousness, but when he saw Katharine, his former schoolteacher, he took her hand and whispered, "I'm not hurt much but I want a long rest."

An hour after Brookins's spectacular fall from grace, Hubert Latham launched his bid for the cup. But the wind had steadily increased throughout the morning so that it "now came whooping in puffy gusts out of the northeast," and at every pylon the Frenchman was blown off course, losing precious seconds as he righted his machine. After lap five he was one minute and eleven seconds down on Grahame-White, and by lap ten the deficit had increased to three minutes twelve seconds. As he started lap fifteen, Latham was more than four minutes behind the Englishman's time, and second place was the best for which he could hope. Then, as he cornered dead man's turn, a flurry of wind caught his left wing and pushed him "directly into a group of automobiles which were parked near the fence by the side of the old running track . . . He passed so closely above their occupants that his motors roared deafeningly in their ears. They dropped out of their cars in panic and chairs went over and men and women fell and ran and scrambled toward the clubhouse for safety." Latham regained control of the Antoinette, but he had had enough; why risk his life when the chance of victory had gone?

Luncheon came and went without any further challenges to Grahame-White's time, though the fifty-thousand-strong crowd didn't appear too perturbed. They were too busy reliving the intense excitement of the morning. What had been the most thrilling moment? they asked one another. The Le Blanc smash? The Brookins crash? The Latham near miss? For many, certainly the reporters, it had been the arrival of Le Blanc in the press stand less than an hour after he had discharged himself from Dr. Ross's care. According to several eyewitnesses, the doctor had been only too pleased to wave good-bye to the Frenchman, after he had "in a passionate outburst of rage and vexation, denounced every one connected with the meeting." Le Blanc had then marched in his blue flying overalls into the press stand with "his head rounded in white linen bandages, a complicated structure of plastering under his chin, plasters over and under his right eye, and the eye itself closed," and continued his tirade against everything and everyone. With his translator clearly struggling to keep up, Le Blanc raved that he had run out of gasoline on his final lap, something that "was all the fault—the utter stupidity—of one of my mechanics," who had failed to fill the second tank to the brim. Had the poor man been discharged of his responsibilities as a result? ventured a nervous correspondent. "My dear young man," snarled Le Blanc, "that was a decision I reached the very instant I hit that pole."

Le Blanc then added in a statement "that was nothing of insinuation but instead a direct accusation, that there had been something of intent in this failure to fill the petrol tank." But the Frenchman, perhaps realizing he had gone too far in bandying about such allegations, refrained from elaborating and instead "walked the length of the grandstand to show he was not injured, and was cheered again and again."

His reception on hangar row was less enthusiastic, particularly when it was learned he was blaming his mechanics for his demise. That was cheap, considered Grahame-White, as a "thoughtful aviator would always examine his craft and oil supply before ascending." What he, and a lot of the other fliers, suspected was that Le Blanc had intentionally carried the bare minimum of gasoline so that his machine would be as light as possible. Then, when he had descended to take the pylon, what fuel he had left ran down into the front of his engine, leaving him, so to speak, high and dry.

But Le Blanc's rash talk of chicanery brought an ironic smile to Grahame-White's face. The same word had sprung to his mind a short while earlier as he sifted through the wreckage of Le Blanc's machine looking for clues as to why the Frenchman's Blériot had been so much quicker than his own when they were supposed to be identical. He was aware of the different propellers, but that shouldn't have accounted for such a discrepancy in speed. Grahame-White had inspected the Gnome engine, but found it to be the same as his. Then he scrutinized the damaged chassis, and suddenly the penny dropped. "I found that the tube which carries the forward supports of the wings on his machine was placed underneath the top fuselage longitudinals," he wrote a short time later, "whereas mine [the tube] was placed on top of the fuselage longitudinals, which made a difference of some four or five inches in the angle of incidence of the wings. And, although my wings were identical and quite as flat as his, his placing of them on the fuselage would naturally make his machine very much faster."

Grahame-White realized that it was "only an accident that occurred to Le Blanc's machine that caused me to learn of the deal he [Blériot] had tried to pull off on me—in other words to furnish me with a machine that was not equal in speed to Le Blanc's." The perfidious Blériot had sold Grahame-White an airplane he knew was inferior to the one he had delivered to his compatriot, and his patriotic deviousness would have succeeded had it not been for the rashness of Le Blanc.

The Belmont Park crowd was becoming fractious, noticed the correspondent from the *World*, because they "could not understand why the other Americans, Hamilton and Drexel, held back. It had passed 3 o'clock and neither of them had come forward to challenge the Britisher's claim to the cup." Worse, from the home fans' point of view, was that Latham and Alec Ogilvie had both gone up again and finished the course, albeit in slow times. As it stood now, first and second place belonged to Britain, with France in third. The United States faced humiliation. Apart from Peter Prunty's announcement an hour earlier that Walter Brookins would be back on his feet in a few days ("black-and-blue, as though he had been beaten with a club, but no bones broken," as Dr. Moorehead told the *New York Times*) there had been scant else to cheer the whole day.

The crowd didn't care that the wind had increased in the last hour and now teetered on the twenty-five-mile-per-hour mark; they had each paid $1 for a ticket—$2 for those in the grandstand—and they demanded action. Yet neither of the American fliers was keen to risk his neck after what he'd seen this morning. But then at three fifteen P.M.—seventeen minutes before the race's cutoff time—Hamilton went up in his 110-horsepower biplane. He was soon down, after one lap, with engine trouble. One of the French fliers rushed up to the American and, tugging at the sleeve of his leather coat, said, "Come, Monsieur Hamilton, I have a Blériot monoplane here for you . . . hurry! Grahame-White's record will stand if you don't." Hamilton thanked the Frenchman but declined the offer, telling him that he had never before flown a monoplane, and in any case, the wind was just too nasty.

It seemed certain that the U.S. challenge for the International Aviation Cup had fizzled out in dispiriting circumstances, until one of the race organizers pointed out that when Brookins crashed, he hadn't actually crossed the start line; in other words, the American team could call upon one of their three reserves. My God, he's right! people shouted, and an official was dispatched to hangar row with instructions to get the first-named replacement, James Mars of the Curtiss team, up in the air at once.

The first of the Curtiss fliers that the official encountered was Eugene Ely, who explained casually that Mars was not there, he was on his way to a meet in Norfolk, Virginia. The official listened dumbstruck as Ely told him what he later repeated to the press, that the failure to select one of the Curtiss planes was "the smallest thing ever done . . . [and] at that late hour we refused to enter the race. Why should one of our machines go in the race as a substitute when it won the race last year?"

With only a few minutes remaining before the race closed, Grahame-White was looking more smug than ever. The Americans had to do something. Drexel had agreed to go up and was warming his engine, but so was James Radley, the third of the British fliers, who had been held in reserve by Grahame-White to counter just such a last-minute challenge.

"Moisant!" cried the officials. "Get Moisant." The revolutionary was in his hangar finishing a meat pie when he was told to take off. "How long have I got?" he asked, already reaching for his aviation togs. Not long enough to stand around talking. The crowd was in pandemonium as they watched the three identical machines—all fifty-horsepower Blériots—preparing to go aloft. Drexel was first to cross the start line at three twenty-five P.M., but by the time he completed his first leaden lap in 3 minutes 38 seconds, neither Moisant nor Radley was in the air. Now they were taxiing across the grass—but time was nearly up. Radley was next in line, but Moisant snuck ahead and took off at three thirty-one P.M. and thirty-five seconds. Radley waited for Moisant to rise to a safe height, then signaled to his mechanics he was ready. But before he could get airborne, Radley saw the timekeeper waving a red flag. He had been timed out—by twenty-five seconds.

Drexel lasted seven laps before he "narrowly missed a chimney top at the eastern end of the field and gave it up as a bad job," and Moisant descended after lap six. He wasn't finished, though, he told officials, he just needed to make an adjustment to his rudder. Forty-two minutes later Moisant was off again, eventually crossing the finish line in one hour fifty-seven minutes.* Allan Ryan was so tickled he forgot his position as general manager of the meet and came flying out of the judges' box, shouting and waving and running toward Moisant. In a minute he had "fairly pulled him from the machine and dragged him protesting into the clubhouse." Pushing Moisant before him, Ryan held up the aviator's hand and hollered, "Here's Moisant! He did it! He's got second place for America! We may have lost the cup, but we showed them we could fly." Then Ryan called for three cheers from everyone in the clubhouse, and the roar that followed, said the *New York Times* reporter, "must have been heard in the grandstand several hundred yards away," even above the strains of "Yankee Doodle Dandy" from the band. The cheers were probably also heard over on hangar row, where Claude Grahame-White was wondering when he would receive the International Aviation Cup. Ever the gentleman, he had so far maintained a dignified silence on Blériot's skulduggery, telling the reporter from the *World* that "the only manner in which I can account for Le Blanc being so far ahead of me . . . is that he was using a different kind of propeller." He was also happy to concede that the Frenchman would have won, if not for his unfortunate mishap on his final lap.

In return, Grahame-White would have appreciated a little more respect for what he'd achieved, but the stench of churlishness drifted through the hangars as darkness fell on Belmont Park. Charles Hamilton let it be known that "Le Blanc is the best track driver in the world . . . Grahame-White would never have been in it except for Le Blanc's accident."

Armstrong Drexel even told the *New York Sun* that the committee should ask the Frenchman for his address "and telegraph the cup over." As for Cortlandt Bishop, well, Grahame-White expected nothing less

---

* His actual flying time was one hour and fifteen minutes, but his time spent on the ground was included in his final total.

than a graceless barb, but was nonetheless taken aback by the Aero Club president's curt assessment of the race: "It was a complete victory for the Gnome engine." The Englishman didn't know whether to laugh or cry.

By the time the committee got round to the presentations, Grahame-White's pique had turned to anger. Why should he be humble in the face of such ungraciousness? He approached the podium with "his debonair swagger," said the *World*, "and with a cigarette hanging on his lips, smilingly received acknowledgements over his victory." Grahame-White shook hands with Allan Ryan, J. C. McCoy, and Cortlandt Bishop, then the conquering hero turned his back on the vanquished and sauntered back to his hangar.

CHAPTER SIXTEEN

It Isn't True, It Can't Be True!

Sunday, October 30, 1910

UNBELIEVABLE, UTTERLY UNBELIEVABLE. Claude Grahame-White threw the newspapers down in disgust as he took breakfast with Sydney McDonald in the Hotel Astor. Hardly a word of praise for his victory, just the hard-luck stories of Le Blanc and Brookins, and the plucky heroics of Moisant. And then there were the damned lies, such as the one in the *New York Globe* describing how Grahame-White had "continued to soar airily over the track . . . not worrying at all over the fall of his two rivals." But he hadn't even been in the air at the time! Still, he said, smiling at McDonald, at least among all the bumpkin reporting, there were one or two gems. Listen to this, in the *New York Sun*. Wilbur Wright, when asked to explain away the disastrous showing of his machine, replied, "We don't believe in speed for its own sake, we don't even think that it is the most important thing. They all go fast enough." Ha! Thank heavens for the *New York Herald*, said the English aviator, admiring his photograph on the front page under the headline MR. GRAHAME-WHITE WINS INTERNATIONAL AVIATION CUP IN A MARVELOUS FLIGHT. He enjoyed the exuberance of the prose, too, particularly the sentence "It was a spectacle spectacularly modern, a spectacle as perfectly typical of the young century as ever was a chariot smashing, horse slaughtering dash around the Coliseum in the most splendid days of Rome."

But what most caught Grahame-White's eye on the *Herald*'s front page—aside from his own photograph, of course—was the small box in the right-hand corner that listed Sunday's schedule. Along with the Hourly Distance and altitude contests (beginning at eleven A.M.), and the three P.M. cross-country flight, the small matter of the Statue of Liberty race was also still to be decided.

After the blazing row he'd had with the Belmont Park committee on Thursday, Grahame-White had pulled out of the race, even asking for the return of his entrance fee, but on Sunday morning an idea began to form in his mind. Le Blanc was in no fit state to fly, and Charles Hamilton's 110-horsepower machine was defective. The Curtiss boys were still sulking, and the Wright team was grounded on account of the Sabbath. He knew that neither Alex Ogilvie nor James Radley fancied the race, which left just a few Frenchmen, Armstrong Drexel, and John Moisant, none of whom had a machine as powerful as his own hundred-horsepower Blériot. It might well be the easiest $10,000 Grahame-White had ever made, and it would be a hoot to see the faces of the Belmont Park committee when he walked off with the spoils for a second time.

Unpopular as he was with the American aviation fraternity and certain sections of the nation's press, Grahame-White remained a big hit with the fans, many of whom were "in a state of perpetual excitement" from the moment he strolled through the front gates of Belmont Park on Sunday morning. Among the dozens of men and women who stalked the Englishman's every move "were some who begged continuously and imploringly to be taken aloft." Young men wore their caps back to front in the Grahame-White style, and old men with fat wallets offered $500 for a five-minute flight. Meanwhile, the correspondent from the *New York Tribune* reckoned that "most any girl would give a lock of her own real hair for a ride" with the handsome flier. But Grahame-White was deaf to all entreaties, and the only woman he seemed to have eyes for was Eleonora Sears, who accompanied him to the clubhouse—oblivious of "the envious green-eyed bunch that hung around the rail"—wearing an elegant brown suit and a large black velvet hat. It hadn't gone unnoticed by the American press that since Miss Sears had met Grahame-White, she had dispensed with her "mannish style" of dress and replaced it with one more suited to a society woman.

Word soon spread along hangar row of Grahame-White's change of heart toward the Statue of Liberty race. The *New York Herald*'s reporter telegraphed the news to his office in Herald Square, and they in turn alerted the *Owlet*, the *Herald*'s dispatch boat anchored in the waters off the Statue of Liberty, and also the wireless station in Fort Wood on Bedloe's Island, the operator of which was none other than Louis Ginsberg of the SS *Trent*, who had become something of a celebrity since his role in saving Wellman and the crew of the *America*.

By noon Belmont Park was bulging with humanity. Nearly seventy-five thousand were on the grounds or peeking through the gaps in the fence where some of the canvas sheets had been removed. The crowd "was not so fashionable" as on Saturday, but they were creating a livelier atmosphere; best of all, for the first time in eight days, the wind was under ten miles an hour. Typical, just typical, thought Arch Hoxsey and Ralph Johnstone, who prowled the length of hangar row like two caged tigers. How they would have loved to be up in the air on such a benign day, challenging for the morning altitude contest, won by René Simon, with a feeble height of 959 feet.

Shortly before one o'clock Clifford Harmon escorted Augustus Post and Alan Hawley along hangar row and introduced the pair to Grahame-White. The three of them watched Harmon fly a couple of laps in his Farman biplane, then Grahame-White put on a show for the balloonists by taking up Sydney McDonald and one of his mechanics. This time the machine made it into the air despite the load, and after a brief spin, Grahame-White landed on the grass outside Harmon's hangar, No. 16. He thanked his friend for the loan of his machine and went off to lunch. Not long after, Harmon followed, telling his mechanics not to bother to return his biplane to its hangar as he would soon be back for another flight.

John Moisant was finishing his own lunch in hangar No. 18 when Harmon disappeared in the direction of the clubhouse. With him were his brother, Alfred, and two of his sisters, Louise and Mathilde, who had recently arrived in New York. The women were still getting used to their brother's being one of the most famous men in America, but they were warming to the idea. They had already watched him finish second to Hubert Latham in the morning's Hourly Distance contest, and now they were helping him prepare for the Statue of Liberty race. "You're going to win," Mathilde told her brother, "I can feel it in my bones."

Moisant was relying, however, on more than female intuition to win the race. In a fifty-horsepower Blériot, his only hope of beating Grahame-White would be to fly the direct route, straight over the city. But Moisant had never before flown over a metropolis and had no idea how it would affect the air currents. Would the currents eddy up, he wondered, "just as spray flies when it hits the wall?" To find out, Moisant called on the two people in the world who knew best: Ralph Johnstone and Arch Hoxsey. Get up high, they told him, out of the reach of the currents that hang over cities and that give the air more holes than a lump of Swiss cheese. On the return leg—and Moisant would have the wind at his back in the afternoon—they advised him to gradually descend and make use of the extra ground speed. They wished him good luck and made to leave, but Johnstone lingered for a moment at the hangar door. He imagined that Moisant's stomach had started to tighten the way his always did. "Just be careful, John," he said, "there's no point in getting yourself killed. No amount of publicity's worth that."

The bomb exploded bang on one thirty P.M. to signal the start of the afternoon's program, and Moisant decided to take his machine round the course for a few gentle laps before he embarked on the Statue of Liberty race at two forty-five P.M. He strode out of his hangar, acknowledging the good wishes of several dozen spectators who had talked their way onto hangar row and stood behind a line of small red flags planted in the grass, beyond which no one but the aviator and his mechanics were allowed. Among the crowd was a correspondent from the *Boston Daily Globe* who had never been as close to an airplane as he now was. He watched in reverential silence as Moisant climbed into his machine and the propeller was engaged. The motor sparked and then . . . was this normal? the reporter wondered. The monoplane began "running over the ground on its chassis, like a great winged bicycle [it] took an involuntary turn to the left and instead of rising crashed head-on into the left wing of Mr. Harmon's biplane." There was a smash, a tearing sound, a splintering, followed by a torrent of profanities. When the *Globe* reporter reached the accident site, he found Moisant "looking like a man who wanted to fight somebody."

The aviator clambered out and inspected his machine. The left wing was smashed, there were two cracks in the tail, and as much was left of the propeller as there had been of Le Blanc's after his meeting with the telegraph pole. The mechanics quickly identified the cause of the collision as a rudder malfunction, but Moisant blamed his misfortune on Harmon for having left his machine unattended on the grass. What are you going to do? asked the *Globe* correspondent. Moisant shrugged dejectedly. "It will cost me about two thousand dollars to fix that machine," he replied, adding that it would be impossible to repair it in time for the afternoon's race.

People had been gathering at various points along the Statue of Liberty route since noon, and by two forty-five P.M. "fully one million persons in all the neighborhoods of the city" were waiting in hope of seeing an airplane. By three o'clock hardly a space was to be had in Brooklyn; there were crowds on the elevated railroad station at Thirty-sixth Street; huge numbers of people were picnicking in Prospect Park, field glasses close at hand among the sandwiches and cakes. Younger, more athletic aviation enthusiasts had secured vantage points atop the Soldiers' and Sailors' Monument at Park Plaza, and chaos reigned in Highland Park, where police were trying to control the excited masses.

Similar scenes occurred in Queens, Jamaica, and Manhattan as the temperature hovered around 45 degrees Fahrenheit. Families were grouped on the walkways of bridges, on the tops of buildings, on the decks of boats. A reporter from the *World* joined the throng at the Battery. How many were there? He wasn't sure, but he guessed around fifteen thousand, though they continued to arrive throughout the afternoon. They came, he wrote, "in automobiles and crested carriages as well as afoot and on street cars . . . from the Aquarium to the Barge Office, high-hatted men and women in rich furs mingled with the habitués of the park in a crowd that extended from the chains along the water's edge to the beaches along the grass." Five thousand people had made the journey from the Battery to the statue on Bedloe's Island, according to the *New York Herald*, and "it was a restless crowd, filled with pleasurable anticipation." A great many had squeezed onto the topmost level of the statue's base, while the more energetic had climbed the spiral staircase inside the statue up to her head. Some carried field glasses, one or two telescopes, a young boy clutched a "bit of a windowpane he had smoked himself," and a group of young women were equipped with opera glasses.

By three P.M. everyone on Bedloe's Island was "turned constantly to the east, from which direction all knew the men of the air must come. The air was clear, the skies bright, the sun gleaming and wind so gentle that the flags of the craft that studded the bay, many of them at anchor, rose and fell listlessly."

Count Jacques de Lesseps and Claude Grahame-White shook hands and returned to their hangars to make their final preparations for their flights to the Statue of Liberty. The Frenchman embraced his sister, then his brother, and at five minutes past three he set off. He circled the ground once, and a second time, then began to climb higher. The spectators in Belmont Park watched him fly west and pondered his route. In the opinion of the *Boston Daily Globe* reporter, he appeared to be "headed straight for the tower of the Singer Building on the lower end of Manhattan Island . . . in a general direction along the Long Island railroad."

Three minutes later Grahame-White was in the air and "was seen to head fully four points of the compass more to the south." Those spectators high up at the back of the grandstand watched him through their field glasses and told each other confidently he was going away from Brooklyn toward Coney Island. For several minutes seventy-five thousand people stood with their hands over their eyes watching as "the broad wings dwindled into mere patches, then grew smaller and smaller until only the keenest eye could follow and hold them in sight, and then they disappeared." Now all the crowd could do was wait, and hope, like members of an arctic party left behind at base as their colleagues struck out for the pole.

De Lesseps was flying toward the yellow captive balloon that he could clearly see silhouetted against a golden sky just near the Statue. He was at two thousand feet and already feeling the cold through his blue jean overalls. Down below on the streets of Brooklyn people gazed up through their field glasses and read the number on the underside of the monoplane's left wing. "Number Six," they cried, and began flicking through their newspapers to the list, which identified it as "Count de Lesseps." They resumed their stare, then suddenly they saw the machine fall.

At the controls of his Blériot the Frenchman was unsure what had happened. Everything had been fine, then all at once his world went black. He felt something running down his face—for an awful moment he thought it was blood, until he tasted the oil in his mouth. Wiping his goggles with his gloves, de Lesseps saw that a joint of his oil-feed pipe had ruptured, and oil was spurting over him like blood from a severed artery. He pulled out of the dive at fifteen hundred feet and maintained a steady altitude. For a few minutes he flew with one hand on the wheel and the other clamped over the broken pipe, but as he neared the Statue, he knew he would need both hands on the controls. He released his grip on the pipe and hoped for the best.

A reporter from the *New York Sun* was in Chinatown when de Lesseps appeared overhead a little before three thirty P.M., and he described the bedlam that ensued as the Chinese poured into the streets in bewilderment. "Some of the men waved their arms in the air and threw back their heads so far that they retained their balance with difficulty. Others rushed to their houses and up the stairs, chattering in what appeared to be terror. Still others raced from one side of a street to the other, gesticulating and trying to tell all within hearing of the great wonder."

The wide-eyed incredulity was just as great on board the battleships *Connecticut* and *North Dakota*, both of which were in the Navy Yard preparing to sail for Europe. Sailors clattered into one another as they ran across the deck looking up in frenzied excitement. Lieutenant Commander Jones, the flag secretary of the fleet, admitted to being "simply fascinated" as he and his fellow officers trailed the two airplanes with their field glasses, telescopes, and even their range finders.

Inside the Statue of Liberty the reporter from the *New York Herald* observed the progress of the machine that had materialized from the south, having soared along the coastline over Coney Island, Benson-hurst, and Bath Beach. As it got closer, the journalist made out a 10 on the underside of the left wing—Grahame-White's number—then the airplane vanished from sight, circling around the statue before heading back the way it had come, "like an eagle to its nest."

De Lesseps followed a couple of minutes later, and everyone within the statue—from the boy with the smoked glass to the girls with the opera glasses—tracked the airplane as it returned "over the housetops of Columbia Heights in Brooklyn, passing a towering church spire here and there, and from a speck in the sky faded into nothingness in the distance."

The moment that the two machines had circled the balloon, the wireless operator on Bedloe's Island telegraphed the news to the *New York Herald*'s offices in Manhattan, which relayed the message by telephone to the newspaper's aviation correspondent sitting in the judges' box at Belmont Park, who opened the door and passed it on to Peter Prunty, the final link in the chain. He picked up the megaphone and announced that de Lesseps and Grahame-White had both successfully completed the first leg of the race. A mighty cheer went up, said the *Boston Globe* reporter, but still "nobody was quite prepared for it when a man looked up over the edge of the grandstand and shouted, 'There he is! Somebody's coming back!'" It was Grahame-White, buzzing homeward at a terrific rate. He touched down in a total time of thirty-five minutes and twenty-one seconds, and de Lesseps followed in a time six minutes slower. Belmont Park became a maelstrom of hats, newspapers, programs, and champagne corks as the crowd celebrated the historic achievement. For the first time in aviation a race had been held over a city; what's more, without mishap, and once again Grahame-White had demonstrated the superiority of the airplane over all other forms of aeronautics in covering the distance in more than a mile a minute. Grahame-White and de Lesseps shook hands, the latter's blue overalls soaked black with oil.

They were collected by a tournament automobile and driven toward the grandstand as Peter Prunty bawled into the megaphone, "He might be an Englishman, but you've got to hand it to him!" The band of the Seventh Regiment began to play "God Save the King," and Grahame-White was called upon to make a speech. He looked almost bashful as he stood on the steps of the judges' box "in his brown aviation suit, grasping in his hand the famous to-be-worn-backward cap that has gone through all his flights in this country." Grahame-White declined to make a speech, but motioned for de Lesseps to join him, and as the two stood side by side, the band struck up the "Marseillaise," and soon the feet of the great crowd banged to the beat of the anthem. The acclaim of the spectators was still ringing in Grahame-White's ears a couple of minutes later, at six minutes past four, when he heard another noise, the sound of a Blériot motor. He watched the plane take off and turn west, toward the Statue of Liberty. Its number wasn't clear—it looked as if it had been painted over another— but it appeared to be 21, John Moisant's.

Not long after Moisant had crashed into the parked biplane of Clifford Harmon, his brother Alfred appeared. He was a little taller, a little older, and a little darker than John, and around his neck he liked to wear "a gold nugget as big as an egg and a long string of gold nuggets as big as filberts for a watch chain." First he checked his brother was all right, then he told him he would get him another plane. Alfred ran down hangar row to No. 8, Le Blanc's shed. Inside were the twisted remnants of his machine, and another Blériot monoplane, a fifty-horsepower model that was about to be disassembled, crated, and shipped back to France. "I am now the own-er of that machine," Alfred advised Le Blanc's mechanics in perfect French. "Put it together as fast as you can and there'll be extra dollars in it for you."

Then he demanded to see Le Blanc. The mechanics shook their heads and told him their boss was back at the Knickerbocker Hotel, sulking. The two Moisants drove to the clubhouse, and from there they put through a call to the Frenchman at his hotel. "I want to buy your craft," Alfred barked down the receiver. Le Blanc might have taken a nasty bang on his head twenty-four hours earlier, but he'd lost none of his faculties. "It will cost you ten thousand dollars," he said of a machine whose true worth was about $2,000. Moisant could feel a "but" coming. "But you know," added the Frenchman, "it was admitted without duty [into Amer-ica] merely for exhibition purposes. If you want to keep it in this country, you'll have to pay the duty. That's five thousand dollars more."

You've got yourself a deal, Moisant told him. Now it was his turn to pull the strings. "Be so good as to come to Belmont Park and assist in fixing up the machine," he said to Le Blanc, "and I'll have a check waiting you—and a bonus, too, if we win."

Le Blanc arrived at three thirty P.M., his head still swathed in bandages. First he inspected, then pocketed, his check for $15,000, then he gave Moisant a crash course in flying his Blériot. Moisant didn't require much tuition; after all, he'd flown across the Channel in a similar model, and all he had to do was "adjust the levers to his own size and height or learn the peculiarities which are a part of every machine."

He was still going through his final preparations as Grahame-White and de Lesseps returned. Making a note of the time he had to beat, Moisant set his compass at his feet and shouted out to the mechanics, "Roll her out, boys!" The *New York Herald*'s reporter watched as Moisant signaled he was ready. He turned and shouted good-bye to his brother and his two sisters, both of whom ran alongside the airplane for a few yards. Then they stopped, linked arms, and watched as their brother's Blériot "rolled only twenty yards and then almost stood on its tail as it swept straight into the air."

The *New York Herald* reporter was still on the grass when Moisant was spotted "high in the air and coming like a shooting star" out of the red sun. The newsman glanced at his watch—four thirty-five P.M. The American aviator had been out for twenty-nine minutes. Near the reporter a group of men, more used to cheering on racehorses, began to work their hands like whips, growling, "Come on, you, Moisant, oh, come on now, boy!" A woman was crying in excitement and her "lace handkerchief was being ripped into strips by her nervous fingers." Outside the Moisant hangar, his mechanics were pumping their fists, screaming, "Go on, John!" and the aviators' two sisters "were running around in circles, looking over the shoulders of those who held stop watches." One of the timers yelled, "He's got two minutes to beat Grahame-White!" and the sisters implored their brother, "Hurry up."

A lavender mist was beginning to roll across the course as the Blériot got closer and closer. Two men tipped a barrel of gasoline onto the grass and set it aflame. In the judges' box the reporter from the *World* noticed that the "hands of the men holding stopwatches began to shake. They were reading the signs from the little gold encased dials of the possibility of an American victory."

Grahame-White was with Eleonora Sears outside his hangar, his face impassive under his back-to-front cap, as he drew on a cigarette. He said nothing as he watched Moisant descend in a spectacular swoop. The American crossed the line, and then, for what seemed like an eternity, the scoreboard remained a mute witness to all the drama. Then the numbers flashed up, beacons in the gloom: ELAPSED TIME: 34 MINUTES, 38 SECONDS. A barely coherent Peter Prunty roared out the result: "John Moisant wins by forty-three seconds," and suddenly the grandstand "seemed filled with mad people, who tossed their arms about each other and shouted the name of Moisant again and again."

"It isn't true," stammered Eleonora Sears, "it can't be true! The figures are not official." In the Wright hangar the brothers were showing a couple of reporters the wreck of the Baby Grand when they heard the announcement. The correspondent from the *New York Telegram* got the fright of his life as Wilbur "gave a yell like a Comanche Indian, jumping at least three feet from the ground and waving his hands in the air. Then he recovered his composure somewhat and, smiling at the reporters, said, 'That's my opinion, boys!' "

A couple of hundred yards away Alfred Moisant was equally euphoric, dancing a jig with a mechanic, while his two sisters hugged anyone and everyone. Then the three of them started to run across the grass toward their brother, who had been hoisted out of his machine, stiff with cold, red and raw, but beaming from ear to ear. As the triumphant aviator was brought back in an automobile, "the crowd made a rush toward him that nearly swept the official timing house from its moorings."

For many minutes Moisant stood in front of the multitude "with his brown eyes dancing and his white teeth flashing in happiness . . . [and] he bowed and bowed and kindly showed his own great pleasure in his triumph." Pinkerton security men battled with spectators as a great chant of "Moisant, Moisant" resounded around Belmont Park. Only a concerted counterattack by the guards cleared a path from the judges' box to the clubhouse, so that Moisant could be carried inside on the shoulders of two race officials, an American flag draped over his shoulders and the band playing yet another rendition of "Yankee Doodle Dandy." After a hot drink to thaw the frozen marrow of his bones, Moisant was reunited with his family and eventually driven back to his hangar.

The *New York Herald* reporter was getting the story of the flight when a knock came on the hangar door and Grahame-White appeared. He entered with a smile and a handshake. "Really very well done, old chap," he said without a trace of malice. "Accept congratulations." The two men shook hands, but before Moisant could say anything, Grahame-White looked down at his adversary and added, "But I'm going out after the statue prize again tomorrow, and I'll surely beat you." The Englishman turned on his heel and left, leaving Moisant a "rankled soul." "How can he beat me when I have already won the prize?" he spluttered to the *Herald* reporter. The newsman chased after Grahame-White to find out. "Are you going to attempt the flight again tomorrow?" the reporter demanded. The Englishman laughed. "You bet! I'll not lay down under a beating like that. If I did, I'd be a Dutchman." Then he reminded the reporter of the rules, or at least the new rules, as promulgated in the bulletin issued by the committee three days earlier: the race was open to any flier for the duration of the tournament, and because of last Sunday's inclement weather, the tournament had been extended for a day, which meant he had until Monday evening. Oh, and another thing, added Grahame-White, nothing in the rules allowed only one attempt. A flier could try for the prize as many times as he liked, and that's what he intended to do.

CHAPTER SEVENTEEN

My Disgust at This Betrayal

Monday, October 31, 1910

THE STAFF OF THE PLAZA HOTEL at the corner of Fifth Avenue and Central Park South had been busy all day, decorating the gold-trimmed ballroom so that the evening's guests would feel at home. It hadn't been easy—with one or two tumbles from chairs and the odd wobbling ladder—but it was done, and the magnificence of the setting now took one's breath away. Hanging from the ceiling among the chandeliers was a replica of the *America II*, with Alan Hawley and Augustus Post visible in the basket, as well as a model of Walter Wellman's airship, *America*, almost as inert as the real thing had been. Around the two cumbersome shapes swarmed a flock of model monoplanes and biplanes, suspended by invisible strands, diving and climbing and swooping.

The flags of America, Britain, France, Switzerland, and Germany festooned the walls and the balcony; the International Aviation Cup and the International Balloon Cup were on prominent display, along with two or three other aeronautic cups; and on the menu cards—written in French, and including such delights as *foie gras, filet de boeuf*, and *mousse aux marrons glacés*—were caricatures of every aviator who had taken part in the Belmont Park tournament.

The guests began to arrive a few minutes before seven thirty P.M., each in evening wear with the heels of their polished leather shoes clicking as they walked across the Plaza's marble-floored lobby toward the ballroom. They were welcomed by a member of the Aero Club of America and offered a glass of Moët & Chandon champagne—Imperial Crown Brut.

Walter Wellman came from the Waldorf-Astoria Hotel, looking none the worse after his recent adventure on the high seas. He shook hands with the Belmont Park committee and recognized one or two faces among those already present. Walther de Mumm was in animated conversation with Alfred Le Blanc and Jacques Faure, perhaps discussing the quality of the champagne, while Samuel Perkins and Arch Hoxsey were admiring the decorations. A trio of German balloonists—Hugo Von Abercron, August Blanckertz, and Leopold Vogt—were comparing notes on their experiences. Wellman knew James Radley and Alec Ogilvie only from their photographs in the newspapers, and the same for René Simon and Roland Garros, the French aviators. Wellman spotted Alan Hawley and Augustus Post, and went over to offer his congratulations; the pair thanked him and inquired after his health. At eight P.M. Cortlandt Bishop, president of the Aero Club of America, asked the guests to take their seats for dinner.

As guests of honor, the winning balloonists were steered toward the top table. Post sat on the flank but Hawley was in the center, between Bishop and General Nelson Miles.

Also present were August Belmont, Colonel Theodore Schaeck—the Swiss balloonist—and John Moisant. Between Schaeck and Augustus Post, however, there was a gap, a hole, what appeared to be a vacant seat. Post could see the name on the place setting: CLAUDE GRAHAME-WHITE. He looked around the ballroom and saw other empty chairs among the three hundred guests. How many? One, two, three . . . at least a dozen. He began to search for faces. Where for instance was his good friend Clifford Harmon? And Armstrong Drexel? And what about Count de Lesseps and Hubert Latham? No Charles Hamilton, no Glenn Curtiss, no Charles Willard. What was going on?

August Belmont rose and thanked everyone for their attendance. He gave a small cough, said the reporter from the *New York Times*, and drew the guests' attention to the number of empty seats. Unfortunately, Belmont told his audience, "there had been so many accidents to the airplanes at the meet that many of the aviators who had to get away before tomorrow had been compelled to stay late at the field, but would come as soon as they possibly could."

By eight P.M. the party at Louis Sherry's restaurant on Fifth Avenue and Forty-fourth Street was in full swing. It was an intimate affair, thirteen in total, but the guests felt a kinship with one another that produced a conversation rich in laughter. Armstrong Drexel was the host, sitting between his brother, Anthony, and Claude Grahame-White. Farther down the table the de Lesseps brothers, Jacques and Bertrand, had a joke translated into French by Hubert Latham, while Charles Hamilton was wreathed in cigarette smoke. Sydney McDonald waved his empty crystal glass and called for more wine, and Charles Willard tried to suppress a giggle as Clifford Harmon retold the story of how John Moisant had come to grief outside his hangar.

As they ate and drank and smoked against a backdrop of tapestries and oil paintings, the men talked over the day's events. Grahame-White had his leg pulled for his crash, though he cared not a jot. He'd still won the Grand Speed Contest, pocketing another $3,000, and he'd come out on top in the Hourly Distance event, his aggregate total of 106 laps over the tournament being six more than . . . whose? He winked and raised his glass in the direction of a laughing Hubert Latham. But the highlight of the day, they all agreed, had been Ralph Johnstone's new record in the Grand Altitude event. What was it again? 9,714 feet. Incredible. He'd smashed the world's record by over five hundred feet; if only he'd managed another 286 feet, he would have won the Aero Club's special prize of $5,000 for the first aviator to break the ten-thousand-feet barrier.

But perhaps that had been Johnstone's greatest achievement, the triumph of his self-preservation over his pride. Who knew, if he'd pushed for those extra 286 feet, might not he have gone the way of Icarus? And don't forget, they told one another, Johnstone had been in a "hysterical" state when he'd landed after his record-breaking ordeal.

As the men refilled their glasses and selected Cuban cigars from the box brought out by the waiter, they kept their eye on the time. At nine thirty P.M. Armstrong Drexel called for the bill. Time to go, gentlemen, he said, the Plaza Hotel awaits.

In between mouthfuls of *filet de boeuf*, John Moisant described to General Miles and Walter Wellman his thirty-six-mile flight round the Statue of Liberty. They had read his account in Monday's edition of the *World*, in which he'd told of how, time and again, he was caught in air currents as he flew over Manhattan, and how, yes, it was true, as he'd rounded the Statue of Liberty, it had occurred to him how appropriate it was that he should be doing so as an American in a French machine, seeing as how the statue had been a gift from France. Of the row with Grahame-White, there was no mention.

Minutes after the *New York Herald* reporter had run back to Moisant's hangar on Sunday evening to confirm that Grahame-White intended to make a second attempt to round the statue, the American began drafting a frantic letter to the Belmont Park committee. He started by saying that the race "called for the fastest flight from Belmont Park to and around the Statue of Liberty and return to aviation field, during the present international meet, dates for which are from October 22 to 30, and officially the meet closed tonight." He then wrote that he had received no official confirmation that the meet would be open on Monday, and in his opinion "if the prize is put up again tomorrow on the ground that the meet has been continued, it might as well be put up for six months more or a year or continued indefinitely."

Moisant took a fresh sheet of paper and began a second letter, this one an official protest against Clifford Harmon and Claude Grahame-White. He accused them of negligence in having left the Farman biplane on the grass, pointing out that "under all the rules of international meets sanctioned by the International Aeronautic Federation, a damaged or crippled machine or one which is being repaired, must be removed to its hangar." This rule had been broken, he concluded, and he trusted the committee would concur.

Moisant hand-delivered the letters to the clubhouse, and the committee sat long into Sunday night discussing the matter. Outside, meanwhile, a handful of reporters waited to hear their decision, among them the *New York Times* correspondent. While he and his colleagues agreed with Moisant that it would be "manifestly unfair for a competitor to receive a second chance," nonetheless they—unlike Moisant—were fully aware that "it had been announced on Saturday that attempts to fly around the Statue might be made on Sunday or Monday."

Eventually J. C. McCoy emerged from the clubhouse and, in the light of the winking lanterns hanging on either side of the door, addressed the newsmen: "The committee announces that the meeting officially ended at the close of flying hours on Sunday, October 30, 1910, as provided in the entry blanks of the program and that the events of this day [Monday, October 31, 1910] are special competitions, distinct from the events of the meeting."

Grahame-White had first heard of the committee's decision early on Monday morning when he arrived at Belmont Park to prepare for his second attempt. Count de Lesseps was also planning another crack at the "Goddess," and James Radley and Emile Aubrun were considering their options. As was his habit, Grahame-White checked the bulletin board and saw the communiqué issued just a few hours earlier. By the time he had finished reading it, his suave sangfroid had melted in a furnace of rage, and Sydney McDonald was doing his best to calm him. A reporter from the *New York Evening Sun* appeared and bore the brunt of the Englishman's fury. "It's a bally injustice, sir," he cried, "that the committee declared the flight at an end after Moisant, an American, had won it last night." It's funny, isn't it, he sneered, that the "committee in excusing its actions in closing the Statue competition said that today's events are not regular on the program. Yet I notice that the grand speed and grand altitude contests will be decided." What will you do, asked the reporter, lodge an appeal? Grahame-White shook his head. Beating Le Blanc was one thing, trying to defeat the Belmont Park committee was as futile as trying to cross the Atlantic in an airship. "What's the use of making protests?" he replied. "They ignore them . . . It's been a succession of injustices and downright unfair treatment for me at Belmont Park, and, you know, I'm dreadful sick of it. Really, they're almost a bunch of bally bandits."

Later on Monday morning Grahame-White had issued a challenge to Moisant to race him around the Statue of Liberty, but the American laughed at the proposal. He knew that second time around Grahame-White would fly the direct route, over Manhattan, and in his hundred-horsepower Blériot he would win with ease. Moisant retaliated by telling reporters he would race Grahame-White "anywhere, at any time, under any circumstance, on equal terms," but in the meantime the Englishman should quit being such "a poor loser."

Shortly before ten P.M. toastmaster Cortlandt Bishop rose to his feet and invited August Belmont to say a few words. The host of the tournament praised the aviators—those present—and reminded them that they were much more than mere entertainers, "for their flights were being watched with much interest by officers of the army and navy, and one day they might be asked to risk their lives for their country, which would be a greater honor than the one they had already attained." After Belmont finished, Bishop introduced to the company Messrs. Hawley and Post, "the men who only a few days ago, after leaving St. Louis, were wandering in the bleak Canadian wilds while two nations were anxiously trying every means for clues of their fate." Bishop presented each man with the gold medal of the Aero Club of America and then, "to ringing applause" he handed over the International Balloon Cup.

Glasses were raised as Bishop presented a gold loving cup to Alfred Le Blanc (whose bandages had been removed save for a square Band-Aid plaster above his right eye) in recognition of his splendid performance in Saturday's international race, then John Moisant was asked to take a bow. "He got the most enthusiastic reception of the whole evening," said the correspondent from the *New York Times*, who listened rapt as Moisant described his trip across the English Channel in August. "He refused, however, to talk about his victory around the Statue of Liberty."

Bishop then called upon Nelson Miles "to say something about the uses that might be made of aviation in war." The general got to his feet and began to talk of the airplane's importance, not just in times of conflict but also perhaps "as a harbinger of peace." As he spoke, a slight commotion came from the back of the ballroom, and in walked Armstrong Drexel, Grahame-White, Hamilton, de Lesseps . . . the whole merry gang of malcontents.

Not long after the three hundred guests had sat down to dinner in the Plaza's splendid ballroom, word began to spread that the real reason for the empty seats was a rival dinner being hosted by Armstrong Drexel at Sherry's restaurant, "which was something of a protest meeting." The aviators present knew all about Drexel's revolt, having been invited to join it themselves, and over the starter of *pomme caprice*, they enlightened their fellow guests as to the reasons behind the uprising.

Earlier in the afternoon Drexel had stormed into the clubhouse at Belmont Park and told Cortlandt Bishop that he no longer wished to be a member of the Aero Club of America. His letter of resignation followed, and he then wired the editors of several leading newspapers in America, Britain, and France to explain his decision. While Bishop wrung his hands in fury at the contents of the letter, the editors rubbed their hands in glee as they read the telegrams. No need to worry how to fill the next day's front page.

Dear Sir

I wish through your columns to protest against the action of the Belmont Park Aviation Committee in refusing to allow Grahame-White, the Englishman, to fly a second time for the Statue of Liberty Prize. Their doing so is contrary to all the traditions of sport and honor, and as an American myself, familiar with the conditions of sport in Europe, I cannot allow an act of such startling unfairness to pass without protest.

Furthermore, by their decision they have barred such fliers as Radley, the Englishman, and Aubrun, the Frenchman, from competing. As a general result it will be freely said in Europe that the Liberty prize was juggled into an American's hands. This will only be the plain truth, according to the conditions of the contest, as understood by the aviators.

I was myself told by Chairman McCoy of the committee in the presence of a witness, that the Liberty prize contest would be open to the end of the meeting, which as he and everyone else knew, was definitely intended to include Monday. He also gave me to understand that the same man could make more than one flight, and that the best time would win. This, too, was the general understanding of the aviators, and no denial of it by the committee can explain or excuse their subsequent action.

The plain fact is that the committee, seeing a chance of winning the prize for an American, went back upon their word, and by closing the contest and the official meeting, stopped two men, Messrs. de Lesseps and Grahame-White, from trying again, and the other fliers from even competing.

My disgust at this betrayal is more almost than I can express. What the feelings of the Englishmen and Frenchmen are could they be induced to speak their mind, I dare hardly imagine. Anyhow, it is my intention to resign immediately from the Aero Club of America, and I hope all American sportsmen will follow my example.

It will of course be understood that I write this letter with no personal bias either for or against Messrs. Moisant and Grahame-White.

I am, yours truly
J. Armstrong Drexel

Cortlandt Bishop's retaliation was swift. He likened Drexel and Grahame-White to grand opera singers, saying "they are jealous and very difficult to manage." However, he slyly added, perhaps this was inevitable as the pair's "nerves are on edge from their flights." As for Drexel's resignation, Bishop told reporters he was disappointed but not that surprised: "Mr. Drexel has lived much of his life abroad although he is a native born American. Perhaps that has something to do with it."

Having resigned from the Aero Club, Drexel then invited his fellow aviators to a soiree of his own at Sherry's, just a couple of blocks away from the Plaza. Count de Lesseps was in—he had already made an official protest of his own at the committee's volte-face—and Latham had also lodged a complaint, questioning the absence of official observers from the pylons in the latter stages of Moisant's flight in the International Aviation Cup race. For all he knew, Moisant might have cut a few corners in the gloom of Saturday evening. Hamilton, Harmon, and Willard accepted, but Glenn Curtiss and Eugene Ely opted for neutrality, which was also the stance of the Wrights. They attended neither dinner and left it up to their team to make their own choices. Walter Brookins was recovering from his injuries, Ralph Johnstone chose to spend the evening with his family, and Arch Hoxsey went to the official dinner, along with James Radley and Alec Ogilvie. British they might have been, but they considered it a breach of etiquette to snub one's host, whatever the reason.

As General Miles addressed the audience, the *New York Times* reporter slipped out of his seat and tiptoed across the ballroom toward Drexel. "Would you explain the reason for the dinner at Sherry's tonight?" he asked in a whisper. "The dinner," said Drexel, talking to the reporter's ear, "was a protest against the action of the committee with regard to Mr. Grahame-White and the Statue of Liberty race. I was exceedingly indignant at it, and I did not feel that I could bring myself to sit down with the other members of the Aero Committee at the official dinner."

When the general concluded his speech, J. A. Blair, one of the committee members, left his seat and welcomed the latecomers. Please, he told them, smiling, sit down. They did, all except Drexel, and Grahame-White "got a thoroughly cordial reception" as he took his place at the top table between Augustus Post and Theodore Schaeck. Cortlandt Bishop got to his feet, and, said the *New York Times* reporter, "a thrill ran through the audience" as he made the official presentation to Grahame-White of the International Aviation Cup, telling him, "In handing you this cup I also in the name of the Aero Club of America challenge you for it. We shall take profit by your example and shall work early and hard for it, and I hope that next year an American will bring it back again."

The pair shook hands and Grahame-White took delivery of the trophy, as well as a check for $13,600—his tournament winnings. He admired the trophy for a moment, in the way he liked to admire himself in the mirror each morning, then placed it carefully on the table. He was in his element now, the center of attention, with three hundred people on tenterhooks waiting to discover if he would turn on the men he had earlier described as "bandits." But Grahame-White was far too much of an English gentleman to give in to his emotion.

He was humble in his gratitude for the victory, but, he wondered, what might have happened had it not been for the "lamentable disaster" that befell Walter Brookins? Then he turned to Alfred Le Blanc and told the audience with fulsome modesty that the Frenchman was "an aviator of far greater experience than I am and has qualities as an aviator which I cannot claim. His ability is far superior to mine."

Next Grahame-White gestured toward two of his fellow companions at the top table, Augustus Post and Alan Hawley. You know, he said, with a sheepish grin, "We aviators are sometimes prone to look down on balloonists, but in view of the performance which recently startled the whole world, our hearts went out to Messrs. Hawley and Post, and we realized that these pilots of balloons cannot be looked down on, for they showed themselves men of courage and audacity, and their sporting and daring attempt which broke all records was a very, very, very fine feat."

The *New York Times* reporter joined in the applause, then listened as Grahame-White brought the speeches to a close by "extending an invitation to all the aviators present to come to England next year for the international meet and he promised them a hearty welcome."

We're Sending Sputniks to the Moon

THERE WAS INDEED a "hearty welcome" for all those who came to Eastchurch, in southeast England, in July 1911 to compete for the International Aviation Cup. But Claude Grahame-White wasn't there to greet them, and nor were most of the aviators who had thrilled the fans at Belmont Park the previous year. Cortlandt Bishop was present and threw a Stars and Stripes around the shoulders of Charles Weymann when he won the cup back for the United States. In second place was Alfred Le Blanc, beaten again, this time by influenza, or at least that was his excuse.

On November 1, 1910, the morning after the acrimonious dinner at the Plaza Hotel, the *New York Herald* used its editorial to reflect on the Belmont Park tournament. Of course, it said, "It is to be regretted that a misunderstanding arose just at the close but that such things were to be expected when men are engaged in eager competition." Of greater pertinence was the significance of the meet, and the *Herald* concluded, "Whatever may be the merits of the controversy, it cannot change the fact that the international aviation tournament this year was the greatest ever held and nothing can detract from the wonderful results or from the powerful stimulus it will give to the development of the art that is to play such a wonderful part in the world's future." The next day, November 2, the *New York Evening Sun* reported that as a result of the recent aviation tournaments in Europe and the United States, the German War Office had ordered airplanes of five different types, including the Wright bi-planes, and "elaborate tests are to be made of these machines and then it is said that the Government will make extensive purchases for the army."

In addition, Britain and France were equipping themselves with fly-ing machines, so it was therefore with no little relief, continued the *Evening Sun*, that General James Allen, fresh from Belmont Park, "rec-ommends the purchase of at least twenty airplanes to be used in regular practice at different parts of the country during the year." These would complement the current American aerial strength of one dirigible and two aircraft.

Less than a fortnight later, General Allen was one of the guests on board the cruiser *Birmingham*, anchored five miles off the Virginian coast, as Eugene Ely took off from the deck and successfully completed the first ship-to-shore flight. In doing so, proclaimed the *Chicago Daily Tribune*, Ely "proved that the airplane will be a great factor in naval war-fare of the future."

Before the year was out, the first successful message had been sent from an airplane to a wireless station midflight, and Phil Parmalee had demonstrated the commercial capabilities of the airplane by transporting a consignment of silk from Dayton, Ohio, to a dry-goods firm in Colum-bus, only sixty-five miles but the first air-freight flight. Also the United States Aeronautical Reserve, established on September 10, 1910, had ex-panded at a prodigious rate, boasting among its members not just military men but "financiers, sportsmen and hundreds of others interested in aero-nautics, from President Taft down to the humblest airplane mechanic."

In an end-of-year article for *Fly* magazine, Glenn Curtiss described 1910 as "a year of triumphant progress," and Louis Blériot enthused that "the airplane as it exists today really stands upon the threshold of the most amazing, sporting and commercial possibilities . . . There is ab-solutely nothing to prevent flight becoming one of the greatest develop-ments in the world's history."

Fly's rival publication, *Aero*, joined in the applause in its editorial of

December 31, 1910: "Perhaps when years pass and the airplane is accepted universally upon its superior merits, when it is admittedly the
King of Transit; when the sight of the flying machine is no rarer than
that of its gasoline motored cousin on the ground; then, let us hope,
some altruistic pioneers will look backwards, remember 1910, and erect
a giant pylon of marble in the memory of the year when aviation came
into its own. Good old 1910!"

The Wright exhibition team traveled to Denver in mid-November 1910
to put on a show. Flying at five thousand feet above sea level was a new
experience for Ralph Johnstone and Arch Hoxsey, but they dazzled the
huge crowds with stunts over the foothills of the Rockies. Walter
Brookins joined in, too, in his first public appearance since his Belmont
Park smash. The morning demonstration on November 17 had been
rapturously received, and in the afternoon the trio were up again,
Brookins and Hoxsey performing a series of death-defying stunts close
to the ground while Johnstone climbed to one thousand feet to demonstrate one of his legendary spiral glides. "He swooped down in a narrow
circle," wrote a reporter from the *Chicago Daily Tribune*, "the airplane
seeming to turn almost in its own length. As he started the second circle,
the middle spur which braced the left side of the lower plane, gave way
and the wing tips of both upper and lower planes folded up as if they had
been hinged."

 Shrieks came from the stands as the biplane started to hurtle toward
the ground. Johnstone was pitched forward out of his seat, but his body
caught on the wires between the planes. His cap flew off and fell from the
sky. One of the aviator's flailing arms grasped a wooden brace, and as
his legs dangled nine hundred feet above the Denver earth, with extraordinary strength and dexterity he pulled himself up so he was standing
between the two planes. The crowd wasn't sure if it was Johnstone's latest trick, but the reporter from the *Tribune* had attended enough aviation
meets to know this was no stunt. He looked up as Johnstone tried to ma-
nipulate the two planes with his hands and feet. For a second the reporter
thought he'd succeeded—perhaps so did Johnstone—"but the hope was
momentary, however, for when about 800 feet from the ground the machine turned completely over and the spectators fled wildly for safety as

the broken airplane, with the aviator still fighting grimly in its mesh of wires and stays, plunged among them with a crash."*

Johnstone lay under his engine, which was enveloped by the white canvas wings, a shroud for the dead aviator. The hordes that had been fleeing paused, turned, then ran toward the wreck. "Frantic for souvenirs," wrote the *Tribune*'s correspondent, "the spoilers quarreled and pulled and tugged among themselves even for the possession of the gloves that had protected Johnstone's hands. These had been torn from his hands by the first of the mob, but even more heartless was the action of one man, who, cheated of any other booty, tore a splinter of the machine from Johnstone's body and ran from the scene, bearing his trophy with the aviator's blood still dripping from its ends."

Brookins and Hoxsey had seen the whole incident, every terrifying, desperate second. Hoxsey was led away from the broken body of his friend, murmuring the same words over and over: "Poor Ralph, poor Ralph."†

In the days following the Belmont Park Meet, John Moisant became the idol of America. The tournament had enriched him to the tune of $13,550 (although the $10,000 for the Statue of Liberty race had been held back while Grahame-White's appeal was taken to the International Aviation Federation), and not a day passed without his appearance in a newspaper or magazine. His life story was told in comic strips, and he became a favorite subject for feature writers. Kate Carew salivated over

---

* A fortnight after the crash Wilbur Wright told reporters Johnstone's death was caused by a "weak wing," and in the opinion of some historians, this accident, so soon after Brookins's crash at Belmont Park, confirmed that "high noon had come and gone in the careers of the Wright brothers," partly because they channeled so much of their energy into lawsuits, they neglected the developmental side of their business. They dissolved their exhibition team in 1911, and the following year Wilbur died of typhoid, aged forty-five. Orville died in 1948, aged seventy-six.

† In September 1911 Johnstone's widow began flying lessons, telling newspapers that her husband had left little money and she needed to "clothe, feed and educate" her son, and she intended to do so by becoming one of the world's first female aviators. However, this ambitious idea came to naught. In 1920 Ralph junior was found shot dead in Florida; local police said it was suicide, but after a four-year campaign by Mrs. Johnstone, a man was convicted of her son's murder.

him in a piece for the *New York American* on November 6: "His head is
round and shapely. His face tapers from the cheekbones to a square chin,
chiseled as if by a sculptor. His mouth is large, full-lipped and very
widely arched—a bold, Roman mouth to match the dark, imperturbable
eyes. You'd look at him twice, dears, I know you would." In short, who
needed Claude Grahame-White?

Moisant capitalized on his fame by forming the Moisant International
Aviators, combining his flying skills with his brother Alfred's finances.
In the long term Moisant planned to open an aircraft factory and manufacture dozens of his aluminum airplanes, but for the rest of 1910 he and
his troupe of aviators—including Roland Garros, René Simon, and Edmond Audemars—toured America thrilling their legions of fans.

In late December they were performing in New Orleans, and John
Moisant had his eyes on a $4,000 prize tabled by the French tire manu-
facturer André Michelin, for the longest sustained flight of the year.
Some of his team, however, were becoming ever more concerned with
Moisant's daredevilry; earlier in the month he'd glided down from nine
thousand feet after suffering a frozen carburetor while trying for the
world altitude record. One of his business managers, Albert Levino, advised him to be more prudent, but Moisant brushed him off, saying,
"There's no danger in making an airplane flight if the machine is properly adjusted before the ascent is made." Don't worry, he told Levino, "I
don't expect to die in an airplane flight."

Moisant woke early on the morning of Saturday, December 31, in more
of a frenzy of activity than usual. He had only a few hours before the window closed on Michelin's prize. He took off at nine fifty-five A.M. from
City Park aviation field in New Orleans, said the correspondent from the
Indianapolis Star, "confident of winning the Michelin Cup record for 1910
as a final triumph to his year of achievement." The reporter was among a
sizable crowd that had already gathered to watch his attempt, and for the
first few minutes they were treated to some of Moisant's most daring stunts
as he warmed up his machine, including "his famous right circle . . . pro-
nounced the most daring feat ever attempted by an airman." They purred
with delight as Moisant swerved suddenly to the left, then the right—then
something went wrong. The machine got caught in one of the holes in the
air, and instead of making the famous right circle, it "pointed its nose di-

rectly at the ground and came down like a flash." The first people to reach the wreckage were a group of railroad laborers; they found Moisant lying in some long grass, without a bruise on his body, and with not the "slightest trace of fear or pain" on his face. His neck was broken and death had been instantaneous.

News of Moisant's death hadn't yet reached California as the passengers stepped off the Pacific Electric trains at the stop for Aviation Field. The sky was gray and overcast, with the same zephyr as there had been in January, when Louis Paulhan so enraptured the spectators. People skipped along the road in merry anticipation as the sounds of the revving motors grew louder. Whom were they looking forward to seeing most? The daring Frenchman Hubert Latham? Boyish but indestructible Walter Brookins? Eugene Ely? Charles Willard? No, they all wanted to see the hometown hero, Arch Hoxsey.

Five days earlier Hoxsey had climbed to 11,474 feet, a new world's record, and one he dedicated to his friend Ralph Johnstone, whose Belmont Park mark had been bettered by a Frenchman called Georges Legagneux in early December. Hoxsey had won back the record for the Stardust Twins, but he'd warned his rivals he'd raise the bar even higher before the year was out. His mother, Minnie, had seen him break the record, as she'd seen him on every day of the meet, but today being Saturday she had a few chores to do before she would be able to travel from her Pasadena home.

Hubert Latham was first in the air in his yellow-winged Antoinette, then James Radley took up his Blériot. Hoxsey was in his hangar making his final preparations for his flight when a friend appeared in the doorway. He was panting and held in his hand a newspaper. "It's an extra," he said between gasps. "Moisant's killed!" The friend told reporters later that Hoxsey took the news "almost listlessly" and said in a barely audible voice, "Poor fellow. He must have become tired out fighting the wind." Hoxsey's friend was alarmed by his reaction and tried to talk him out of flying that day, but the aviator shook his head and smiled. As his machine was trundled out of its hangar, Hoxsey turned to his friend and put a reassuring hand on his shoulder: "If it's after me, it'll get me any other place as well as here."

Walter Brookins stood in front of the press stand chatting to some reporters as Hoxsey's biplane rose into the air. Hard to credit, isn't it, he
said, that Arch was here in January as a spectator, and now eleven months
later he's the star turn.

They watched as Hoxsey began to ascend in his familiar long spirals,
and Brookins gave a running commentary on his friend's altitude. Guess
he's at five thousand feet now, six thousand feet, seven thousand feet.
Brookins turned to answer a question from a reporter, and as he did,
someone in the crowd let out a scream. "Brookins whirled round at the
sound of the cry," wrote the reporter from the *Colorado Springs Gazette*,
and as the biplane dropped from the sky, ". . . he uttered but one word,
'God,' his legs gave way and he fell into the roadway. Although he had
been in several serious accidents himself, he rose thoroughly unnerved
and cried like a child. At the time the field announcers were rushing up
and down, shouting through their megaphones: 'No cause for alarm.
Hoxsey is all right.' But Brookins was not convinced. 'That's a lie,' he
shouted back at one of the announcers. 'Hoxsey's dead. I know it.' And
again he burst into tears."

They wouldn't let Brookins near the crash site. Kind arms ushered him
away. Latham had been the first to reach Hoxsey, and Latham now sat in
his hangar, silent and white and trembling. The sight of Hoxsey impaled
on the wooden strut, his legs contorted under his body, the crushed rib
cage, the blood seeping from under the shattered goggles . . . Latham's
mind was seared with the image.

A squad of mounted police patrolled the field, driving away those
who wished to ransack Hoxsey's corpse the way the Denver crowd had
Johnstone's, while other spectators angrily demanded a refund when the
organizers canceled the rest of the day's events. Glenn Curtiss watched in
silence, then, turning to his mechanics, he said, "Tear down the bunting,
lower all the flags."

Reporters besieged the home of Minnie Hoxsey for the rest of the day,
hoping for a few words. They waited on the porch, well wrapped up against
that chill zephyr, and "every little while could be heard the suppressed
sounds of sobbing." Finally, when she had run out of tears, Mrs. Hoxsey
emerged from the gloom of her house. "I wish I had gone up with Arch,"

she said. "Then I would have died with him. All along I have been in dread he would someday meet with accident, but I rather he would have been killed outright than crippled for life. For, knowing my son as I did, I feel certain he would have lived a life of torment had he been compelled to have gone through life maimed and helpless." One of the reporters, greedy in his ghoulishness, wanted to know if she would be visiting the undertaking rooms to view her son's body. She stared long and hard into the reporter's eyes: "I shall not look on his dead form. I wish to remember him as he was—cheerful, loving, and smiling."*

Claude Grahame-White heard the news of the double tragedy from his hospital bed in Dover, where he had lain since December 18, after a horrific accident that shattered his leg and ankle, slashed open his temple, and reduced his airplane to "matchwood." In chasing a $20,000 prize for the longest nonstop flight from England to the European mainland, Grahame-White had crashed into a stone wall on takeoff. He was helped in his recuperation by the charming bedside manner of Pauline Chase, who had returned to England with him in early December. Miss Sears? A delightful young woman, he had told reporters quayside in New York, but she was just a good friend, at least as far as he was concerned. Marry Miss Chase? "Oh, dear, dear. Stop your spoofin'!" he'd said, laughing.

A Grahame-White quip, now that was a rarity in the weeks that had followed the Belmont Park kerfuffle, although admittedly there'd been precious little to smile about for the Englishman since that roistering good evening at Sherry's. He'd become Public Enemy Number One in the eyes of the American press, with the *Philadelphia Inquirer* accusing him of "mighty poor sportsmanship," the *New York Morning Telegram* labeling him "foolish, unsportsmanlike and grasping," and the *New York Town Topics* ridiculing him in a poem called "Discontent":

> Britons never shall be slaves
> Britain h'always ruled the air

---

* Arch Hoxsey's death was later attributed to heart failure, and it was assumed he was dead by the time his airplane hit the ground. His mother, who had received $50 a month from her son, was given an annuity by the Wrights.

> Blimey, and it ain't quite fair
> Why she shouldn't rule the air
> I've a challenge for the world
> Everywhere the same I've hurled
> Blast yer eyes, come get in line
> Guided by these rules of mine.

The hostility had eventually died down, but then, on the eve of his departure from New York, Grahame-White was informed that the Wrights had filed suit against him. He was summoned to appear before a circuit court judge on December 4 and told to bring with him details of his earnings in the three months he'd been in America. As for his airplanes, the port authorities in New York had been ordered to embargo them the moment he tried to ship them back to Europe. Grahame-White was livid and he impugned the Wrights' integrity to the papers because "they had promised they wouldn't make trouble." But he wasn't that surprised, he added, as "the Wrights are frightened. I've scared them so bloody well that they are terrified. I'm their most formidable competitor and they know it."

Grahame-White let it be known that if there was any trouble at New York, he'd contact his friend the British ambassador, in Washington, but behind the threats he moved with alacrity to outwit the Wrights; he sent his machines home on a freighter from Philadelphia, then booked his passage from New York at the very last minute. He left on board the *Mauretania*, not only with Pauline Chase, booked to play Peter Pan for another season, but with checks totaling $82,000 (approximately $1,312,000 today). That didn't include the $10,000 for the Statue of Liberty race, a sum he vowed to pursue with the same dogged endurance that he'd exhibited in winning the International Aviation Cup at Belmont Park.

The conquering hero was feted upon his return home. Photographs of Grahame-White posing with the International Aviation Cup adorned the London papers, and in one, the *Evening Times*, he hinted at skulduggery. Leaving aside the question of the Belmont Park organizers and their tinkering with race rules, the Englishman found it "unaccountable" that Moisant had beaten his time to the Statue of Liberty when he was flying a markedly inferior airplane to his own. "The same judges [who had changed the rules] acclaimed him the winner, and as having beaten my time by forty seconds. This in a thirty-five-mile flight is a narrow margin." The inference was clear: Grahame-White believed that the judges had knocked off a few minutes from Moisant's time so that their man would win.

A year later, in December 1911, Grahame-White returned to America, this time alone. He and Pauline Chase had drifted apart six months earlier, and while the aviator had remained tight-lipped on the subject, she was happy to inform reporters from her suite in London's Savoy Hotel that she had "concluded that Mr. Grahame-White could not compensate me from retirement from the stage."[*]

To Chase's evident dismay, Grahame-White had plowed most of his earnings from 1910 into forming the Grahame-White Aviation Company, and into establishing London's first aerodrome, at Hendon, on the northern outskirts of the city.

Given his many business commitments throughout 1911, Grahame-White had done precious little flying. One or two exhibitions here and there, but he'd been unable to find the time to participate in the International Aviation Cup race, and in the United States, the Wrights kept him grounded when he returned at the end of the year. Although a judge had thrown out one of the brothers' suits—the one that demanded a full accounting of Grahame-White's earnings in 1910—on the issue of the airplane patents the judge was waiting for a panel of experts to report back before delivering his verdict.[†]

Not that Grahame-White minded his aerial embargo when he arrived in New York in December. On the passage out from England he had got talking to a beautiful American socialite named Dorothy Taylor, and by the time they docked, they were in love. In between calling on old friends such as Armstrong Drexel, Clifford Harmon, and Eleonora

---

[*] Chase married into a wealthy British family in 1914, swapping the stage for the home and raising three children. She died in England in 1962 aged seventy-six.

[†] Not until January 1914 did the Wrights finally win their patent suit against all other aircraft manufacturers. However, companies such as Glenn Curtiss's exploited several legal loopholes without prosecution, and in 1917 (by which time Orville Wright had sold his company), when the USA entered World War I, the American aviation industry finally forgot its differences and began to work together.

Sears—with whom he attended a charity ball in Madison Square Garden*—Grahame-White wined and dined Miss Taylor and had his proposal of marriage accepted.

His spat with the American press had long since been forgotten—particularly since his appeal against Moisant's victory in the Statue of Liberty race had been successful†—and he happily consented to have lunch with Walter Brookins on December 30 as guests of the *World*. The venue, appropriately, was the Plaza Hotel, where fourteen months earlier he and Cortlandt Bishop had glared at each other over the International Aviation Cup. Brookins and Grahame-White had never been good friends, but a warm camaraderie prevailed between them as they shook hands like two old soldiers at a regimental reunion.

Brookins, like Drexel, no longer flew. Hoxsey's death had made him realize that Charles Hamilton was right when he'd said, "We'll all be killed if we stay in this business." As for news of other aviators, Brookins informed Grahame-White that Eugene Ely and Tod Shriver were dead, and Hamilton had suffered a nervous breakdown.

The purpose of the lunch was to hear the men's thoughts on the future of aviation, and the *World*'s reporter listened intently as the aviators chatted over their food, frequently pausing to smoke cigarettes "with the long drawn inhalation of the devotees." The question that the newspaper wanted them to answer above all others was, would transatlantic air journeys happen? "I would like to make a bet with anyone that in twenty years' time we will be flying across the Atlantic Ocean in fifteen hours," said Grahame-White, taking a sip from his wineglass. "Fifteen hours?" replied Brookins in what the newspaper described as a doubtful tone. "Yes," asserted Grahame-White, "and by that I mean also that it will be

---

* Sears never married but devoted her life to sporting attainments, winning nearly 250 trophies. As a tennis player she reached the third round of the Wimbledon tennis championships in 1923, and in 1928 she became the first women's squash champion. She died in 1968 aged eighty-seven.

† Grahame-White won his appeal on the grounds that the original rules had stated that every competitor must have flown for one continuous hour prior to entering, which neither Moisant nor de Lesseps had achieved. He collected the check for $10,000 (plus $334 interest) from President Taft at a dinner of the Aero Club of America in January 1912.

a regular service carrying passengers back and forth between London and New York. It will surely be done long before that time." Brookins remained skeptical, and later, over dessert, when Grahame-White began talking about airplanes traveling "175 miles or thereabouts an hour," Brookins "halted the flights of fancy with observations along strictly practical lines." Further good-natured disagreement occurred when the reporter steered the discussion toward aviation's role in any future war. Brookins considered the latest German Zeppelin dirigible a most "dreadful" weapon, but Grahame-White reckoned it would soon be rendered obsolete, adding that he was "so optimistic about the airplane in warfare that I fear my views do not agree with most people of today. In fact, I have made it a rule of late to avoid speaking about the uses of the airplane in warfare to avoid being laughed at. People don't realize the importance of this branch of the military service. It is enough to say that the airplane's field in military and naval work is unlimited."

"It's incredible," said the old man in a voice unscratched by the passage of time, "that here we are sending up sputniks to the moon, and yet the first airplane flight in Europe was as recent as 1906." The writer agreed, and in an unobsequious tone pointed out that much of the startling progress was down to men like him, Claude Grahame-White, and the other brave pioneers. Who was left now? he asked, and Grahame-White's memory traveled slowly back over the years. Not Armstrong Drexel, who had died a few months prior in March 1958, after a life abundant with achievement. A decorated war hero (the First World War, in which Grahame-White had flown bombers against German targets, and in which Roland Garros had distinguished himself as a fighter ace), Drexel had for many years been one of London's most successful bankers. Walter Brookins had passed away not that long ago, too, in 1953, but the rest were long dead.

Like Garros, Count Jacques de Lesseps had flown in the French air force during World War I, but unlike Garros, de Lesseps had survived, for a few years at least. In 1927 he'd vanished during a survey flight over the Gulf of St. Lawrence; his body was recovered some weeks later, so at least his wife—Grace McKenzie—and his two children had a body to mourn. René Simon and René Barrier had both died in flying accidents in the 1920s, but not Monsieur Le Blanc—dear old Alfred—who never did manage to get his hands on the International Aviation Cup, and who succumbed to illness in 1921. Glenn Curtiss had also died in his bed from complications following appendicitis surgery in 1930. The Wrights' bête noir went to his grave with a reputation as America's greatest aircraft manufacturer, having founded the Curtiss Aeroplane and Motor Company. He had been a pioneer of the seaplane, and his H-12 flying boat was used by the British during the war. Then, in 1919, Curtiss's NC-4 flying boat became the first aircraft to successfully cross the Atlantic, in a voyage that included a stop in the Azores. Although Curtiss's involvement in the aviation industry effectively ceased in the 1920s, his company merged with the Wrights' to become the Curtiss-Wright Corporation in 1929. During World War II they produced, among others, the Curtiss-Wright C-46 Commando transport plane and the Curtiss P-40 Warhawk fighter.

Tuberculosis had claimed Charles Hamilton in 1914, but in truth he'd been dead long before that, since the day he'd been admitted to the madhouse. And Hubert Latham, with whom Grahame-White had enjoyed such a splendid dinner at Sherry's, had never flown again after Hoxsey's death. Instead he had returned to his first love, big-game hunting. The odds were better. But in the summer of 1912, deep in the Congo, Latham was trampled to death by a buffalo.

Latham's legacy was the same as that of all the other aviators who had been killed in the nine short years since Orville and Wilbur Wright had proved it possible that man could fly: their courage had silenced the world's skepticism and proved that the air was indeed conquerable—in an airplane. Perhaps it was tragically appropriate that as news of Latham's death reached the United States, Melvin Vaniman embarked in the *Akron* on another attempt to cross the Atlantic Ocean in an airship. The dirigible had just crossed the New Jersey coastline when it exploded. Neither Vaniman nor any of his four crew members survived.

Despite his vigorously stated belief in the efficacy of the airship in the days following the *America* debacle, Walter Wellman never again took to the skies. The rest of his days passed by uneventfully, though the happy occasions—such as the marriage of his daughter Rebecca to Fred Aubert— were balanced by spells of misery, such as his short prison term in 1926 for failure to pay a $250 debt. Wellman died of liver cancer in 1934, the same decade in which the world decided that dirigible aviation had no serious future.

Two years after Wellman's death, Alan Hawley died at age sixty-eight. His passion for balloon flight had cooled after his experiences in the Canadian wilderness, but in its place had grown an intense ardor for the airplane, following his visit to Belmont Park. Hawley was elected president of the Aero Club of America in 1913, and over the next six years he was at the forefront of the drive to incorporate aircraft into the U.S. military. As well as being one of the organizers of the Lafayette Escadrille—the squadron of American airmen who flew in the French air force during the First World War—Hawley also campaigned for the establishment of an aerial reserve corps of the National Guard.

Right up until his death in 1936, Hawley remained good friends with Augustus Post, who, like his former pilot, had shown no inclination to continue ballooning after the 1910 victory. Instead Post, once he'd got his divorce out of the way, wrote and lectured extensively on aeronautics, and for a while in the 1920s, he edited a journal called *Aero Mechanics*. In November 1949 his photograph appeared in the newspapers when he led a campaign for the resurrection of the International Balloon Race, ten years after its demise. The goatee was still there, though with a seam of gray, the eyes shone with vitality, and age hadn't withered his turn of phrase. "There's really no sensation in the world like that of floating between the earth and the heavens with the winds of the world," he explained to a reporter, having enjoyed a brief flight in a free balloon as part of his campaign. "Some of my friends claim you can create the same feeling by partaking of four very dry martinis on an empty stomach—but I don't believe it." Post died three years later aged seventy-eight, and though the balloon race wasn't reestablished in his lifetime, it has been held annually since 1983.

Grahame-White died in August 1959, two days before his eightieth birthday, and a few weeks before the publication of his biography. His death went largely unreported around the world, most notably in Britain, where he had long since been forgotten. For years he had lived in Monte Carlo—enjoying the sun and the sea, and the casinos—and his involvement in aviation had ended shortly after the war when he sold the

Hendon aerodrome to the British government for approximately $2 million. He'd never needed to work again, but he went into the real estate business with spectacular results.

After his death Grahame-White's vast collection of scrapbooks were donated to the Royal Air Force Museum, and among all the clippings and photographs was a column from the *Chicago Daily Tribune*, published two days after Ralph Johnstone's death in November 1910. It wasn't written as an epitaph for Johnstone, but it could have been, just as it could have been an epitaph for Grahame-White, Hoxsey, Moisant, Latham, Le Blanc, de Lesseps, and all the other pioneers who, in the early years of the twentieth century, set sail from earth to explore a new world.

> The love of excitement, of fame, of money; the desire to step softly around a sleeping danger, to place a hand on death and vault over it, to tiptoe over destruction and have a multitude watch the act; the ambition to go into the unknown, to test sensations which timid persons could never know—these were the incentives mixed with others governing quiet men of no spectacular accomplishments, seeking merely the perfection of a new science, the full outlines of a new discovery.
>
> Such men were on the five vessels of Fernando Magellan when they cast off from their moorings in the Guadalquivir on Aug. 10, 1519. Such men were on the solitary *Victoria* when that surviving and circumnavigating ship dropped anchor in Seville on Sept. 9, 1522.
>
> Such men were with Vasco da Gama when he sailed from Lisbon to find his way around the Cape of Good Hope and on the Malabar coast; such men were with John Cabot when he found the Newfoundland coast; were with Jacques Cartier when he sailed up the St. Lawrence; were with Drake when with the loot of Spanish ships in his hold he found the northern Pacific coast and took the western route home.
>
> Such a crowd as that which saw Johnstone's fall gathered along the banks of the Guadalquivir on Aug. 10, 1519, when Magellan's ships got under way, a wonder-stricken crowd, prepared for new astonishments, gaping wide-eyed and open-mouthed at the men

who were to feel their way through the unknown into new worlds. Such crowds in Cadiz, Seville, Lisbon, saw the straggling return of ships with strange treasures and wonderful narratives.

The parallel should not be forced, but one finds the characteristics of an earlier age of daring and discovery reproduced in the present one, the same desires and ambitions controlling with results not dissimilar. The martyrdom of the victims may not be conscious and thinking, but the failure which sends one aerial navigator to his death may point to an undiscovered defect in his mechanism, a flaw at which inventiveness has hesitated until stimulated.

The dead, whatever may have been the incentives which sent them into danger, are giving themselves to the cause which seeks ultimate control of a new highway.

ACKNOWLEDGMENTS

Researching a book from an era with no living eyewitnesses is lonely. With no friendly folk happy to talk over a cup of tea and a slice of cake, my only companions are my fellow researchers, silent and serious, in archives and libraries around the world. Nonetheless, the time I spent in the National Air and Space Museum Archives in Suitland, Maryland, was enlivened by the lunchtime conversations with all the staff, whom I found to be not only convivial, but courteous and knowledgeable. Likewise, the staff at the RAF Museum in Hendon, London, went out of their way to be of assistance. My heartfelt thanks to these two venerable institutions.

My research was also aided by the diligence of the staff at the New York Public Library, the Colindale Newspaper Library, the British Library, and the Victoria and Albert Museum.

Kristin Ecuba warrants special praise for translating several documents from German into English with such rapidity and skill, and my agent, Gail Fortune, deserves a hearty pat on the back for her conviction and sound advice.

Lastly I thank my publisher, George Gibson, and my editor, Michele Lee Amundsen, who with their faith and foresight allowed this book to take wing.

Gavin Mortimer
Montpellier, August 2008

NOTES

Prologue: The Biggest Events Are Yet to Come
1   "mere zephyr of breeze that floated": *Ogden (UT) Standard*, January 10, 1910.
2   "An understanding of what holds an airplane": *Chicago Daily Tribune*, September 26, 1910.
2   THE BIGGEST EVENTS ARE YET TO COME: *Weekly Sentinel*, January 19, 1910.
3   "dissipated any doubt that the fragile": *Ogden (UT) Standard*, January 10, 1910.
4   "We can't do anything with that Frenchman": *Indianapolis Star*, January 11, 1910.
4   "there was a sudden shout and out of the gulley": Ibid.
5   "Paulhan was cheered madly": *Boston Daily Globe*, January 11, 1910.
5   COMPANY READY DISCUSS EXHIBITION BUSINESS SERIOUSLY: "Ladies & Gentlemen, the Aeroplane," *Air & Space*, May 1, 2008.
6   "That the bidding will be high": *Oakland Tribune*, January 21, 1910.
6   "They are ennui": *Weekly Sentinel*, January 19, 1910.

Chapter One: It's Europe or Bust
8   "Perhaps we'll make a trial flight first": *Fort Wayne Daily News*, October 15, 1910.
8   "Not much you won't!": Ibid.
9   "The crowd, constantly augmented in numbers": Ibid.
11 "That there is in it some risk to life is apparent": Walter Wellman, *The Aerial Age: A Thousand Miles by Airship over the Atlantic Ocean* (Keller, *1911*), *272*.
11 "Lightning may strike the ship and fire the hydrogen": Ibid., 273.
11 "Our lifeboat is hung with": Ibid., 274.
12 "now let those landlubbers who are afraid": Murray Simon's log, quoted in Wellman, *Aerial Age*.
13 "greatest all-round aviator in the world": *New York Herald*, September 15, 1910.
15 "ascetic, gaunt American with watchful, hawklike eyes": Graham Wallace, *Claude Grahame-White* (Putnam, 1960), 32.

15 "It's a flying machine, isn't it?": Ibid., *41*.

18 "I've no time to waste on duffers": Obituary of Pauline Chase, *Daily Mail* (London), January 5, 1962.

18 "rather massive but handsome": *Penny Illustrated Paper*, November 26, 1910.

19 "gave in and took-off in a foul mood": Wallace, *Claude Grahame-White*, 81.

19 "I am confident of being able": Ibid., 96.

19 "is possessed of a fine athletic figure": Wallace, *Claude Grahame-White*, 98.

20 "If you want your lady-loves' hearts": Ibid., 102.

20 "the society girl who plays polo": *Chicago Daily Tribune*, September 9, 1910.

21 "had to play tennis in the broiling sun": Ibid.

21 "It was perfectly heavenly!": Wallace, *Claude Grahame-White*, 107.

22 FROM BOSTON FRIENDS, IN ADMIRATION: Ibid., 107.

23 "If I should say what I really think": *New York Sun*, October 17, 1910.

23 "I hate to make a prediction": *St. Louis Post-Dispatch*, October 16, 1910.

24 "The credit is due to the biplane": *Globe-Democrat*, October 16, 1910.

25 "It may be that the Wrights have succeeded": *St. Louis Post-Dispatch*, October 16, 1910.

25 "He is quite the most 'showy' in his personality": Ibid.

26 "Stardust Twins": *New York Sun*, October 28, 1910.

27 "It is a beastly work of art": *St. Louis Post-Dispatch*, October 15, 1910.

28 "In the midst of the tumult": *St. Louis Post-Dispatch*, October 16, 1910.

28 "The airplane is doing great things": *Globe-Democrat*, October 16, 1910.

Chapter Two: Let's Stick by the Ship

31 "All did nobly": *St. Louis Post-Dispatch*, October 16, 1910.

31 "ran about shouting and yelling": Wellman, *Aerial Age*, 297.

32 "out of the darkness and mist": Ibid., 299.

32 "I don't suppose they had heard about us": Ibid., 346.

33 "It's a pity to see that": Ibid., 349.

34 "Let's stick by the ship": Ibid., 308.

34 "This crew seems to be made up": Ibid., 350.

36 "loved the limelight": *New York Times*, December 13, 1910.

37 "How nicely it works!": *Century Magazine*, October 1910.

38 "the envelope appeared to take": *New York Times*, October 12, 1908.

38 "as if some great giant was hurling": *Century Magazine*, October 1910.

39 "It is inexplicable to me": *Fort Wayne Sentinel*, October 23, 1908.

39 "the length of the appendix": *Fort Wayne Sentinel*, October 12, 1908.

39 "The successful make-up of a team": *Century Magazine*, October 1910.

40 "While we were passing above Noble County": *St. Louis Post-Dispatch*, September 20, 1910.

41 "Your Fifth Avenue and the constant stream of pretty women": *New York Herald*, October 16, 1910.

42 "I will try the machine for you": *New York Herald*, October 16, 1910.

42 "The cash prizes amount to $72,300": *New York Sun*, October 16, 1910.

43 "So great is the interest in the secrets": *New York Herald*, October 16, 1910.

43 "Germany has now in military service 14": *New York Times*, February 14, 1910.

44 "German military experts are visionaries": *Baltimore American*, June 12, 1910.

45 "A few oranges or confetti bombs": *Boston Sunday American*, September 11, 1910.

45 "Eventually the airplane will be the feature in all wars": Wallace, *Claude Grahame-White*, 110.

45 "and made one of his sensational sweeping dives": *New York Herald*, October 17, 1910.

Chapter Three: A Sort of Bleeding to Death

48 "The wind has eased considerably": Wellman, *Aerial Age*, 352.

48 "about 400 miles east of the Hampton roads": Ibid., 317.

49 "The *America* airship will die from sheer exhaustion": Ibid., 355.

50 "millions of stars are twinkling": Ibid., 358.

51 "For the same amount of premium": *New York Herald*, October 18, 1910.

52 "covered and inclosed amphitheater, where an exhibition": *New York Times*, September 18, 1910.

54 "Sysonby's ghost stood at the far turn of Belmont Park": *New York Herald*, October 18, 1910.

55 "I took up flying as a hobby eight or nine months ago": *Daily Mirror*, August 17, 1910.

55 "I found my way by compass entirely": *Daily Mail*, August 17, 1910.

55 "That's what took me straight to Amiens last night": Ibid.

56 "cheerfulness of temperament": *London Daily Graphic*, September 14, 1910.

56 "I have been treated right royally here in England": *London Evening Standard*, September 7, 1910.

58 "You'll have to find out about that from somewhere else": *New York City Globe*, October 12, 1910.

58 "They have guessed many times that I was Mexican": Ibid.

58 "I do not expect to win any prizes in the Belmont Park": *New York Sun*, October 9, 1910.

58 "made entirely of aluminum and steel": Ibid.

58 THE REVOLUTIONIST FROM SAN FRANCISCO: *San Francisco Chronicle*, October 8, 1910.

62 "That's one of the greatest troubles with airplanes today": *New York City Globe*, October 12, 1910.

62 "There is no great mystery or great difficulty about": *St. Louis Post-Dispatch*, October 13, 1910.

62 "since his arrival in this country have been of extraordinary interest": *New York City Post*, October 13, 1910.

63 "He's lucky he didn't break his neck": *St. Louis Post-Dispatch*, October 17, 1910.

63 "it is easier to learn to make the spiral": Ibid.

65 "a quart of whisky, four quarts of assorted wines": The descriptions of the provisions carried by each basket appeared in the *St. Louis Globe-Democrat*, October 17, 1910.

66 "It's at least forty percent luck": Ibid.

66 "We are good to stay up seventy or eighty hours": *St. Louis Post-Dispatch*, October 25, 1910.

67 "must be something like the proverbial": Augustus Post, "A Fall from the Sky," *Century Magazine*, October 1911.

68 "17 miles northwest of St Louis": An abbreviated version of the logbook kept by Augustus Post appeared in the *New York Herald*, October 28, 1910.

68 "My God, it's a pretty sight, brother!": Augustus Post wrote an account of the voyage for the December 1910 issue of *Century Magazine*.

Chapter Four: Will Launch Lifeboats and Trust to You

69 "As soon as the sun comes out today": Wellman, *Aerial Age*, 360.

69 "Why not draw water and fill one": Ibid.

70 "So help me God": *New York World*, October 20, 1910.

70 If you're being "nutty": *New York Sun*, October 20, 1910.

70 "continued to come from beneath the black": Ibid.

71 "We do love our airship, but, oh, you *Trent!*": Wellman, *Aerial Age*, 361.

71 "Do you want our assistance?": The *New York World*, October 20, 1910, reproduced the text of the entire communication between the *Trent* and the *America*, which was also published in Walter Wellman's account of the voyage, *The Aerial Age*.

72 "every man in the crew at work now": *New York Sun*, October 20, 1910.

73 "knocking a hole in the forward air chamber": Wellman, *Aerial Age*, 364.

74 "Good old *America*, farewell": This quote appears in *Aerial Age*, 334, and although not attributed to the lecture given by Wellman aboard the *Trent*, mentioned in the *New York Daily Sun*, October 20, 1910, I have imagined it to be an approximation of what he told his audience with characteristic melodrama.

75 "Nothing so excruciatingly funny as the action of this machine": This description appeared in *Aero* journal and was reproduced in Wallace, *Claude Grahame-White*, 84.

75 "I will demonstrate the efficiency": *New York Herald*, October 19, 1910.

76 "In the lines and the chassis they are essentially": Ibid.

78 "we suddenly struck a zone of air": *St. Louis Post-Dispatch*, October 22, 1910.

78 "After a sheer drop of six thousand feet there came a brief halt": Ibid.

78 "We were within a hundred feet of the surface": Ibid.

78 "Our attempt to land was fraught": Ibid.

79 "exhibited their usual panic with noisy sounds": *Century Magazine*, December 1910.

80 *America II passed over this place*: *St. Louis Post-Dispatch*, October 24, 1910.

Chapter Five: We Are in Bad Country and Grave Danger

83 "examined it and found that some patches": *New Orleans Picayune*, October 22, 1910.

83 "I pulled the valve and we descended with terrific force": *St. Louis Republic*, October 20, 1910.

84   "The lonesomeness and darkness of the place were appalling": Ibid.

85   "for had it not been for this lucky sighting": An account given by Leon Givaudan and quoted on the Web site www.pionnair-ge.com.

85   "growling and snapping and looking all too anxious for prey": *St Louis. Post-Dispatch*, October 22, 1910.

86   "Highest altitude, 5700 feet": *New York Herald*, October 19, 1910.

87   "while to the south beautiful soft mists": *Century Magazine*, December 1910.

87   "this is the chance of a lifetime": Ibid.

88   "Both realize that we are in bad country": Ibid.

88   "made a mental survey of the country": Ibid.

89   "the sun broke through the thick mist": *New York Herald*, October 20, 1910.

89   "fairly tore them to pieces in their eagerness": *New York World*, October 20, 1910.

90   "think we know how a ship to achieve such a voyage": *Popular Mechanics*, December 1910.

90   "Such a ship will come as surely": *New York Sun*, October 20, 1910.

90   "The experiment speaks for itself": Ibid.

90   "He sailed forth into unknown perils": *Evening Sun*, October 19, 1910.

91   "tends to confirm the growing conviction": *St. Louis Post-Dispatch*, October 20, 1910.

92   "They were sure there was going to be": *St. Louis Post-Dispatch*, October 19, 1910.

92   "We will be married next spring in London": *New York Herald*, October 19, 1910.

94   "Now listen to me": Wallace, *Claude Grahame-White*, 108.

94   "the monoplane was seen to dip suddenly": *New York Herald*, October 20, 1910.

94   "It was sheer carelessness and lack of forethought": Ibid.

95   "Why, nobody ever gets hurt flying!": *Mansfield (OH) News*, October 20, 1910.

Chapter Six: Progress Slow and Exhausting

96   "After talking things over and discussing": *Century Magazine*, December 1910.

97   "the woods were putting on a dress of unearthly loveliness": Louis Hémon, *Maria Chapdelaine* (Kessinger Publishing, 2004).

97   "awakened by the falling of the limb of a tree": *Century Magazine*, December 1910.

98   "This is the balloon 'America II,' pilot": Ibid.

98   "covered with a mass of rotten stumps": *New York Herald*, October 28, 1910.

99   "I thought the log was solid": *St. Louis Globe-Democrat*, October 28, 1910.

100 "an experience which I do not care to repeat": *St. Louis Republic*, October 20, 1910.

100 "on the edge of civilization": Ibid.

102 "I intend to enter most of the general events": *New York Herald*, October 21, 1910.

102 "very, very angry over the incident": *St. Louis Post-Dispatch*, October 26, 1910.

103 "Of one thing the public may be sure": *New York Herald*, October 21, 1910.

Chapter Seven: Wait Until Orville Comes

105 "got a wetting so that we had to go out": *Century Magazine*, December 1910.

105 "The northern lights lit up the horizon": Ibid.

107 "last sighted Tuesday sailing over Lake Huron": *St. Louis Post-Dispatch*, October 21, 1910.

107 "No name since Columbus": *New York Times*, October 23, 1910.

108 "calumny and abuse while we were forced to await": Ibid.

108 "One of the things demonstrated": Ibid.

108 "Any person that attempts the highly": *Chicago Daily Tribune*, October 22, 1910.

109 "Arch Hoxsey in a Wright biplane": *New York Herald*, October 22, 1910.

109 "heavily-built and good-natured man": *Collier's Weekly*, November 26, 1910.

110 "another cofferful of American dollars": *New York Evening Observer*, June 8, 1910.

111 "but not a man connected with the Wrights": *New York Herald*, October 22, 1910.

111 "Wait until Orville comes": Ibid.

111 "bird of prey:" Terry Gwynn-Jones, *The Air Racers* (Pelham, 1983).

111 "the world owed them a bounty": Seth Shulman, *Unlocking the Sky* (Perennial, 2002).

111 "Keep out of my air!": Ibid.

111 "The Wright Company has given guarantee": *Aero*, September 14, 1910.

112 "found that the wings had been severely crushed": *New York Herald*, October 22, 1910.

113 "We have traveled with that machine": Ibid.

Chapter Eight: An Epoch-Making Event

114 "it is believed that they landed on Wednesday": *Times* (London), October 22, 1910.

115 "Have landed thirty-two miles northeast": *Oshkosh (WI) Daily Northwestern*, October 22, 1910.

116 "officials of the Aero Club of America": *St. Louis Post-Dispatch*, October 22, 1910.

116 "with the weather so cold that at times": *Gettysburg Times*, October 28, 1910.

116 "Hawley's leg hurt him so severely": *Century Magazine*, December 1910.

117 "talked over the events of the voyage": Ibid.

117 "to bring back a muskrat from their trip": This anecdote is described in the *New York Herald*, October 29, 1910.

118 "At the dawn of the opening day of the great": *New York Herald*, October 22, 1910.

118 "airmen have a habit of working": *New York Sun*, October 22, 1910.

118 "coining their heroic feats at our expense": *New York City Review*, October 22, 1910.

119 "At 50 feet the biplane appeared to have": *New York Herald*, October 23, 1910.

121 "All our suits for infringement of patent": *Washington Post*, October 23, 1910.

121 "confident that the courts of America and European": Ibid.

121 "no Blériot, Curtiss, Farman, or in fact": Ibid.

121 "that they didn't think the Curtiss planes": Sherwood Harris, *First to Fly* (Simon & Schuster, 1970).

121 "were taught by the Wrights that the Curtiss": Ibid.

122 "The cup will remain in America": *New York Herald*, October 23, 1910.

122 "The exact dimensions of the new": Ibid.

123 "The Curtiss racer, on the other hand": Ibid.

123 "He calls a 'single surface' airplane": *New York Sun*, October 23, 1910.

124 "Whether it will fly well—or fly at all": Ibid.

124 "vendors who hawked programmes": *New York Evening Sun*, October 22, 1910.

125 "Popular with the man who owns the eatables": *New York Sun*, October 23 1910.

125 "apricot-colored polo coat and bell-shaped": Most of the New York papers devoted considerable space to the sartorial taste of the city's high society, but the *New York Herald*, the *New York World*, and the *New York Sun* were the most avid.

126 "became so excited": *New York Sun*, October 23, 1910.

127 "strongly opposed to flying over cities": *New York Evening Sun*, October 12, 1910.

127 "The prize will be open to all competitors": Ibid.

128 "on account of cutting slightly inside a pylon": *New York Herald*, October 23, 1910.

128 "growing smaller and smaller": Ibid.

129 "so blinded by rain that he couldn't make": Ibid.

129 "has won for him a host of friends": Ibid.

Chapter Nine: Tears Started to Our Eyes

130 "Each of us realized without mentioning": *Century Magazine*, December 1910.

130 "Dear God, the best friend of all": *Boston Daily Globe*, October 29, 1910.

131 "Our ambitions, which had been at rather": *Century Magazine*, December 1910.

131 "There was plenty of driftwood and birch-bark": Ibid.

131 ALL SAFE. 1230 MILES: *St. Louis Post-Dispatch*, October 23, 1910.

132 PERKINS OF BOSTON AND GUERICKE SAFE: *Boston Globe*, October 23, 1910.

132 "dropped eighteen thousand feet in nine minutes": *New York World*, October 26, 1910.

132 "literally had to cut our way through the underbrush": Ibid.

132 "we heard wolves and other wild animals": Ibid.

132 "had seen tracks of very large animals": *New York Times*, October 30, 1910.

133 "the wild Nipigon country": *New York American*, October 23, 1910.

133 "winter has already begun in Canada": *St. Louis Post-Dispatch*, October 23, 1910.

133 "flying in a wind is rather in the position": Claude Grahame-White and Harry Harper, *The Aeroplane* (Jack Publishers, 1914).

134 "the unfortunates who were promenading": *New York Sun*, October 24, 1910.

134 "dressed in a severely plain costume": *New York Herald*, October 24, 1910.

135 "the steering wheel jammed me back": *New York Times*, September 11, 1910.

135 "I really believe that this game has gotten": *Popular Mechanics*, December 10, 1910.

135 "I see the crowd below me looking upward": "Fatalism of the Fliers," *Century Magazine*, November 1912, posthumously quoted Ely.

135 "what they want are thrills": *San Antonio Light & Gazette*, December 4, 1910.

136 "he needed all his caution": *Washington Post*, October 24, 1910.

137 "a man who keeps his head can never be injured": Wallace, *Claude Grahame-White*, 39.

137 "accused the committee of attempting to deceive": *Cincinnati (OH) Post*, October 24, 1910.

Chapter Ten: A Death Trap

139   "the celebrated mountain police will begin": *Syracuse (NY) Post Standard*, October 24, 1910.

140   "We have no idea of the location of the *America II*": *St. Louis Republic*, October 24, 1910.

140   "which would carry it east of Lake Superior": *St. Louis Post-Dispatch*, October 24, 1910.

140   "It is within the range of possibilities that: *Chicago Daily Tribune*, October 24, 1910.

141   "gave an exclamation of surprise": *Century Magazine*, December 1910.

141   "was to be used as a wedge in getting bark": Ibid.

142   "Post, if anyone asks me what heaven is": Ibid.

142   "I had not gone far when I saw a cache": Ibid.

142   *No admission without business*: Ibid.

142   *Oct. 24, 1910. Alan R. Hawley and Augustus Post*: Ibid.

143   "with a smart fire burning in the stove": Ibid.

143   "The international course as it has been laid": *New York American*, October 24, 1910.

144   "If I were to tell the truth about the track": *New York Herald*, October 24, 1910.

144   "Most emphatically do I say": *New York Sun*, October 24, 1910.

144   "tried to make that turn at the acute angle": Ibid.

144   "Mr. Curtiss had to fly over houses and trees": *New York Herald*, October 24, 1910.

145   "aviators who fly above certain adjacent properties": *New York Sun*, October 24, 1910.

145   "childish:" Ibid.

145   Ryan picked up a copy of the *New York*: The confrontation between Ryan and the head of security is constructed from reports carried in the *New York Sun*, October 24, 1910, the *New York Evening Sun*, October 24, 1910, and the *New York World* of the same date.

146   "Mr. [Cortlandt] Bishop again went over the course": *New York Sun*, October 25, 1910.

147   "a navy blue suit with the skirt": Ibid.

147   "leather with several inches of padding": Ibid.

147   "which are built around murders or suicide": *New York Evening Mail*, October 21, 1910.

148   "with a bow and a smile, cut off an animated": *New York World*, October 25, 1910.

150   "The Four Hundred had at last discovered a new": *New York Evening Mail*, October 24, 1910.

150   "the crowd watched fascinated and motionless": *New York World*, October 25, 1910.

151   "the softly moving lips of Wilbur Wright": *New York Herald*, October 25, 1910.

151   "and if my luck held, I'd break the gliding record": Harris, *First to Fly*, 165.

153   "plodded unsteadily over the field to his hangar": *New York World*, October 25, 1910.

153   "It was beastly cold": *New York Sun*, October 25, 1910.

153   "When she first leaves the ground": Ibid.

153   "No policeman in Central Park would stand": Ibid.

154 "plane was dancing right down the": Ibid.

155 "He's up!": Ibid.

155 "Aviation is so contrary to all our hitherto conceived": *Warren (PA) Evening Mirror*, November 11, 1910.

156 "roared around the course twice like an eighteen": *New York Evening Sun*, October 25, 1910.

Chapter Eleven: Here Are Two Men in a Boat

157 "supplying information leading": *St. Louis Post-Dispatch*, October 25, 1910.

158 "I concede that as the situation now stands": *Albany (NY) Evening Journal*, October 25, 1910.

159 "a bark canoe, on the south side of Sotogama": *Century Magazine*, December 1910.

159 "He was facing the mountain north": Ibid.

160 "Another night has passed with no sign": Ibid.

160 "Come out, Post! Here are two men in a boat": Ibid.

160 "We dropped here in a balloon": Ibid.

160 "they had suffered much misery": Ibid.

161 "We will take you up the river": Ibid.

161 "We have not had anything": Ibid.

161 "It is remarkable how different": Ibid.

162 "whipped out the pistol and pointed": Ibid.

163 "Count de Lesseps handles his machine with such confidence": *New York American*, October 26, 1910.

164 "the foreign birds and their mechanics": *New York Sun*, October 26, 1910.

165 "you can't tell whether Orville is": *New York Sun*, October 26, 1910.

165 "When I have time, I will turn out propellers especially": *New York Herald*, October 26, 1910.

165 "The innate fault of the single-plane machine is its weakness": Ibid.

166 "I don't know. I can't tell yet": *New York Sun*, October 26, 1910.

166 "conversed gently but earnestly with his pupil": Ibid.

166 "Yesterday was Wright Day all right": "Ladies & Gentlemen, the Aeroplane," *Air & Space*, May 1, 2008.

167 "height of about 4,000 feet and to the east of the aviation": *New York Sun*, October 26, 1910.

167 "Wow, that was cold": *New York American*, October 26, 1910.

168 "I am encouraging the War Department to take": *New York Herald*, October 26, 1910.

168 "The sight of the auto chugging over the hillocks": *New York Evening Sun*, October 26, 1910.

169 "the rivalry between the English-speaking and French": Ibid.

169 "That is, I merely": The confrontation was described in full in the *New York Sun*, October 26, 1910.

Chapter Twelve: Are You These Gentlemen?

172 "The big yellow gas bag is down": *New York Herald*, October 26, 1910.

173 "Now all you have to do is follow": *Century Magazine*, December 1910.

173 "It will be three days' work for us": Ibid.

173 "With light hearts we hastened forward": Ibid.

174 "sure we were thought to be visitors": Ibid.

174 "The wire is broken": Ibid.

174 "Are you these gentlemen?": Ibid.

174 LANDED PERIBONKA RIVER. LAKE CHILAGOMA: Several newspapers, including the October 27 editions of the *New York World*, *New York Herald*, and *New York Times*.

175 "Well, I hope you had the same good luck": *St. Louis Globe-Democrat* reproduced the exchange between Post and Guay on October 28, 1910.

176 Post agreed to speak to the reporter: The lucky—or rather, canny—reporter who met Post and Hawley in Chicoutimi had his report syndicated to a raft of newspapers, though in this case I quote from the *New York Times*, October 27, 1910.

177 "was disappointed but not surprised": Ibid.

177 "breeziest race track now in use": *New York Times*, May 5, 1905.

177 "for a daily promenade around the track": Wallace, *Claude Grahame-White*, 117, and *St. Louis Republic*, October 26, 1910.

177 "air chauffeur": *New York Sun*, October 26, 1910.

178 *"Aviation is vexation"*: Wallace, *Claude Grahame-White*, 117.

178 "most effective in preventing and overcoming the effects": *South Wales Post*, August 28, 1910.

178 The evidence was right there in front: The *New York World*, *American*, and *Herald* all ran prominent photographs of Sears and Grahame-White on October 26, 1910.

179 "person on the box did not lose himself": *New York Sun*, October 27, 1910.

179 "I'm crazy about it and I came down": *New York Evening Mail*, October 26, 1910.

180 "Hardly had the two conspicuous": *New York World*, October 27, 1910.

181 "there is no further cause for controversy": *New York Herald*, October 27, 1910.

181 "brought disappointment to the calamity:" *New York Evening Sun*, October 27, 1910.

182 "There goes the winner of the big race!": Ibid.

182 "Seven seconds better in each lap than": *New York Herald*, October 27, 1910.

183 "raised their voices in excited arguments as one": *New York Sun*, October 27, 1910.

183 "Where are they?": Ibid.

183 "and a black form was seen flitting across": Ibid.

183 "it was only after an hour of brisk rubbing": Ibid.

183 The dining room of the Hotel Astor: The *New York Herald*, October 28, 1910, carried a report on the aviation craze sweeping the city.

Chapter Thirteen: There's Always a Chimney for a Man to Hang On To

185 "began sending messages to all points": *Chicago Daily Tribune*, October 27, 1910.

186 "He wins the cup!": *New York Herald*, October 27, 1910.

186 "My God": *New York World*, October 27, 1910.

186 "For two weeks before leaving for": *New York Herald*, October 27, 1910.

186 "Overjoyed": *San Francisco Chronicle*, October 27, 1910.

186 "Indications are that you have beaten": *Chicago Daily Tribune*, October 27, 1910.

186 "immediately dropped the telephone receiver": *New York Times*, October 27, 1910.

188 "I am frank in saying that I never expected to see": *New York World*, October 27, 1910.

189 "believing that he had won the race": *Century Magazine*, December 1910.

189 "may join in the last days of our meeting": *St. Louis Globe-Democrat*, October 28, 1910.

189 "There was never a time when I considered": *Chicago Daily Tribune*, October 28, 1910.

190 "We made a good landing in the trees": Ibid.

190 "I can stand a good deal of pain": Ibid.

190 "it's lost in a good cause": *Boston Daily Globe*, October 28, 1910.

191 "she reached Belmont Park with Claude": *New York Evening Mail*, October 27, 1910.

191 "You newspapermen are a nuisance!": Ibid.

192 "prevaricators": Ibid.

192 "revoked its rule that all aviators taking part": *New York Herald*, October 28, 1910.

192 "I took out my Farman biplane on Sunday": *New York Sun*, October 27, 1910.

193 "certain death": *New York Sun*, October 27, 1910.

193 "after considerable dipping and diving": *New York Herald*, October 28, 1910.

193 "he had the moral support in his protest": *New York Herald*, October 28, 1910.

193 "There's always a chimney for a man to hang on to": *New York Sun*, October 27, 1910.

194 "journeyed his way around the curves by": *San Francisco Chronicle*, October 28, 1910.

194 "had an offer of $750 by the management to fly": *New York Sun*, October 28, 1910.

194 "he hadn't even soiled his collar": *St. Louis Post-Dispatch*, October 28, 1910.

195 "flitted the air with whirling autumn leaves": *San Francisco Chronicle*, October 28, 1910.

195 The accident to Baldwin: Described in the October 28, 1910, edition of the *New York Sun*.

195 "to whom he is supposed to be engaged": *New York Sun*, October 28, 1910.

195 "a long session, productive of several heated arguments": *New York Times*, October 28, 1910.

196 "For nearly three hours": Ibid.

196 "The failure to select a representative": Ibid.

Chapter Fourteen: I'll Be Able to Give the Wrights a Good Race

197 "asked how four figures would look": *New York Herald*, October 29, 1910.

197 "Nothing doing": *New York Evening Mail*, October 28, 1910.

197 "reluctantly left their beds in the stateroom": *Boston Daily Globe*, October 29, 1910.

198 "Peroxide!": *New York Evening Mail*, October 28, 1910.

198 "Well, it's a secret": Ibid.

198 "Nature fakirs!": Ibid.

198 PLEASE ACCEPT THE ASSURANCES OF OUR: *New York Herald*, October 29, 1910.

198 "but I shall also have a look around": Ibid.

199 "people learned who was present on the train": *Boston Daily Globe*, October 29, 1910.

199 "he shared the pride of all Americans": Ibid.

199 "A clean shirt each": Ibid.

199 "justified in shooting himself": Ibid.

199 "There was one incident about our trip": Ibid.

200 "finally won his consent": Ibid.

200 "Mr. Hawley is not a man of emotional": Ibid.

200 "just a strong gripping of hands": *New York World*, October 29, 1910.

200 "to equip its [coastal] life saving stations": Ibid.

200 "their contribution to the romance of adventure": Ibid.

200 "It must not be supposed that the balloon": *New York Herald*, October 28, 1910.

201 "aerial drifting competition": *New York Daily Globe*, October 27, 1910.

201 "seemed nervous when he was welcomed": *New York Times*, October 29, 1910.

202 "You cannot imagine how it feels": Ibid.

202 YOU OWE ME NO THANKS FOR THE ASSISTANCE: *St. Louis Post-Dispatch*, October 29, 1910.

202 "Keep your seats. You are men of action": *Boston Daily Globe*, October 29, 1910.

202 "would make a chapter in himself": *St. Louis Post-Dispatch*, October 16, 1910.

203 "raised his hand for the helpers": *New York Evening Sun*, October 28, 1910.

203 "His monoplane banked gracefully": Ibid.

203 "Oh, I think I'll be able to give": Ibid.

204 "I must again on principle respectfully": Ibid.

206 "The engagement was not announced": *New York Evening Mail*, October 28, 1910.

206 "I am in no position to say anything about": Ibid.

207 "he would probably make the trip": *New York Evening Sun*, October 28, 1910.

207 Elsewhere, the table of Mr. George Huhn Jr.: *New York Evening Sun*, October 29, 1910.

207 "he encountered an unusually strong head": *New York Herald*, October 29, 1910.

208 "as he neared the enclosure he dropped": Ibid.

208 "Tell you what, boys": *St. Louis Post-Dispatch*, October 29, 1910.

209 "It was just like shooting the chutes": Ibid.

Chapter Fifteen: I'm Not Hurt Much but I Want a Long Rest

211 "There were almost 1,000 determined aero": *New York Globe*, October 30, 1910.

212 "You want more than a blur as a souvenir": Ad that appeared in the *New York Evening Mail*, October 28, 1910.

212 "Room!" shouted the first guard: *New York Sun*, October 31, 1910.

212 "Under the rules, the Gordon Bennett Cup": *New York Times*, October 29, 1910.

213 "There's nothing she can't do": Henry Villard, *Blue Ribbon of the Air* (Smithsonian, 1987).

214 "Curtiss got away with the cup at": *New York Evening Sun*, October 29, 1910.

216 "There was an instant turning of faces": Ibid.

216 "were clocking him carefully watching every shift": *New York Herald*, October 30, 1910.

217 "There was no one who watched Mr.": Ibid.

217 "Lee Blank": *New York Tribune*, October 31, 1910.

218 "its motor humming a fierce": *New York World*, October 30, 1910.

218 "as a hound would chase a fox": Ibid.

219 "as he went persistently on": Ibid.

219 "feel the woodwork of the monoplane heating": *New York Herald*, October 30, 1910.

221 "Le Blanc was shot forward": *New York Sun*, October 30, 1910.

221 "crumpled up into a smashed bundle of wreckage": *New York Herald*, October 30, 1910.

222 "threw his arms around the policeman": *New York Sun*, October 30, 1910.

222 "tall, lithe, boyish-face of Walter": *New York World*, October 30, 1910.

223 "and in a dense dust cloud it turned tail": *New York Sun*, October 30, 1910.

223 "and tore it from his head": *New York Times*, October 31, 1910.

224 "I'm not hurt much but I want a long rest": *New York Sun*, October 30, 1910.

224 "his head rounded in white linen bandages": *New York Herald*, October 30, 1910.

225 "My dear young man": *New York World*, October 30, 1910.

225 "that was nothing of insinuation": *New York Herald*, October 30, 1910.

225 "thoughtful aviator would always": *Boston Post*, November 13, 1910.

225 "I found that the tube which carries the": *Aero*, November 23, 1910.

226 "only an accident that occurred to Le Blanc's": *Boston Post*, November 13, 1910.

226 "could not understand why the": *New York World*, October 30, 1910.

226 "Come, Monsieur Hamilton, I have a Blériot": *New York Times*, October 30, 1910.

227 "the smallest thing ever done": *Brooklyn Daily Eagle*, October 30, 1910.

228 "narrowly missed a chimney top": Ibid.

228 "fairly pulled him from the machine": *New York Times*, October 30, 1910.

228 "the only manner in which I can account for Le Blanc": *New York World*, October 30, 1910.

229 "his debonair swagger": Ibid.

Chapter Sixteen: It Isn't True, It Can't Be True!

230 "We don't believe in speed for its own sake": *New York Sun*, October 30, 1910.

230 "It was a spectacle spectacularly modern": *New York Herald*, October 30, 1910.

231 "most any girl would give a lock": *New York Tribune*, October 31, 1910.

233 "You're going to win": *Evening Mail*, November 1, 1910.

233 "Just be careful, John": Gwynn-Jones, *The Air Racers*, 56.

233 "running over the ground on": *Boston Daily Globe*, October 31, 1910.

234 "looking like a man who wanted to fight somebody": Ibid.

234   "It will cost me about two thousand": Ibid.

234   "in automobiles and crested carriages": *New York World*, October 31, 1910.

235   "it was a restless crowd, filled with": *New York Herald*, October 31, 1910.

235   "turned constantly to the east, from which direction": Ibid.

235   "headed straight for the tower": *Boston Daily Globe*, October 31, 1910.

235   "the broad wings dwindled into mere patches": Ibid.

237   "nobody was quite prepared for it": Ibid.

237   "He might be an Englishman": *New York Herald*, October 31, 1910.

238   "I am now the owner of that machine": *New York World*, October 31, 1910.

238   "It will cost you ten thousand": Ibid.

239   "Roll her out, boys!": *New York Herald*, October 31, 1910.

239   "Come on, you, Moisant": Ibid.

239   "lace handkerchief was being ripped": Ibid.

240   "hands of the men holding stopwatches": *New York World*, October 31, 1910.

240   "seemed filled with mad people": *Philadelphia Press*, October 31, 1910.

240   "It isn't true": *New York World*, October 31, 1910.

240   "gave a yell like a Comanche Indian": *New York Telegram*, October 31, 1910.

240   "That's my opinion, boys": Ibid.

240   "the crowd made a rush toward": *Boston Daily Globe*, October 31, 1910.

240   "with his brown eyes dancing": *New York World*, October 31, 1910.

241   "Really very well done, old chap": Ibid.

241   "If I did, I'd be a Dutchman": Ibid.

Chapter Seventeen: My Disgust at This Betrayal

242   Hanging from the ceiling among the chandeliers: Many newspapers carried descriptions of the Plaza Hotel event, but the *New York Times* and *New York Herald* of November 1 had the most comprehensive accounts.

243   "there had been so many accidents": *New York Times*, November 1, 1910.

244   "hysterical": *New York Herald*, November 1, 1910.

245   "called for the fastest flight from Belmont Park": *New York Times*, October 31, 1910.

245   "under all the rules of international meets": Ibid.

246   "it had been announced on Saturday": Ibid.

246   "The committee announces that the": *New York Evening Sun*, October 31, 1910.

246   "It's a bally injustice, sir": Ibid.

246   "What's the use of making protests?": *Pall Mall Gazette* (London), November 1, 1910.

247   "anywhere, at any time": *New York Herald*, November 1, 1910.

247   "poor loser": *New York Evening Journal*, November 1, 1910.

247   "for their flights were being watched": *New York Herald*, November 1, 1910.

247   "the men who only a few days ago": Ibid.

247   "He got the most enthusiastic reception": *New York Times*, November 1, 1910.

248   "which was something of a protest meeting": Ibid.

248   "I wish through your columns to protest": Transcripts of Drexel's letter were repro-

duced in many newspapers around the world, such as the *New York Times* on November 1, 1910.

249   "they are jealous and very difficult to manage": *New York Evening Journal*, November 1, 1910.

250   "Would you explain the reason for": *New York Times*, November 1, 1910.

250   "In handing you this cup": Ibid.

251   "an aviator of far greater experience": Ibid.

251   "We aviators are sometimes prone to": Ibid.

251   "extending an invitation to all the aviators": Ibid.

Epilogue: We're Sending Sputniks to the Moon

253   "proved that the airplane will be a great": *Chicago Daily Tribune*, November 15, 1910.

253   "financiers, sportsmen and hundreds": *Pekin (IL) Tribune*, October 22, 1910.

253   "a year of triumphant progress": *Fly*, January 1911.

254   "He swooped down in a narrow circle": *Chicago Daily Tribune*, November 18, 1910.

255   "Frantic for souvenirs": Ibid.

255   "high noon had come and gone in the careers": Harris, *First to Fly*, 219.

255   "Poor Ralph, poor Ralph": *Orange County Times-Press*, November 22, 1910.

255   "clothe, feed and educate": *Des Moines Daily News*, October 1, 1911.

256   "His head is round and shapely": *New York City American*, November 6, 1910.

256   "There's no danger in making an airplane flight": *New York Times*, January 2, 1911.

256   "confident of winning the Michelin Cup": *Indianapolis Star*, January 1, 1911.

256   "pointed its nose directly": Ibid.

257   Hoxsey was in his hangar making: The encounter in Hoxsey's hangar was described in "Fatalism of the Fliers," *Century Magazine*, November 1912.

258   "Brookins whirled round at the sound": *Colorado Springs Gazette*, January 1, 1911.

258   "Hoxsey's dead. I know it": Ibid.

258   "Tear down the bunting, lower all the flags": *Indianapolis Star*, January 1, 1911.

258   "I wish I had gone up with Arch": *Coshocton (OH) Daily Times*, January 2, 1911.

259   "I shall not look on his dead form": Ibid.

259   "Oh, dear, dear. Stop your spoofin'": *Cedars Rapids (IA) Evening Gazette*, December 1, 1910.

259   "Foolish, unsportsmanlike and grasping": *New York Morning Telegram*, November 1910.

259   "Britons never shall be slaves": *New York Town Topics*, November 5, 1910.

260   "they had promised they wouldn't make trouble": *Warren (PA) Evening Mirror*, November 30, 1910.

260   "The same judges acclaimed him the winner": *London Evening Times*, December 9, 1910.

261   "concluded that Mr. Grahame-White could not compensate me": *Lima (OH) Daily News*, May 22, 1911.

262   "We'll all be killed if we stay in this business": Villard, *Blue Ribbon of the Air*, 76.

262   "I would like to make a bet": The discussion between Walter Brookins and Claude Grahame-White, and a third aviator, Harry Atwood, was reproduced verbatim in the *New York World*, December 31, 1911.

263   "here we are sending up sputniks to the moon": Wallace, *Claude Grahame-White*, 27.

265   "There's really no sensation in the world": *New York Herald Tribune*, November 14, 1910.

265   "Some of my friends claim you": Ibid.

266   "The love of excitement, of fame, of money": "Martyrs of the Air," *Chicago Daily Tribune*, November 19, 1910.

Appendix: The neck or snout of the balloon envelope for venting expanded gas.

Ballast: Anything used to stabilize and equilibrate a vessel. The competitors in the 1910 International Balloon Cup race carried cloth bags filled with sand.

Barograph: An instrument that records the changes in atmospheric pressure on a roll of paper without the use of fluids such as mercury. For this reason it's also known as an aneroid (without fluid) barometer.

Barometer: A word derived from the Greek words for weight and measure. A barometer is an instrument that uses mercury to measure the pressure of the air due to the weight of the column of air above.

Dirigible: From the French word for "to guide," it was also the early name for an airship, a lighter-than-air craft that uses gas to rise and propellers and rudders for propulsion and steering.

Drag rope: A long, weighted rope that can be trailed from a balloon and used as ballast in influencing the rate of ascent and descent.

Elevator: A control surface on the tailplane of an aircraft allowing it to climb or descend.

Envelope: The fabric of a balloon that encloses the gas. Nowadays balloon fabric is made from nylon or polyester, although in the early days silk was the norm.

Equilibrator: A derivative of *equilibrate* meaning "to balance"; the name given to the ballast carried on Walter Wellman's airship *America*.

Guy rope: A rope, wire, or chain used to anchor or steady an object.

Plane: A flat surface and the early-twentieth-century name for an airplane's wings.

Pusher: The name given to any airplane in which the propeller and the engine were situated behind the aviator.

Rip cord: A cord extending from a long strip sewn into the balloon material near its upper shoulder called a ripping panel. Pulling the cord rips away the panel, releasing the gas and causing the immediate descent of the balloon.

Terracing: An early aviation technique for landing in blustery conditions whereby the airplane flies forward horizontally for one hundred yards, for example, drops vertically for one hundred yards, flies forward horizontally for one hundred yards, and so on.

Wing warping: The system devised by Wilbur Wright of twisting the wings of an airplane to raise or lower the tips, thereby allowing the aviator to achieve roll control. The system entailed bracing the tips of the wings with wires that the aviator manipulated from his seat.

SELECTED BIBLIOGRAPHY AND SOURCES

Books

The Aerial Age: A Thousand Miles by Airship over the Atlantic Ocean by Walter Wellman. Keller, 1911.

The Air Racers: Aviation's Golden Era, 1909–1936 by Terry Gwynn-Jones. Pelham, 1983.

The Bishop's Boys: A life of Wilbur and Orville Wright by Tom Crouch. Norton, 1990.

Blue Ribbon of the Air: The Gordon Bennett Races by Henry Villard. Smithsonian Institution, 1987.

Claude Grahame-White by Graham Wallace. Putnam, 1960.

Cruisers of the Air: The Story of Lighter-than-air Craft by C. J. Hylander. Macmillan, 1931.

Dictionnaire universel de l'aviation by Bernard Marck. Tallandier, 2005.

The Eagle Aloft: Two centuries of the balloon in America by Tom Crouch. Smithsonian, 1983.

First to Fly by Sherwood Harris. Simon & Schuster, 1970.

500 fahrten im freiballon by Hugo Von Abercron. R. C. Schmidt & Co., 1929.

Heroes of the Air: A book for boys by Claude Grahame-White and Harry Harper. Oxford University Press, 1918.

J. M. Barrie and the Lost Boys by Andrew Birkin. Constable, 1979.

Learning to Fly: A practical manual for beginners by Claude Grahame-White and Harry Harper. Macmillan, 1916.

Maria Chapdelaine: A Tale of the Lake St. John Community by Louis Hémon. Kessinger, 2004.

Memories by Harry Preston. Constable, 1928.

Notable Flying Men by the staff of *The Motor*. Temple Press, 1910.

Pionniers de l'aviation by Louis Blériot. Hachette, 2004.

The Romance of Ballooning by Edita Lausanne. Viking Press, 1971.

Skycraft by Augustus Post. Oxford University Press, 1930.

The Story of the Aeroplane by Claude Grahame-White. J. B. Lippincott, 1911.

The Story of the Airship by Hugh Allen. Goodyear Tire & Rubber Company, 1931.

Unlocking the Sky by Seth Shulman. HarperCollins, 2002.

Collections

National Air and Space Archives, Washington, D.C.
Wilfred Beckert scrapbook
Alexander Graham Bell scrapbooks
Frank Coffyn scrapbook
Glenn Curtiss Collection
Early Aeronautical Newsclippings
(Alexander Graham Bell)
Collection
The Moisant family scrapbook

RAF Museum, Hendon, London
The Grahame-White papers

Victoria and Albert Museum, London
Pauline Chase papers

New York Public Library
The Augustus Post papers

Newspapers

Albany Evening Journal
Baltimore American
Billings Gazette
Boston Daily Globe
Boston Post
Boston Sunday American
Brooklyn Daily Eagle
Cedar Rapids Evening Gazette
Chicago Daily Tribune
Cincinnati (OH) Post
Colorado Springs Gazette
Coshocton Daily Times
Daily Graphic
Daily Mail
Daily Mirror
Daily Northwestern
Daily Sketch
Des Moines Daily News
Dover Standard
Dublin Herald
Fort Wayne Daily News
Fort Wayne Sentinel
Gettysburg Times
Indianapolis Star
Knoxville Journal
Le Journal (Paris, France)
Lima Daily News
London Evening Standard

London Evening Times
Manchester Guardian
Mansfield News
New Orleans Picayune
New York American
New York City Review
New York Evening Mail
New York Evening Observer
New York Evening Sun
New York Globe
New York Herald
New York Morning Telegram
New York Post
New York Sun
New York Times
New York Town Topics
New York World
Oakland Tribune
Ogden Standard
Orange County Times-Press
Pall Mall Gazette
Pekin (IL) Tribune
Philadelphia Press
Post Standard
San Antonio Light & Gazette
San Francisco Chronicle
South Wales Post
St. Louis Globe-Democrat

St. Louis Post-Dispatch
St. Louis Republic
Times (London)

Warren Evening Mirror
Washington Post
Weekly Sentinel

Journals/Magazines

Aero (London)
Aero, America's Aviation Weekly
Aeronautics
Air & Space
Century Magazine
Civil Service Gazette (UK)
Collier's
Field (UK)
Flight: Official Organ of the Royal Aero
  Club of the UK

Fly
Lady's Pictorial (London)
L'Aero (Paris)
Motor Car Journal (London)
Penny Illustrated Paper
Popular Mechanics
Tatler
Time
Variety

Chasing Icarus is Gavin Mortimer's sixth book. His most recent, *The Great Swim*, was published in 2008 by Walker. He has also written numerous books for children and contributed articles to a wide range of publications.